THE BLACKWELL
DICTIONARY OF
Social
Policy

Edited by

PETE ALCOCK
ANGUS ERSKINE
MARGARET MAY

Social Policy Association

Blackwell
Publishers

Copyright © Blackwell Publishers Ltd 2002
Editorial matter and arrangement copyright © Pete Alcock,
Angus Erskine and Margaret May 2002

First published 2002

2 4 6 8 10 9 7 5 3 1

Blackwell Publishers Ltd
108 Cowley Road
Oxford OX4 1JF
UK

Blackwell Publishers Inc.
350 Main Street
Malden, Massachusetts 02148
USA

Library of Congress Cataloging-in-Publication Data has been applied for

ISBN 0-631-21846-7 (hardback); 0-631-21847-5 (paperback)

British Library Cataloguing in Publication Data

A CIP catalogue record for this book is available from the British Library

Typeset in 10.5 on 12.5 pt Sabon
by SNP Best-set Typesetter Ltd., Hong Kong
Printed in Great Britain by MPG Books Ltd, Bodmin, Cornwall
This book is printed on acid-free paper.

Contents

Contributors and Editors

Contributors

KA   Karl Atkin, Senior Lecturer in Ethnicity and Primary Care, Centre for Research and Primary Care, University of Leeds

PA   Pete Alcock, Professor of Social Policy and Administration, University of Birmingham

BB   Barbara Bagilhole, Reader in Equal Opportunities in Social Policy, University of Loughborough

SB   Sue Balloch, Professor in Health and Social Care, University of Brighton

GC   Gary Craig, Professor of Social Justice, University of Hull

JC   Jochen Clasen, Professor of Comparative Social Research, University of Stirling

SC   Sangeeta Chatoo, Centre for Research and Primary Care, University of Leeds

HD   Hartley Dean, Professor of Social Policy, University of Luton

AE   Angus Erskine, Senior Lecturer in Social Policy, University of Stirling

DG   Dan Goodley, Centre for Disability Studies, University of Leeds

DEG   David Gladstone, Senior Lecturer in Social Policy, University of Bristol

HG   Howard Glennerster, Professor of Social Administration, London School of Economics

MH   Malcolm Hill, Professor for the Child and Society, University of Glasgow

MEH   Meg Huby, Senior Lecturer in Social Policy, University of York

MJH   Michael Hill, Visiting Professor of Social Policy, Goldsmiths College, University of London

HJ   Helen Jones, Senior Lecturer in Social Policy, Goldsmiths College, University of London

RL   Ruth Lister, Professor of Social Policy, Loughborough University

AM   Alan Murie, Professor of Urban and Regional Studies, University of Birmingham

DM   Deborah Mabbett, Lecturer in Government, Brunel University

HM   Hannah Morgan, Centre for Disability Studies, University of Leeds

JM   Jane Millar, Professor of Social Policy, University of Bath

MM   Margaret May, Principal Lecturer in Social Policy, London Guildhall University

TM   Tony Maltby, Senior Lecturer in Social Policy, University of Birmingham

MP   Mark Priestley, Centre for Disability Studies, University of Leeds

RMP   Robert Page, Reader in Democratic Socialism and Social Policy, University of Birmingham

SP   Sheila Paul, Public Health Project Officer, Camden and Islington Health Authority

DWS   Duncan Scott, Senior Lecturer in Social Policy, University of Manchester

CU   Clare Ungerson, Professor of Social Policy, University of Southampton

Editors

Pete Alcock   Professor of Social Policy and Administration, University of Birmingham

Angus Erskine   Senior Lecturer in Social Policy, University of Stirling

Margaret May   Principal Lecturer in Social Policy, London Guildhall University

Editorial Advisory Board

Acknowledgements

The editors should like to thank Sarah Falkus and all the staff at Blackwell Publishers for their support and forbearance during the production of the text. It proved to be a much more extensive, and intensive, task than we had (perhaps naively) initially anticipated. We should like to thank the Social Policy Association for their support in partnering Blackwell in the commissioning of the book and in securing the support and co-operation of so many expert contributors. We should also like to thank the Editorial Advisory Board for their support, advice and helpful suggestions – this Dictionary is undoubtedly a better book as a result of their efforts. And finally we should like to thank our contributors for agreeing to supply draft text, for keeping to deadlines (in part at least), and for co-operating so helpfully with the difficult editorial process of securing consistency and complementarity within such a wide-ranging undertaking. Of course, only we can take full responsibility for the final product. We hope that the considerable work involved in producing this Dictionary will succeed in making the tasks of those who use it that much easier.

Pete Alcock, Angus Erskine and Margaret May

Introduction

A Dictionary of Social Policy

This book is a new venture in Social Policy publishing. Dictionaries and encyclopedias providing definitions and descriptions of key terms and concepts exist in many academic subject areas and provide important sources of reference for students and practitioners. However, there has so far never been a comprehensive and authoritative dictionary of Social Policy in the UK. This compilation provides such a resource.

The Dictionary was commissioned by Blackwell Publishers to accompany the *Student's Companion to Social Policy*. As with the Companion, it has been produced in collaboration with the Social Policy Association, the professional body representing academics and researchers in the field of Social Policy. The support provided by the Association and the extensive range of Social Policy experts to which this secured access have ensured that this Dictionary is an authoritative and representative guide to the subject. It has been designed and produced by the same editors who worked on the Companion: Alcock, Erskine and May. Their experience and standing has ensured that the Dictionary builds on the successful foundation laid by the Companion.

The entries included in the text have been prepared by a group of Social Policy experts, selected by the editors, all of whom are active teachers and researchers and prominent members of the Social Policy Association. The text has also been guided by advice from an Editorial Advisory Board of senior Professors and Readers, who provided comments on the proposed list of entries and the completed draft of the final text. The aim is to provide a clear and accessible guide to the major terms and concepts that students and practitioners are likely to encounter in studying Social Policy. It is the perspective of the committed but relatively uninformed new reader that has been used to determine both the selection of entries, and the style and focus of definitions and descriptions. Inevitably this has required a number of important editorial decisions about the scope and scale of coverage, which are outlined below.

What is Included in the Dictionary?

The Dictionary has been written by British academics and produced primarily for a UK Social Policy audience. It is likely to be of interest to scholars and practitioners in a number of other countries which share a similar intellectual and policy-making framework with the UK, notably the US, Canada, Australia, New Zealand and most of continental Europe. But the book is not an international Social Policy text and does not seek to provide coverage of many of the specialist concepts and traditions found in other countries, including those mentioned above. Nevertheless the study and development of Social Policy are no longer narrowly national activities – comparative analysis, policy transfer and supranational developments are now core features of research, teaching and practice. Thus the Dictionary does seek to provide a guide to those major terms and concepts derived from the activities of supranational and international agencies which impact on policy development and practice in the UK. Such a limited comparative and international dimension was a deliberate feature in the selection of entries and the recruitment of some contributors and Editorial Advisory Board members.

The entries selected focus on the subject of Social Policy itself. However, delineating the boundaries of academic subjects and therefore deciding upon those areas which are, or are not, within those boundaries is a complex, and inevitably a contested, activity. Nevertheless boundaries must be drawn. Other dictionaries and encyclopedias exist to serve related subject areas, such as Sociology, Politics and Social Work; and thus this volume intentionally does not include terms that might more usually be associated with those subjects. Students working across, or on the margins of, subject boundaries may therefore find that they have to refer to more than one source for some definitions or descriptions. The focus of this text, on Social Policy narrowly conceived, means that the coverage provided here is unique and does not duplicate or challenge other subject guides. This is a virtue that justifies the careful selection made.

A number of other important considerations have led to some potential entries, or classes of entries, being excluded from the text:

- Key individuals have been included, but only where they have played an important role in the development of the study or application of Social Policy and are therefore likely to be encountered by students studying in the area. Furthermore only those individuals who were deceased at the time of the final editing have been included.

- The names or titles of organizations and agencies have not been included. These are the property of these organizations and they may have views about how they are described. These organizations are also subject to an inevitable process of change as they grow, decline or change direction, which means that any guide that includes them may quickly become outdated.

- Statutes and government reports have also been omitted. The decisions on which of these to include would be difficult. A list of current statutes and reports would rapidly become outdated; and any list of past publications would be likely to be a long one with many included even though they had been superseded by later legislative or policy changes. Lists of statutes and other legislative measures can be found in government publications, specialist directories or in legal texts dealing with particular policy areas. They are therefore not included here.

- Definitions of technical terms used within specific policy areas, such as details of social security benefits, medical conditions or diagnoses, or elements of educational curriculum, are also excluded. This level of detail is too specific for an introductory guide, and readers can resort to more specialist texts for access to such material.

Although the above categories have been excluded from the list of entries, contributors have been asked to make reference to particularly important organizations or reports where appropriate. This also applies to mention of living individuals who are closely associated with the genesis of certain terms or concepts. However, the book does not contain any references to other texts or other authors. To include these would have extended the scale and scope of coverage significantly and would have altered the book from being a quick source of reference to something more like an academic text. More general introductory Social Policy texts, including the Companion, do include such references and readers wishing to pursue a more detailed exploration of issues should therefore resort to these.

The entries that have been included nevertheless vary significantly in scale and scope. Some terms are more important and more extensively used than others; many concepts can only adequately be explained by providing some history and context to their use and by discussing the varied and specific aspects of their development and use. Thus the entries vary between

- longer entries, or key issues, where background and context and different uses and applications are discussed;
- brief discussions of major terms, where some explanation and occasional examples accompany the definition;
- short descriptions of minor terms, where a more concise dictionary-style definition is provided.

How to Use the Dictionary

The entries in the Dictionary are listed in alphabetical order. This makes it easy for readers to locate the discussion or definition of the term that they are looking for. Where terms are also mentioned or discussed to a significant extent within other entries, cross-references are provided, for example: see COMMUNITY DEVELOPMENT. In some cases the entry itself will simply be a cross-reference to another term, and the substantive discussion in the referred entry will provide a description or definition of both terms.

Thus the expectation is that readers will approach the text with a term or concept that they have come across or been referred to, which they are uncertain about the meaning or use of. If it is a Social Policy term then you should find an appropriate entry here, perhaps with specific cross-references to other related entries. In consulting entries, of course, readers may come across other terms and concepts which are themselves the source of separate entries, and to which you may wish to make reference. All terms that have separate entries have thus been identified in the text by the use of SMALL CAPITALS, and you can readily identify these and consult with these entries if desired. In places two or more consecutive terms have been highlighted such as USER CHARTERS. In cases such as this you should look under both USER and CHARTER. In other cases, words which contain the same root have been highlighted, such as THATCHERITE or SOCIAL DEMOCRATS; in these cases you will find THATCHERISM or SOCIAL DEMOCRACY as the relevant entry. Where a term may be close to an entry which should be consulted, it is also placed in small capitals; thus SECONDARY SCHOOLING is in small capitals but you will only find an entry for SECONDARY EDUCATION.

It perhaps goes without saying therefore that this is not a book to be read from cover to cover. It is intended as a resource and a source of reference to be carried through Social Policy study and to be consulted whenever and wherever queries about meaning or usage of terms arise. It will thus provide a resource over time and it has been designed and constructed to limit the inclusion of terms or definitions that will rapidly become outdated or disappear. Of course no text can stand still in a changing world. This is perhaps particularly the case in the field of Social Policy; but by avoiding the inclusion of technical, statutory and organizational details the book provides a guide to policy which should outlive the rapidly changing ideas and initiatives of particular politicians and policy makers. You, the readers, will be the final judges of how far this goal has been achieved.

A

Abel-Smith, Brian (1926–1996)

One of the most renowned figures in post-1945 SOCIAL ADMINISTRA-
TION, who first came to prominence with his incisive analysis for
the Guillebaud enquiry into the cost of the NATIONAL HEALTH SERVICE
(*The Cost of the National Health Service in England and Wales*, with
RICHARD TITMUSS, 1956). He was assistant lecturer (1955), lecturer
(1957), reader (1961) and Professor of Social Administration (1961) at
the LSE. He is best remembered for his joint publication *The Poor and
the Poorest* (with Peter Townsend, 1965), which demonstrated that
POVERTY had persisted despite the post-1945 WELFARE reforms. He
acted as a special adviser to both the 1964–70 and 1974–9 Labour governments. In the 1970s and 1980s his work became more international
in focus and he visited over sixty countries as a World Health Organization consultant. Julian Le Grand noted in one obituary: 'There are
few academics who have changed the world – and even fewer who have
changed life for the better. Brian Abel-Smith was one of that select
group.' His other publications include *The Hospitals 1800–1948* (with
Robert Pinker, 1964) and *An Introduction to Health: Policy, Planning
and Financing* (1994). (RMP)

Abortion policies

The termination of pregnancy is governed in Britain by the 1967 Abortion Act. This makes an abortion legal if it is performed by a registered
medical practitioner after two independent medical practitioners have
agreed to the termination. The main grounds are that the continuance
of the pregnancy would cause physical or mental risk to the health of
the woman, or her existing children, greater than if the pregnancy were
terminated. The upper time limit (since 1990) is 24 weeks pregnant,

with some exceptions beyond this. There have been several attempts to change the abortion law since 1967, notably in 1998 when a significant reduction in the upper time limit was proposed (and defeated). The 1967 Act has been criticized by many FEMINISTS because there is no RIGHT to an abortion on request (as there is in several other European countries). The medicalized approach, where the decisions lie with doctors, can also cause delays and access to NATIONAL HEALTH SERVICE abortion services varies across the country. Many abortions are therefore performed in private clinics. About one-quarter of all conceptions in England and Wales are terminated by abortion, rising to two-fifths of conceptions among women under 20 years old. (JM)

Access to welfare

A notion derived from the need to establish principles for deciding who should receive welfare BENEFITS and services when resources are limited. At the most general level it is generally agreed that access to welfare should be based upon the principle of meeting NEED. However, there is considerable disagreement as to how NEEDS should be defined and met. This revolves around whether ELIGIBILITY for BENEFITS and services should be based on

- legal RIGHTS or the DISCRETION of professionals and officials to determine NEED and/or DESERT;
- UNIVERSALISM or SELECTIVITY – through MEANS TESTING or other forms of TARGETING;
- CONDITIONALITY, which can take the form of behavioural requirements such as job-seeking, or of contribution conditions as under SOCIAL INSURANCE.

There are two issues of growing significance. First is the position of nonnationals who face increasingly restrictive IMMIGRATION, ASYLUM and SOCIAL SECURITY laws, which define their access to welfare on the basis of their immigration or residence status. Second is the debate as to how far USERS should be involved in determining the rules that govern access to welfare. (RL)

Accountability

Relates to the ways in which the providers of welfare services are responsible both for the services they provide and to the people to whom they provide them. For policy makers, public servants and welfare agencies, being accountable means, on the one hand, having to give an account of themselves and, on the other, being held to account for what they do. The concept is complex because accountability is capable of being achieved at a variety of levels and in a variety of ways. It is also a contested concept. For example, some commentators would argue that public accountability is a form of 'stewardship' that entails moral principles that are inherently inimical to the prevailing political process. Others would argue that a genuine process of democratic renewal should transcend the issue of accountability by EMPOWERING CITIZENS directly to shape the welfare services they require.

Within the WELFARE STATE there have traditionally been two main strands of accountability: one relating to the political executive, the other to officials and professionals. The first entails electoral and parliamentary accountability (sometimes called the 'Westminster model'). This contends that elected politicians who assume executive responsibility as central government ministers or LOCAL GOVERNMENT committee chairs, are accountable for the discharge of their duties to parliament or to the local council respectively. In turn, these bodies are periodically accountable to the electorate (which has the power to vote in an alternative administration). The second entails bureaucratic and professional accountability (sometimes called the 'public administration model') and contends that civil servants and LOCAL GOVERNMENT officers are accountable through a hierarchical system of line-management, while professional staff (such as medical personnel) are accountable for their performance to the professional bodies that accredit them.

Additionally, service providers are financially and legally accountable. In recent times, central government departments have been accountable to the all-party Public Accounts Committee and the National Audit Office, while LOCAL GOVERNMENT is accountable to District Auditors and the Audit Commission. The substantive decisions of the political executive and public administrators are susceptible to judicial review in the courts. There are additional mechanisms, in a number of fields of welfare provision, by which the recipients of services or BENEFITS may APPEAL against individual decisions to specially constituted administrative TRIBUNALS or can complain to specially appointed OMBUDSPERSONS.

Recent political trends and the inherent complexity of government, according to many commentators, have resulted in a crisis of accountability for the WELFARE STATE. On the one hand, power over key aspects of local welfare expenditure and provision has become increasingly centralized and the sheer scope of ministerial responsibility is such that, arguably, it is now more of a fiction than a reality. On the other hand, paradoxically, responsibility for decision-making in many fields of welfare provision has become increasingly fragmented as it is passed to bodies such as indirectly accountable agencies, non-elected QUANGOS or charitable or commercial organizations. At the same time, however, new concepts of accountability have been emerging.

The most significant of these – the related concepts of contractual and market accountability – have been associated with the rise of NEW PUBLIC MANAGERIALISM, which, since the 1980s, has substantially displaced the public administration model throughout much of the WELFARE STATE. This sort of accountability derives in part from the inherent efficiency that is supposed to flow from the introduction of COMPETITIVE TENDERING, QUASI-MARKETS and/or PURCHASER/PROVIDER SPLITS and from the opportunity that such innovations present for introducing explicit performance targets into contracts for welfare services. With this notion of accountability came a number of innovations:

- LEAGUE TABLES were introduced by which the performance of service providers could be scrutinized and compared.
- New processes were developed by which the performance of professional practitioners could be AUDITED.
- Service USER CHARTERS by which PUBLIC SECTOR service providers were to be made accountable to their 'customers' in a broadly similar way to that in which PRIVATE SECTOR providers must respond to consumer demand in a free market.
- Consistent with this approach, new COMPLAINTS procedures (as distinct from the APPEALS processes that characterize the public administration approach) have been introduced in several areas of welfare provision.

The MANAGERIALIST approach to quality and accountability, first pioneered under Conservative governments, has been embraced by Labour which, through the development of its BEST VALUE regime, aims to sustain a culture of continuous improvement of management in welfare services. At the same time, however, Labour is seeking new ways to consult CITIZENS at the local level through CITIZENS' JURIES and community fora and, through its various ACTION ZONE initiatives, to involve a range of STAKEHOLDERS in more directly participative mechanisms. The DEVOLUTION of selective powers to the Scottish Parliament, the Welsh Assembly, the Northern Ireland Assembly and the Greater

London Authority and Mayor similarly represents a reversal of previous trends towards CENTRALIZATION, although further devolution to the English regions seems at the time of writing to be unlikely. None the less Britain remains essentially a unitary state for which, in an era of complex GOVERNANCE, accountability remains a problematic issue. (HD)

Action research

See EVALUATION

Action zones

Areas of DEPRIVATION TARGETED by central government initiatives for special funding to encourage PARTNERSHIP and project working with marginalized groups in local areas. Examples include Health Action Zones, Education Action Zones and Employment Action Zones. The Action Zones are linked to other AREA-BASED INITIATIVES (such as Sure Start and NEW DEAL FOR COMMUNITIES) through planning in LOCAL STRATEGIC PARTNERSHIPS. (SB)

Active citizenship

The concept of active CITIZENSHIP requires individual CITIZENS to consider their obligations to society alongside their RIGHTS. At its broadest, all are invited to volunteer time and money, donate blood and organs. More narrowly it has become the focus of a number of project-based schemes, mainly targeted upon the young and long-term adult unemployed, to promote employment or community activity, often through co-operation with VOLUNTARY SECTOR agencies. Different versions of active CITIZENSHIP have been promoted by politicians of different persuasions; for example, CONSERVATIVES tend to emphasize the individual, while centre-left parties talk of collective SOLIDARITY. (DWS)

Acts

Substantive legal statutes passed by a legislative body, imposing duties or obligations on public bodies, and/or constraints upon or BENEFITS to

CITIZENS (hence in the United Kingdom Acts of Parliament). More specific regulations or STATUTORY INSTRUMENTS may amplify them. (MJH)

Adoption policies

Adoption is a legal arrangement whereby a court transfers the parental RIGHTS and responsibilities of a child's original birth parents to an adoptive couple or individual. In the UK married couples and single people may adopt, but not unmarried couples. Often the adopters do not know the child previously, but a significant proportion of adoptions involve stepchildren. Grandparents, other relatives and FOSTER CARERS may also adopt. In much of Western Europe a high proportion of adoptions concern children brought in from other countries, particularly Asia and Latin America. British adoption policies in the 1970s and 1980s concentrated on within-country adoption of LOOKED-AFTER CHILDREN. As it became more common for young lone mothers to keep their babies instead of relinquishing them for adoption, increasingly children placed for adoption are older and have DISABILITIES or emotional/behavioural problems. In response, various post-adoption support and counselling services have developed. Since the 1990s inter-country adoption has become more common. Another major trend has been towards openness, i.e. some kind of contact between the birth and adoptive families after adoption. This usually consists of sending or exchanging letters, cards, photos or gifts, but sometimes face to face contact occurs. (MH)

Adult education

An umbrella term encompassing provision for continuing education and self-development beyond the compulsory school-leaving age. Pioneered by voluntary organizations such as Mechanics Institutes and the Workers Educational Association, the university extension movement and LOCAL AUTHORITIES, traditionally it has been offered through distinct centres or courses either within or independent of institutions of FURTHER and HIGHER EDUCATION. Recent decades have seen increasing diversification as UNIVERSITIES, colleges and adult education establishments have extended the types of courses available. New public and private suppliers have also entered the field, many (such as the Open University and the University for Industry) based on individualized or distance learning. Currently provision extends across a wealth of recreational, academic and vocational subjects, ranging from 'interest-based' studies such as those offered by the University of the Third Age, to assistance with basic skills, support for further academic study and continuing professional development. These may be studied on a full- or part-time basis and are usually fee-based, though a variety of fiscal and other measures, including learning accounts, are available for some, as are exemptions for the unemployed or retired. Many courses do not lead to accreditation, but there is increasing emphasis on award-bearing provision as well as opportunities for LIFELONG LEARNING. (DEG)

Adult services

The section of local SOCIAL SERVICES DEPARTMENTS dealing with the provision of PERSONAL SOCIAL SERVICES to adult USERS and USER groups. (PA)

Adverse selection

A special type of MARKET FAILURE, which applies to any type of insurance market, but is especially important in the case of private insurance for health and LONG TERM CARE. For markets to work efficiently there has to be good information available to both the buyer and the seller. Individuals buying health insurance or LONG TERM CARE are likely to know more about their RISKS of being sick than an insurance company, and it is not in their interests to divulge this – a situation of adverse selection. However, insurance companies and other providers may take steps to reduce potential bad risks, resulting in CREAM SKIMMING. (HG)

Advice centres

The term is applied to local agencies that provide advice to the public, such as Citizens' Advice Bureaux (CAB) and other independent advice centres; housing, consumer and WELFARE RIGHTS advice services run by LOCAL AUTHORITIES; and more specialized agencies such as law centres and housing aid centres. (HD)

Affirmative action

Policies and procedures aimed to rectify past imbalances and ensure fair participation by under-represented groups at all levels in the labour market. Such arrangements have been successfully supported by legislation in the USA and to some extent in Northern Ireland. EQUAL OPPORTUNITIES legislation in Britain, however, is generally based on a different approach. In relation to ethnicity, for instance, the 1976 Race Relations Act forbids direct DISCRIMINATION ('less favourable treatment on racial grounds') in employment; indirect DISCRIMINATION (conditions which fewer members of a racial group can comply with); and most forms of POSITIVE DISCRIMINATION (e.g. a policy of only selecting minority ethnic staff for appointment or promotion to REDRESS existing DISCRIMINATION). As with measures regarding the employment of women and disabled people, it does, however, allow for positive action, for example in the provision of training facilities TARGETED at particular ethnic or other excluded groups.

This stance, essentially aimed at stopping negative employment or other practices, contrasts with that adopted in the US under various federal Affirmative Action Programs and CIVIL RIGHTS legislation. In terms of ethnicity, for example, the main elements of affirmative action for an employer include analyses of actual and potential workforces for specific roles in terms of local majority and minority populations, race awareness training for personnel, appropriate training for under-represented groups, and appropriate, carefully targeted recruitment procedures. Affirmative action is thus much wider than POSITIVE DISCRIMINATION as practised in the UK. However, following the 1997 Treaty of Amsterdam and in line with the European Union Fair Treatment Directive, the definition of and protection against DISCRIMINATION has been strengthened in the UK and policies to further amend EQUAL OPPORTUNITIES requirements are also in train. (GC)

Ageism

Stereotypical beliefs and practices, related to the ageing process and originating in the biological variation between people. Ageism condones and legitimates the use of chronological age to systematically deny resources, status, power and social opportunities that others enjoy. It results in expressions of fear, loathing and rejection often associated with old age and growing old in contemporary society. (TM)

Aggregation

Refers to the treatment of all the sources of income and wealth of a family or household as one single resource for all members – all income is aggregated into one pot. This is of particular importance in the application of MEANS-TESTS where ENTITLEMENT to benefits is calculated on a family basis, with the effect that the income of one family partner will be taken into account in assessing the potential ENTITLEMENT of another. For other purposes, for instance tax and NATIONAL INSURANCE, family members are treated separately with individual liabilities and entitlements. See DISAGGREGATION. (PA)

Allocation policies

A class of decisions made by government or some other agency to apportion money or other scarce resources like professional staff or new buildings to given purposes or areas. For instance, central government allocates money between services in the public spending round – called the COMPREHENSIVE SPENDING REVIEW. Allocation to different areas also takes place, sometimes according to established formulas, such as proposed by the RESOURCE ALLOCATION WORKING PARTY (RAWP). (HG)

Alternative medicine

Usually defined as forms of medical practice and treatments (such as osteopathy, acupuncture, aromatherapy and homeopathy) not traditionally practised by the established medical professions in the UK. However, these and other forms of COMPLEMENTARY MEDICINE are increasingly being used alongside conventional approaches; hence the term is open to change, as its definition depends upon the views of leaders of orthodox medicine and upon what state health services will support. (MJH)

Altruism

An act can be said to be altruistic when an individual voluntarily gives help to a stranger without expectation of reward. Altruism is clearly distinguishable from both selfishness (in which one undertakes a course of action for personal gain at the expense of another) and self-interest (in which one seeks a personal benefit without 'harming' others in the process). It also needs to be distinguished from duty (in which helpful actions are undertaken out of a sense of obligation),

RECIPROCITY (where help is offered on the basis of mutual support) and restitution (where help is offered to make good a previous omission or shortcoming).

Anthropologists have drawn attention to the fact that unconditional giving should not be assumed to be altruistic. Gifts can be used to affirm the status of the giver or be used to bind individuals and communities into long-term reciprocal relationships.

Historically, it was often assumed that altruism was the key motivating force for CHARITABLE or VOLUNTARY forms of welfare. However, this viewpoint has been challenged on the grounds that such aid might equally well be provided to maintain class divisions or control the poor. Similar criticisms have been levelled at those who have argued that the growth of state welfare during the twentieth century reflects an evolving humanitarianism.

It has been suggested that the establishment of the post-1945 WELFARE STATE in Britain owed much to the upsurge in selflessness that occurred during the Second World War. In the face of enemy attacks, people were more willing to help strangers (as evidenced in the evacuation scheme) and adhere to the principle of fair shares for all, which underpinned the system of rationing. The growing demand for a more equitable postwar society was seen as one of the outcomes of this value shift. Certainly, the popular acclaim accorded to the BEVERIDGE Report and the victory of the Labour Party committed to UNIVERSAL state welfare provision in the 1945 general election lends substance to this approach.

For RICHARD TITMUSS, UNIVERSAL state welfare services were morally superior to atomistic, bilateral commercial activity. Unilateral provision served to engender greater degrees of SOLIDARITY, altruism and toleration. In *The Gift Relationship* TITMUSS sought to demonstrate how the highly effective voluntary blood donor system operating in Britain could only be understood by reference to the establishment of a NATIONAL HEALTH SERVICE, which offered treatment to all on the basis of medical NEED rather than ability to pay. He contrasts this approach with the commercial blood donation system in the USA, which suppressed expressions of altruism and functioned in a less efficient way.

TITMUSS has been criticized for his over-optimistic views of human nature. Commentators have emphasized the need to recognize that self-interest is of key importance in terms of understanding human motivation. This has given rise to considerable debate over the question of whether state welfare systems should be organized on the assumption that CITIZENS are self-interested rather than altruistic. In addition, questions have been raised as to whether it is possible for the WELFARE STATE to engender greater levels of altruism within a competitive market society. (RMP)

Ancillary services

Support services such as cleaning, laundry and catering traditionally provided in-house by health, education and other authorities. Against strong trade-union resistance, governments in the 1980s and 1990s sought to increase private provision of these services through the introduction of COMPETITIVE TENDERING and market testing. More recently the emphasis has been on securing providers, public or private, which offer BEST VALUE. (SB)

Annual Employment Survey (AES)

Replaced the CENSUS OF EMPLOYMENT, which was last carried out in 1993. Data from sampled workplaces are fed into an estimation process that enables results to be produced for the whole business population. The results take the form of aggregate statistics. (JC)

Annuity

Any yearly grant or payment can be called an annuity, but the term usually refers to payments made by PENSION providers to beneficiaries of an annuity contract. The contract provides INSURANCE against the risk of living to an old age, as the annuity is payable until the death of the beneficiary (or a dependent partner). In PERSONAL PENSIONS annuities are purchased on RETIREMENT with the money accumulated in a PENSION FUND. Insurance companies invest the fund to pay for the annuity. Its value depends partly on LIFE EXPECTANCY and partly on the rate of return insurers can earn on the fund. (DM)

Appeals

Methods of REDRESS by which an individual may make a legal challenge to an official decision, such as the refusal of a SOCIAL SECURITY BENEFIT or of a place in a particular school. RIGHTS of appeal are created by statute and are only available in relation to certain kinds of legal decisions. (HD)

Area-based initiatives

Generic term used to refer to the wide range of programmes introduced at the end of the twentieth century to support REGENERATION and SOCIAL INCLUSION activity in areas with high levels of social DEPRIVA-TION. Examples include ACTION ZONES, sure start, NEW DEAL FOR COMMUNITIES and the Single Regeneration Budget (SRB). (PA)

Assessment

NEEDS assessment is a key activity for those who determine the ELIGI-BILITY of individuals for services. It is required, for example, under the 1990 National Health Service and Community Care Act for any person appearing in need of COMMUNITY CARE services. A financial assessment is used to determine the level of CHARGES. (SB)

Asset-based welfare

Measures such as the Child Trust Fund, the Saving Gateway and individual development accounts aimed to encourage individual saving and wealth-building and enable those on low incomes to build up their resources. Initially developed in the USA, it is increasingly being promoted in the UK and other societies as part of the attempt to widen opportunities and foster SOCIAL INCLUSION as well as encourage contingency planning. (MM)

Assisted places scheme

Introduced by the Conservative government in 1980 to ENABLE able children from less wealthy backgrounds to attend INDEPENDENT SCHOOLS, with their fees being remitted in relation to parental income. It was criticized for transferring pupils and resources from the state to the PRIVATE SECTOR and abolished by the Labour government in 1997. (DEG)

Asylum

Term derived from the Greek and used since the seventeenth century in the UK to signify a secure place of refuge or shelter, particularly for those institutionalized with severe MENTAL HEALTH problems (hence 'lunatic asylum'). Now applied to REFUGEES from political victimization seeking political asylum within another national jurisdiction. Here, technically, 'asylum' is the permission to remain given to a person recognized as a REFUGEE under the 1951 United Nations Convention. (GC)

Asylum Seekers

Those formally seeking political ASYLUM or refugee status but where a host country has yet to make a decision on their status. They differ from REFUGEES in that the latter individuals or households have had their refugee status endorsed by a host government, giving them associated long-term residence status and, usually, CITIZENSHIP RIGHTS. Asylum seekers have no right to employment, BENEFITS or permanent housing and are dependent on temporary and varying forms of support, often experiencing destitution. (GC)

Attlee, Clement Richard (1883–1955)

After spending part of his early adulthood as a social worker and as secretary of Toynbee Hall (1910), Attlee became a lecturer at the LSE (1912–23). He was the first Labour mayor of Stepney (1919) and served as a Labour MP for Limehouse from 1922–50. He was leader of the Labour Party from 1935 to 1955 and Prime Minister from 1945 to 1951. During his premiership, the first in which Labour had an overall majority, the foundations of the modern WELFARE STATE were put into place. He presided over the introduction of a comprehensive NATIONAL INSURANCE scheme and the establishment of the NATIONAL HEALTH SERVICE. His determination to press ahead with DEMOCRATIC SOCIAL-IST reforms in an age of austerity says much about his political acumen and his steadfast determination to improve the condition of the people. (RMP)

Audit

A procedure for checking the income and expenditure of organizations to ensure that both are properly entered into the accounts and that no individual is misusing these. In the case of UK government departments, the National Audit Office undertakes this process. The Audit

Commission audits LOCAL AUTHORITIES and the NATIONAL HEALTH SERVICE. (HG)

Autonomy

From the Greek *autos/nomos* meaning 'self-rule', belief in autonomy has been used to oppose the political power of the state as well as to provide a basis for the exercise of power by professionals and other occupational groups. It has been argued that all power relations involve both autonomy and DEPENDENCE, as even the most autonomous actor is in some degree dependent and the most dependent retains some autonomy.

Individual autonomy of action has been defined as a key 'trait' of professional groups, particularly those well-established professions such as medicine and law. In caring professions the autonomy of some groups, such as NATIONAL HEALTH SERVICE consultants, is criticized for lack of ACCOUNTABILITY for unprofessional action, while that of others, such as SOCIAL WORKERS and nurses, is more restricted by hierarchical management structures.

Participatory democracy, USER EMPOWERMENT and PARTNERSHIP working, principles in the current modernization of LOCAL GOVERNMENT, all involve power sharing and require a redefinition of professional autonomy to allow service USERS more CHOICE and independence. While giving more power to USERS is bound to take some power away from professionals, those who see power as a relational, rather than a 'zero-sum' concept, argue that redistributing power should only challenge, not destroy, professional expertise. (SB)

B

***

Barnett, Samuel Augustus (Canon) (1844–1913)

The founder and inaugural warden of Toynbee Hall in the East End of London in 1884, which was intended to provide opportunities for privileged UNIVERSITY undergraduates to mix with working-class people for their mutual benefit. Barnett's early enthusiasm for the individualistic ideas of the CHARITY ORGANIZATION SOCIETY gradually waned as he became convinced of the need for a greater degree of state intervention if the SOCIAL PROBLEMS of the age were to be resolved. (RMP)

Basic income

An alternative form of SOCIAL SECURITY provision intended to replace provision based upon SOCIAL INSURANCE or MEANS-TESTING. Basic income is also sometimes known as CITIZEN'S INCOME, GUARANTEED MINIMUM INCOME or SOCIAL DIVIDEND. The principle is that the BENEFIT should be paid to all members of society, irrespective of status or income. It would be administered by the state and financed out of taxation on earned income or wealth. If such a basic income were sufficient to provide enough for a subsistence or participation income then paid employment would effectively be optional for CITIZENS, although such a level of BENEFIT would require very high levels of taxation on any earned income. If the basic income were lower then individuals would need to supplement it with earnings, savings or other BENEFITS. A limited or partial basic income scheme would be easier to introduce but would not entirely replace current SOCIAL SECURITY BENEFITS. CHILD BENEFIT is in effect a current example of a partial basic income for children, or their CARERS. (PA)

Beacon status

A title, supported by extra funding, awarded to LOCAL AUTHORITIES and other service providers denoting the high standard of their provision and their role as a model for others to emulate through a range of dissemination, consultancy and PARTNERSHIP arrangements. (MM)

Benchmarking

A method of securing continuous organizational and service improvement through the identification and incorporation of good practice. Originating in private industry, it increasingly applies to public agencies, particularly through BEST VALUE requirements. It involves providers comparing their performance both with similar agencies, including those deemed 'market leaders', and the overall criteria set by government with a view to demonstrably and continuously enhancing provision, reducing differentials and securing high quality. (MM)

Benefits

A generic term used to refer to the payments made to CLAIMANTS under the SOCIAL SECURITY scheme. Different types of benefit are paid at different levels to different groups of claimants. See BEREAVEMENT ALLOWANCES, CATEGORICAL, CHILD, CONTINGENT, CONTRIBUTORY, EARNINGS-RELATED, FLAT-RATE, INCOME-RELATED, INDEXING OF, IN-KIND, NON-CONTRIBUTORY, SURVIVORS, WIDOWS/WIDOWERS.

Bentham, Jeremy (1748–1832)

One of the leading philosophers and reformers of his age, Bentham developed the theory of UTILITARIANISM (the greatest happiness for the greatest number) and endeavoured to apply this doctrine to various aspects of public life. By the meticulous collection of evidence he believed that it was possible to determine whether a particular institution was conforming to this principle.

His ideas on POVERTY and the POOR LAW, which were explored in his book *Pauper Management Improved* (1798), underpinned the New POOR LAW of 1834. Believing that individuals will always seek to maximize their pleasure while avoiding pain, Bentham sought to curb POOR LAW dependency by the adoption of the principle of LESS ELIGIBILITY and the introduction of the WORKHOUSE test.

While Bentham was a firm supporter of LAISSEZ-FAIRE in the economic sphere he was persuaded by the merits of interventionism in the social arena. Indeed, for Bentham, individualist and collectivist approaches were compatible with UTILITARIANISM.

Bentham's belief that it was possible to create the good society by means of appropriately designed laws and well-functioning institutions led him to advocate a range of autocratic measures, not least his panopticon prison scheme. In later life he became more receptive to the virtues of representative democracy. (RMP)

Bereavement Allowances

Short-term benefits paid to widows and widowers below pensionable age to enable them to cope with the immediate costs of the loss of a spouse. (MM)

Best Value

A statutory duty placed on all LOCAL AUTHORITIES from 2000 to pursue continuous improvement and deliver services to clear standards (covering both cost and quality) by the most economic, EFFICIENT and EFFECTIVE means available. Replacing the narrower requirements of compulsory COMPETITIVE TENDERING, it obliges them to establish clear objectives and PERFORMANCE INDICATORS, annual improvement plans and a five-yearly review cycle. Services have to be reviewed according to four criteria (the 4 Cs). Authorities have to 'consult' with local CITIZENS and USERS; 'compare' performance with their own and national indicators and those of similar providers; 'challenge' the need for and form of current provision; and 'compete' by testing its EFFICIENCY and EFFECTIVENESS relative to statutory and non-statutory alternatives, establishing which offers best value. They are also required to develop a more PARTNERSHIP-based approach and take cognizance of issues of EQUITY and SUSTAINABILITY.

Best Value principles also apply to other public bodies and, through PARTNERSHIP and contracting arrangements, also affect non-statutory agencies. They are central to government policies for modernization and renewal and the REGULATION of public services. (MM)

Bevan, Aneurin (1897–1960)

Born in Tredegar in South Wales, Bevan became a miner at the age of
13, combining this with work as both a councillor and chairman of the
South Wales Miners' Federation Lodge. He was an Independent Labour
and then Labour MP for Ebbw Vale from 1929–60. Briefly expelled
from the Labour Party in 1939 for supporting the formation of a
Popular Front, he rejoined in 1940, becoming Minister of Health in
1945. His greatest achievement was unquestionably the establishment
of the NATIONAL HEALTH SERVICE, which he realized by nationalizing
the hospitals, buying off opposition (most notably the consultants) and
forging an uneasy concord with the GP-dominated British Medical
Association (BMA). His record as Minister for Housing has attracted
criticism, not least because of his unwillingness to compromise quality
for quantity. Although he fell well short of his ambitious house-
building target, his success in overseeing the construction of a million
affordable dwellings of a good standard for lower-income families was
a considerable feat. He became Minister of Labour and National Service
in 1951 but resigned over the issue of NATIONAL HEALTH SERVICE
CHARGES in the same year. His fundamentalist SOCIALIST beliefs, not
least his insistence on the importance of nationalization, which he set
out in his book *In Place of Fear* (1951), led to serious disagreements
with reformers such as GAITSKELL, who eventually defeated him in the
party leadership contest of 1955. (RMP)

Beveridge, William Henry (1879–1963)

After graduating from Oxford in 1901, Beveridge decided not to follow
a legal or academic career. Instead he pursued his interest in the scientific resolution of SOCIAL PROBLEMS. He accepted an offer from Canon
BARNETT to become sub-warden of Toynbee Hall (the Oxford SETTLE-
MENT in East London). At Toynbee Hall he was attracted to the Webbian
(see WEBBS) notions of a NATIONAL MINIMUM and administrative
reform. He became a firm advocate of old age PENSIONS and free school
meals and accepted the need for government action to tackle UNEM-
PLOYMENT. Towards the end of 1905 he joined the *Morning Post*
as a leader writer and published a stream of articles on social and
economic questions of the day. A visit to Germany during this period
confirmed his belief in the importance of both LABOUR EXCHANGES
and SOCIAL INSURANCE as a means of combating UNEMPLOYMENT.
Shortly after advancing the case for the introduction of such policies in

evidence to the Royal Commission on the Poor Law (1905–9), Beveridge was invited by Winston Churchill, the Liberal President of the Board of Trade, to help in the preparation of new legislation on UNEMPLOY-MENT as a non-established civil servant. Working with LLEWELLYN SMITH, he helped to draw up the Labour Exchanges Act of 1909 and Part II of the National Insurance Act of 1911. Beveridge became a permanent civil servant in 1909, rising to the rank of assistant secretary (1913). Subsequently he helped in the drafting of the Munitions of War Act (which was heavily criticized by trade unionists because it constrained the rights of workers) and new UNEMPLOYMENT Insurance legislation.

Beveridge's less than cordial relations with the trade union movement resulted in a move from the new Ministry of Labour to the Ministry of Food in 1916. In 1919 he accepted an invitation from SIDNEY WEBB to become Director of the LSE. In his new post Beveridge succeeded not only in attracting scholars such as Laski, Hobhouse, TAWNEY, Robbins and HAYEK to the school, but also in securing funds for an expansion in activity. While successful in ensuring that the LSE became an influential centre for the social sciences his high-handed administrative style and unyielding commitment to positivism brought him into conflict with many academics. According to his biographer, Jose Harris, there was a general sense of relief when he accepted an appointment as Master of University College Oxford in 1937.

At the outbreak of war in 1939 Beveridge cherished the hope that he might be invited to play the key role in the control and direction of labour. However, it was not until 1940 that he was invited by Ernest Bevin to carry out a survey of the government's requirements for labour and, subsequently, to devise a list of reserved occupations. Beveridge's desire to take full control in the direction of civilian labour was dashed by Bevin. Bevin believed that Beveridge had effectively disqualified himself from such a role by his hostility towards the trade unions during the First World War. Accordingly, Beveridge was asked to head an inter-departmental inquiry into the co-ordination of SOCIAL INSURANCE and allied services in June 1941. Beveridge quickly overcame his disappointment at being sidelined in this way and used this opportunity to set out his own long-term vision for SOCIAL POLICY. After eighteen months of detailed research and consultation, he published his report on *Social Insurance and Allied Services* in December 1942. Beveridge advocated the scything down of the five giants of idleness, ignorance, disease, squalor and want by means of a free NATIONAL HEALTH SERVICE, FAMILY ALLOWANCES, and a universal SOCIAL INSURANCE scheme to cover all of the main RISKS CITIZENS faced from the cradle to the grave. Beveridge was adamant that his proposals would only prove effective if the government was committed to the maintenance of FULL EMPLOYMENT – an issue he dealt with at length in his companion volume *Full Employment in a Free Society* (1944).

According to his biographer Harris, Beveridge's report on SOCIAL INSURANCE with its 'mingled tone of optimism, patriotism, high principle and pragmatism exactly fitted the prevailing popular mood'. Coming shortly after the Allied victory at El Alamein the report was greeted with acclaim by the general public (sales topped the 70,000 mark just a few days after publication), but the official reaction was noticeably cooler. Although the coalition government supported the proposals in broad principle, it was felt that further detailed scrutiny by a civil service committee was necessary. Beveridge was dismayed by the government's tepid response and decided that he could best promote his plan by entering the world of politics. He resigned his post at Oxford and entered parliament as Liberal MP for Berwick-upon-Tweed in 1944. He failed to keep his seat at the 1945 election and subsequently went to the House of Lords.

Beveridge was critical of the incoming Labour government's approach to SOCIAL INSURANCE, in particular its decision to provide PENSIONS immediately at a substantially lower level than he had recommended, thereby undermining the principle of adequacy. His desire for collectivist solutions to problems such as POVERTY and UNEMPLOYMENT was tempered by his support for market activity and the need to preserve personal and constitutional FREEDOMS. For example, his strong commitment to state interventionism in economic affairs in the early 1940s needs to be contrasted with his championing of VOLUNTARY ACTION, not least by the FRIENDLY SOCIETIES. (RMP)

Bills

Measures under consideration by a legislature that become ACTS on completion of all the legislative stages. In the UK this means being passed by both houses of parliament and receiving the royal assent. (MJH)

Birth rate

See FERTILITY RATE

Bismarck, Otto von (1815–1898)

German Chancellor between 1871 and 1890. With the aim of weakening an increasingly influential labour movement he introduced the first ever compulsory state SOCIAL INSURANCE schemes in the 1880s, consisting of health insurance (1883), accident insurance (1884) and invalidity and old age PENSION insurance (1889). (JC)

Blue Book

An obsolete generic term for major UK government reports, which were traditionally published in a blue cover. (MJH)

British Household Panel Survey (BHPS)

A multi-purpose panel survey of each adult (16+) member of a sample of about 5,000 households in the UK that started in 1991. Since then respondents have been reinterviewed every year, including those who form new households. Since 1994 it includes a separate interview for children aged over 11. (JM)

British Social Attitudes Survey

A large-scale sample survey of public attitudes normally carried out annually by Social and Community Planning research with core funding from Sainsbury Family Charitable Trusts and additional funding from various sources, including government departments. It produces data on attitude change and a varying range of social issues. (MJH)

Budget Standards

See POVERTY

Building societies

Financial institutions whose activities were originally focused around housing and which continued to have a major part of their activity related to lending for house purchase and funding for REGISTERED SOCIAL LANDLORDS. The original building societies were terminating societies, set up to enable people to build their own homes. They became permanent, retaining a mutual status in which their investors were shareholders and no dividends or properties were distributed. They had a strong focus on the small saver and the house purchaser, and an extensive range of local high street branches. In the 1980s new legislation and REGULATION arrangements put building societies in a position where they could compete on equal terms with banks and in subsequent years a number of the largest building societies have converted to banks and ceased to be mutual organizations. These banks are no longer building societies. The building society movement is consequently smaller but retains its historical attributes of mutuality and support for housing and retail banking. (AM)

Bureaucracy

A term encapsulating the structuring of organizations and their activities along clearly defined hierarchical and functional lines. Decision-making powers are concentrated in the upper level and staff allocated to different ranks according to their tasks and responsibilities, accountable to their superiors and subject to codified rules and procedures. For the early twentieth-century founders of state welfare it appeared intrinsically superior to the discretionary DESERT-based approach characteristic of the POOR LAW and contemporary VOLUNTARY WELFARE. Offering a predictable and impartial means of administering and delivering BENEFITS and large-scale services efficiently and uniformly, it became the organizational norm for central and LOCAL GOVERNMENT. Though such structures were also common in large companies, public bureaucracies were increasingly criticized from the 1980s. USER groups questioned their supposed neutrality and lack of ACCOUNTABILITY. NEO-LIBERAL and PUBLIC CHOICE analysts highlighted broader inflexibilities and the inefficiencies resulting from the absence of competition, arguing that services were provider- rather than USER-driven and asserting the superiority of market mechanisms. Such criticisms have contributed to the ongoing restructuring of public service bureaucracies along MANAGERIALIST lines and the introduction of tighter regulatory frameworks. (MM)

Bureau-professionalism

An organizational structure characteristic of many state welfare agencies, based on combining the administrative advantages of BUREAU-

CRACY with the employment of specialist professional staff. The former facilitated publicly accountable, standardized provision, the latter offered an expert-based means of assessing USER NEEDS and dispensing appropriate treatment. Though the balance between the two varied from service to service, with professional DISCRETION being more extensive in the NATIONAL HEALTH SERVICE than other areas, the combination was held to safeguard consumers and meet their NEEDS effectively. It was also held to engender a strong public service ethos. Like BUREAUCRATIC processes and PROFESSIONALISM more generally, it has been criticized by NEW RIGHT analysts and USER groups who challenged both its EFFI-CIENCY and the notion of disinterested, consumer-oriented provision. (MM)

Butler, Richard Austen (1902–1982)

Elected as a Conservative MP in 1935 and appointed as President of the Board of Education by Churchill in 1941, Butler introduced the 1944 Education Act that attempted to increase opportunity for working-class children by making academic merit, rather than ability to pay, the main selection criterion for SECONDARY EDUCATION. Although Butler held many prominent government posts he was to prove unsuccessful in his two bids to lead the Conservative Party. (RMP)

Butskellism

The term first appeared in the *Economist* in 1954. It was argued that the economic policies being pursued by the then Conservative Chancellor BUTLER had become virtually indistinguishable from those of the shadow minister HUGH GAITSKELL. Subsequently the term was used to describe the so-called consensus between the Conservatives and the Labour Party over such issues as FULL EMPLOYMENT, economic interventionism and the WELFARE STATE. It remains a matter of contention as to how deep this agreement was, not least because of the deep divisions within each of the parties. This consensus began to unravel in the early 1970s as the Conservatives under Edward Heath adopted more distinctive free-market economic policies and advocated a greater degree of SELECTIVITY in the area of social policy. This shift away from the post-1945 consensus became more marked after Margaret Thatcher took over the leadership of the Conservative Party in 1975. (RMP)

C

Care management

This was known as case management before the National Health Service and Community Care Act 1990. Typically a care manager works with an individual to assess their NEEDS, plan a care package, and monitor and review arrangements once in place. In some LOCAL AUTHORITIES, however, ASSESSMENT and other care management functions have been separated. (SB)

Care managers

Employees, usually with SOCIAL WORK training, of LOCAL AUTHORITY SOCIAL SERVICE DEPARTMENTS in England and Wales (and their equivalents in Scotland and Northern Ireland) responsible for people in need of continuing or LONG TERM CARE. Their work involves assessing NEED, constructing a care package in consultation with the USER (and where appropriate the CARER) through marshalling services from the MIXED ECONOMY OF WELFARE and assessing the USER's ability to pay for these. (CU)

Care order

In England and Wales a court may make a care order, which transfers to a LOCAL AUTHORITY certain parental responsibilities for a child and the power to determine where the child lives. The primary ground for making a care order is that the child is suffering or is likely to suffer significant harm. (MH)

Carers

Providers of care for adults and children. Traditionally the term denoted individuals who carry out unpaid INFORMAL CARE and, in the British literature, usually referred only to the care of people with special needs. However, recently the use of the term has begun to shift. First, carers are increasingly perceived as those who deliver care to all people who need it. In this sense, they are – typically – mothers of young children. Hence debates about CITIZENSHIP are increasingly concerned with the ways in which 'care' in general, and mothering in particular, can be integrated into an inclusive WELFARE STATE. Second, it is increasingly also applied to those who are paid to care, either by a USER or by a public or non-statutory agency. Nevertheless, the term always includes those who look after people living in their own or in their carers' homes. These carers are very often related to the people they care for, and normally provide the care for no financial reward. Third, while such caring (and caring more broadly) is still a predominantly female responsibility, quantitative national sample surveys have shown that almost as many men as women undertake unpaid care, but women undertake personal care much more than men. (CU)

Case management

See CARE MANAGEMENT

Categorical benefits

BENEFITS are categorical when one of the ELIGIBILITY criteria is membership of a category. The categories used in determining BENEFIT eligibility usually relate to some identified cause of NEED or income shortfall, such as UNEMPLOYMENT, DISABILITY, old age, or the presence of a child or children in the household (as with CHILD BENEFIT). (DM)

Census of Employment

From 1971 to 1993 this provided data for the UK, including the level and distribution of employment, regional labour market information, the gender distribution of employment and the prevalence of full- and part-time jobs. It was based on a large sample size census and has been replaced by the ANNUAL EMPLOYMENT SURVEY. (JC)

Census of Population

Most countries conduct regular population counts to establish basic demographic data and elicit other information about their populations. In the UK such surveys date back to 1801 and are held every ten years. (MJH)

Centralization

Britain has a unitary state in which the only powers that may be exercised by regional or LOCAL GOVERNMENT are those that have been expressly delegated or granted to them by parliament. In turn the executive (the Prime Minister and cabinet) is able to exercise considerable control over the parliamentary process and agenda. In spite of an important trend towards greater WELFARE PLURALISM, the last part of the twentieth century saw increased centralization. On the one hand, central government took steps ever more directly to control LOCAL GOVERNMENT spending. On the other, the office of the Prime Minister began to accrue ever-greater autonomy. Since 1997 the government has embarked on a policy of regional DEVOLUTION and a number of PARTNERSHIP initiatives involving LOCAL GOVERNMENT. However, critics argue that ultimate political power remains firmly centralized and while the processes of GOVERNANCE may have become more diffuse, central government continues to dictate the terms on which welfare is produced and organized. See also DECENTRALIZATION. (HD)

Chadwick, Edwin (1810–1890)

Secretary to the UTILITARIAN philosopher Jeremy BENTHAM and subsequently a civil servant responsible for the reform and early administration of the New POOR LAW, and the development of PUBLIC HEALTH services. He was also influential in developing the registration of population data and the introduction of competitive entry examinations for the civil service. (DEG)

Chalmers, Thomas (1780–1847)

An influential Scottish churchman, political economist and powerful advocate of the moral superiority of voluntary support of the poor. His views on individual help, MUTUAL AID and district visiting, developed in a deprived parish in Glasgow, were influential in the work of the CHARITY ORGANIZATION SOCIETY. (DEG)

Charges

Payments made for ACCESS to a public service, such as PRESCRIPTION CHARGES for medicines prescribed by a doctor. Charges are also made for many LOCAL AUTHORITY PERSONAL SOCIAL SERVICES such as HOME HELPS. Charges differ from a market price in the open market. They are usually below cost and may be subject to a MEANS-TEST. Certain types of USER are often exempt, for example people over 60, the long-term sick and those on INCOME SUPPORT are exempt from PRESCRIPTION CHARGES. The aims of charging are varied. They may be used to raise revenue, to discourage frivolous use, or for symbolic reasons to indicate that the government is concerned about public spending. They have disadvantages. They may deter people from using the service they need. The fact that they are subject to an income test means that a family may have to pay more for a whole range of services as they try to increase their income or move back into work, creating a POVERTY TRAP. See also PRESCRIPTION CHARGES. (HG)

Charity

Generally a positive concept implying a love of humanity, but popular sayings such as 'cold as charity' and 'I don't want your charity' reflect experiences which can be demeaning and unpleasant as well as expressions of good will. Tensions within both the concept and the practice are long-standing; in early Christian thought on this matter there were two broad schools, the one embracing open, unconstrained love and the other anxious to discriminate in favour of 'true' NEED and the work ethic. The subsequent REGULATION and development of charitable activity reflects these different interpretations and their relationship to different interest groups in society. For example, the religious tradition has led to the growth of a wide range of organizations committed to the direct relief of suffering and POVERTY. Similarly, humanitarian and religious philosophies, particularly during nineteenth-century industrial growth, shaped a growing number of 'foundations' responsible for funding research and action with a charitable focus.

The state has intervened, since the 1601 POOR LAW Act, to define, register and monitor charities, in part to focus the notion of charity concern with the very poor, itinerants and HOMELESS, but also to limit the political actions of registered charities. Thus charity is legally defined to apply to organizations set up to promote

- the relief of POVERTY;
- the advancement of education;
- the advancement of religion;
- other purposes beneficial to the community.

By and large the British charity laws are more restrictive than most, although the operationalization of these criteria and popular perception of them are often markedly divergent. For example, many fee-paying INDEPENDENT or PUBLIC SCHOOLS enjoy a charitable status often first granted centuries ago.

Legal definition of charitable status is important because it leads to significant tax exemptions and privileges. LOCAL AUTHORITIES must allow at least 80 per cent relief from the uniform business RATE on a building such as a community centre, while individual and corporate donations to charities qualify for relief from INCOME TAX. However, registered charities are also subject to REGULATION and control, in particular by the Charity Commission.

The registration of organizations as charitable involves three basic types, each with its own constitution.

- Trusts, where large numbers of people need not be involved, and management can be vested in trustees; for example, the provision of aid to specific types of animal or bird, or to particular categories of people such as REFUGEES.
- Unincorporated Institutions, where membership is central, as in a parent–teacher association or a village hall.
- Company limited by guarantee, where the legally separate company can hold property and enter into a variety of legal relationships; an example here might be a committee representing a grouping of charities established to coordinate aid during large-scale disasters.

Estimating the numbers of registered charities is a hazardous business; for England and Wales the Charity Commission will provide a figure of about 185,000. In Scotland, legislation specifically addressing the REGULATION of charities is less than ten years old, and so the figure of

25,000 is thought to be an overestimate. Northern Ireland has no official register; the main INTERMEDIARY AGENCY estimates 5,000 organizations defined as voluntary, but uses different criteria from its counterparts on the mainland.

As increasing numbers of individuals and organizations use the concept of 'charity' to confer legitimacy on their activities – from a door-to-door salesman to an international for-profit company appearing on a national television fund-raising event – the potential for FRAUD is increased. REGULATION may be resisted and there are continuing grounds for concern about the transparency and ACCOUNTABILITY of the regulatory bodies themselves, but it is equally clear that their presence is increasingly necessary. (DWS)

Charity Organization Society (COS)

Founded in 1869 as a 'society for organizing CHARITY and repressing mendicity' (begging), it had declined considerably by the time of welfare reforms of the early twentieth century. It provides a window into the potential roles and dilemmas of a charitable agency attempting to operate in a co-ordinating way. COS was particularly concerned with 'scientific charity'. It was a forerunner of SOCIAL ADMINISTRATION and SOCIAL POLICY, promoting the idea that dimensions of social NEED could be mapped so that more appropriate policies and practices could then follow. It was also in the vanguard of the foundation of SOCIAL WORK as a profession. There was a strong moral dimension to its scientific CHARITY. COS sought to ensure that FRAUD or abuse of services was identified and outlawed. (DWS)

Charter

Describes a declaration of RIGHTS. Generally, such declarations – when they are formal – are more symbolic than specifically enforceable in nature, though the term is also sometimes used rhetorically to characterize the RIGHTS provided by a piece of substantive legislation. The great historical charters – like Magna Carta – have been primarily concerned with civil liberties and political rights. However, there are three kinds of formally constituted charters that are concerned with social rights and SOCIAL POLICY. First, there are certain international documents: the Council of Europe's SOCIAL CHARTER of 1961; the United Nations' International Covenant of Economic, Social, and Cultural

Rights made in 1966 pursuant to the Universal Declaration of Human Rights; the European Union's Charter of Fundamental Social Rights of 1989. Second, at a national level, there is the 'CITIZEN's Charter' announced by the British Prime Minister John Major in 1990, following which a number of periodically updated national charters – such as the NATIONAL HEALTH SERVICE Patients' Charter – have set out the performance standards to which various public services aspire. Third, many LOCAL AUTHORITIES publish similar charters – such as tenants' charters – informing people of their rights to services, to complain and/or to be consulted. (HD)

Chartism

A short-lived working-class political reform movement of the 1830s and 1840s which embodied the notion that political reform was essential to social improvement. Its central demands – full adult male suffrage, vote by secret ballot and the payment of MPs – were set out in a People's CHARTER. (DEG)

Child Benefit

A universal TRANSFER payment made by governments to parents or guardians towards the upkeep of their dependent children. Most developed countries, except the USA, pay some child benefit. Payment levels vary greatly between countries. Often the rate varies with birth order or the age of the child. In the UK Child Benefit replaced FAMILY ALLOWANCES in 1978. (MH)

Child care

First, child care may refer to services that provide daytime care of pre-school children, often while their parents are working. In this sense, child care covers day NURSERIES, nursery schools and classes, CHILDMINDERS, and playgroups. Providers include LOCAL GOVERNMENT, voluntary agencies and private individuals or organizations. Some NURSERIES and groups give priority to physical care or play, while others emphasize an educational role. Increasingly children's centres or family centres seek to combine all these functions. Family centres may also offer classes, groups or individual support for parents, mainly mothers.

Second, child care has been the traditional term in Britain and elsewhere for what is usually termed child welfare in North America. This mainly focuses on children who are LOOKED AFTER on a 24-hour basis in FOSTER CARE or RESIDENTIAL CARE, as well as those who are ADOPTED. Attention is also given to preventative arrangements providing family support so that the need for children to be placed away from home is reduced. In Britain the legal responsibility for such CHILDREN'S SERVICES lies with LOCAL GOVERNMENT (Health and Social Services Boards in Northern Ireland). (MH)

Child protection

Coined in the 1980s to denote the responses of public agencies to child abuse by members of the child's family or other CARERS. In the UK SOCIAL WORK services are the lead agency in responding to suspected abuse, with duties to safeguard the child's welfare and to provide appropriate services. The police usually also have a role to investigate whether a crime has been committed. Health professionals and teachers make significant contributions to identification, ASSESSMENT and support. A series of well publicized inquiries in the 1970s and 1980s led to changes in legislation and practice, which emphasized rescue of children thought to be at serious risk of severe physical injuries or neglect. Subsequently, attention shifted to child sexual abuse, with views varying on its extent and the best ways of responding. Research showed that many families were subject to investigations that neither identified abuse, nor provided positive services. Consequently, policy shifts took place at central and LOCAL GOVERNMENT levels, which sought to 'refocus' services towards family support. Revelations of past and current physical and sexual abuse in FOSTER and RESIDENTIAL CARE have prompted measures for registration of known abusers, screening applicants and whistle blowing. (MH)

Child support

Payments made for the upkeep of a child following the divorce or legal separation of that child's parents. In nearly all Western countries parents and sometimes other relatives are legally obliged to support their children, whether or not they are living with them. When non-resident parents (usually fathers) do not provide financially for their children, there is a high risk of POVERTY. Moreover, the state may then become responsible for maintenance. Various court and/or administrative systems have been established to try to enforce parental payments. A number of countries have fixed national scales related to the income of the payer, but elsewhere the amounts to be paid are calculated on a DISCRETIONARY basis according to each case. Sanctions include compulsory deduction of earnings and imprisonment. The UK Child Support Agency introduced in 1991 has been criticized for making excessive demands on some fathers, failing to relieve the material disadvantage of LONE PARENT families and causing distress. (MH)

Childminder

Someone who looks after another person's child during the daytime. Normally the parents are working and are charged a fee, though LOCAL AUTHORITIES may meet the costs in specified circumstances. Nearly all childminders are women. They are required to register and fulfil minimum safety and care conditions. (MH)

Children's Hearings

Scotland has a Children's Hearings system with similar functions to those of youth or juvenile courts in most other countries, but operating more informally. ACCESS to the hearings is made via a CHILDREN'S REPORTER, who investigates referrals and has DISCRETION to decide whether a case should be pursued. Children may be referred because of concerns about their care or protection, offending, behaviour or school non-attendance. If the facts of the case are disputed, a court determines these. When the grounds of referral are accepted or proven, a panel of three lay members makes the decision about what should happen. Panel members are recruited from the general public and need have no formal qualifications. They do undertake training for the role. To consider the case and make their decision, the panel meets with the child, parents and other relevant persons in an informal setting. The paramount consideration is the child's welfare. It may be agreed that voluntary measures are sufficient, but the panel is empowered to make a supervision requirement or order. The child will then receive compulsory supervision and support at home or be required to live in FOSTER or RESIDENTIAL CARE. (MH)

Children's homes

See RESIDENTIAL CHILD CARE

Children's Reporter

See CHILDREN'S HEARINGS

Children's rights

On account of their perceived vulnerability and lesser competencies compared with adults, children do not have certain political and social RIGHTS, such as the right to vote, marry, work full-time or drive. Their differential status is also recognized in rights specific to children, with corresponding duties laid on parents or governments. Protective rights mean that measures should be taken to safeguard children from cruelty, abuse, neglect and exploitation. Provision rights relate to services promoting survival, material security, health and education. Participatory rights require that children's views be taken into account, particularly in decisions that directly affect them. The United Nations Convention on the Rights of the Child, containing 54 Articles, was adopted by the United Nations General Assembly in 1989 and has subsequently been ratified by the great majority of nation-states. The Convention applies to everyone below the age of 18 (unless majority is reached earlier under national law). The Convention stipulates that respect for children's rights should not discriminate according to a child's characteristics or background. When judicial, administrative and welfare bodies make decisions with respect to children, the child's best interests shall be the primary consideration. Some countries have an OMBUDSMAN or Children's Commissioner to promote children's rights. (MH)

Children's Service Plans

LOCAL AUTHORITY SOCIAL SERVICES DEPARTMENTS in the UK are obliged by law to produce and review a CHILDREN'S SERVICES Plan at fixed intervals. Other statutory and voluntary services are expected to contribute to the plan, which includes information about local NEED, services provided and planned, and about relevant finances. (MH)

Children's services

The section of LOCAL AUTHORITY SOCIAL SERVICES DEPARTMENTS responsible for CHILD CARE and CHILD PROTECTION. (PA)

Choice

A characteristic of free-market exchange is that, ideally, consumers can choose from a wide range of competing products and services and their selections send providers a clear signal that they are – or are not – offering what people want. Traditionally the options available to public service USERS were limited or non-existent. Recent governments have attempted to increase alternative provision both within state services and the wider MIXED ECONOMY OF WELFARE. Concerns remain, however, that the most articulate or well-informed are likely to ACCESS the best services. (HG)

Christian democracy

A major influence on SOCIAL POLICY formation and SOCIAL POLICY development in continental European countries such as Germany, Belgium and the Netherlands. There are three core elements of Christian democratic thought:

• the possession of an elaborated body of (Catholic) social doctrine;
• a political ethic based on notions of SOCIAL INTEGRATION, class compromise, political and social mediation, accommodation and pluralism;
• a religious inspiration which historically enabled Christian democracy to appeal to voters from various social backgrounds, and has governed its internal and external emphasis on politics of mediation and accommodation. (JC)

Christian socialism

Has similar and yet somewhat different meanings in Great Britain and the US on the one hand, and in continental European countries on the other. In Germany, Italy, the Netherlands and Belgium, Christian socialism originated in the form of Catholic working-class unions which stressed co-operation between classes and class reconciliation, without neglecting religious and cultural responsibilities. In line with CORPORATIST ideals their organization was originally guild-like, that is with workers and employers co-operating within a single sectoral association. In Great Britain and the US the term stands for a kind of SOCIALIST movement in the nineteenth century which resulted from the clash between Christian ideals and the effects of capitalism. After the failure of CHARTISM Christian socialists in England promoted labourist associations and their collaboration with the church against capitalism. Their traditions were carried on by the FABIAN Society, by adherents of GUILD SOCIALISM, and by several Roman Catholic groups. (JC)

Church schools

See DENOMINATIONAL SCHOOLS

Citizens

See CITIZENSHIP

Citizen's income

Partial BASIC INCOME scheme where a more limited payment to individuals would operate as a replacement for tax allowances for income earners and a partial BENEFIT payment for non-workers. (PA)

Citizens' juries

An emerging consultative technique by which to involve lay people and service USERS in decision-making. The original concept entailed the selection of 12–16 people to hear expert evidence and draw conclusions. The term is also applied to some local survey techniques, involving larger panels. (HD)

Citizenship

A contested concept, lacking a single agreed definition. In T. H. MARSHALL's classic exposition, which has been highly influential in social policy, it consists of a number of elements:

- Membership of a national community in both the formal sense, embodied in the legal RIGHT to hold a passport, and in the substantive sense of the ability fully to participate in that community.
- The RIGHTS and obligations that flow from that membership.
- EQUALITY of status.
- An ideal that can act as an inspiration and as a measuring rod of progress, particularly today for marginalized groups and NEW SOCIAL MOVEMENTS.

MARSHALL's exposition of citizenship stands in the liberal tradition, which emphasizes the individual and his or (more recently) her RIGHTS. Here, citizenship is understood as a status. Marshall extended the liberal notion of citizenship rights beyond the civil and the political to include social rights. This is the aspect of citizenship that traditionally has been the main focus of SOCIAL POLICY.

There is also an older citizenship tradition, civic republicanism. Originating in Ancient Greece, this represented a practice, enshrined in a civic duty (on free men) to participate in the political life of the community. In contemporary policy young people's participation is increasingly an issue, leading the government to introduce compulsory citizenship education. However, today the greater emphasis is on other forms of citizenship obligation, reflecting in part the priorities of COMMUNITARIANISM. Active citizenship, through VOLUNTEERING, is one expression of this. Even more crucial is the emphasis on paid work obligations as a condition of citizenship that is dominant in policy development in many WELFARE STATES.

An emphasis on the responsibilities of citizenship can also be found in some of the NEW SOCIAL MOVEMENTS. For instance, the green movement promotes ecological citizenship, which asserts the responsibilities of humans to the environment and planet and to future generations. Some FEMINISTS assert the importance of care as a responsibility of citizenship, which should not be undervalued in relation to paid work obligations.

FEMINISM has provided one of the most powerful challenges to established citizenship theory. Whereas traditionally citizenship theory has emphasized citizenship as a force for inclusion, feminists and others have focused on the ways in which it acts as a force for exclusion. In both the civic republican and liberal traditions, citizenship was predicated on the exclusion of women. Citizenship was conceived of as pertaining to the public sphere, identified with the male; women were identified with the domestic private sphere, and therefore deemed unsuited for and incapable of citizenship. Their work in the domestic sphere facilitated men's active participation as citizens in the public sphere, a pattern which, to a lesser extent, still holds today, as women still take the main responsibility for care and domestic work in the home.

The historical pattern of the extension of civil, political and social rights identified by MARSHALL pertained to men not women. It was only gradually, and with considerable struggle, that women won the same rights as men, and then not always in the same order. Even today, women often have inferior ACCESS to social citizenship rights where, as in the UK NATIONAL INSURANCE system, they reflect male employment patterns.

It is not only FEMINISTS who have criticized traditional constructions of citizenship as exclusionary. Other groups such as black people, disabled people and gays and lesbians have challenged their second-class citizenship status. In doing so, these groups have also, sometimes implicitly, sometimes explicitly, been using citizenship as a yardstick to demonstrate that they are not enjoying the equal status that citizenship promises. In some cases they have gone further, arguing that the yardstick itself needs to be refashioned, better to reflect their particular NEEDS and perspectives. In other words they have challenged a notion of citizenship that uses a white, able-bodied, heterosexual male of working age as its norm and standard. Critical citizenship theorists attempt to rearticulate citizenship to address its exclusionary dimensions and promote a genuine UNIVERSALISM that can take account of diversity and difference.

Citizenship theory has tended to focus on the processes of inclusion and exclusion within the boundaries drawn and regulated by nation-states. This nation-state-bounded conception is under challenge in the face of growing numbers of ASYLUM SEEKERS and migrants, excluded at national borders, as well as other factors prompting a more internationalist perspective, such as GLOBALIZATION and ENVIRONMENTALISM. The notion of European citizenship has also taken on greater salience, and been promoted in the EU, with the status of 'Citizens of the Union' enshrined in the Maastricht Treaty. Within the UK DEVOLUTION is also raising questions of citizenship and national identity. See also ACTIVE CITIZENSHIP (RL)

Civil rights

One of the three principal kinds of RIGHTS that make up the rights of CITIZENSHIP. They encompass civil liberties (such as the right to life, freedom of religion and expression, etc.) and legal rights (for example, to own property or enforce contracts through the courts). (HD)

Civil society

Institutional and social relationships which are located outside the state. At the most general level, civil society is not so much about tangible institutions as the different 'spaces' wherein combinations of PRIVATE, VOLUNTARY and INFORMAL SECTORS interact.

There are different views about the advantages and disadvantages of civil society. Neo-CONSERVATIVES wish to expand their version of civil society by emphasizing individualistic values and goals; state BUREAU-CRACY is to be distrusted and self-interest encouraged. The central features are of self-reliance and private property rather than collective association and public services.

SOCIAL DEMOCRATS insist that a vital role of civil society is to nurture and safeguard the CITIZEN against corporate abuse of power (by the state and commercial interests), allowing for a much stronger state presence. The latter is a necessary condition of democratization, for unless a powerful agency (the state) guarantees (by defining and maintaining) civil society, there is a danger that disruption and disorder will become cumulative and endemic.

The intellectual left (including MARXISTS) promote civil society from an oppositional stance, arguing that PARTICIPATION in civil society merely serves a latent function as a means of deflecting attention away from the economic sphere.

Civil society has become more prominent in academic and political debate at the beginning of the twenty-first century, in part because of distrust of both market and state approaches to policy provision. (DWS)

Claimant

As most SOCIAL SECURITY BENEFITS have to be claimed by recipients, the term captures the pro-active nature of BENEFIT receipt, as a result of which some do not TAKE-UP all their RIGHTS TO BENEFIT. (PA)

Classic welfare state

See WELFARE STATE

Clinical governance

A statutory duty placed on all NATIONAL HEALTH SERVICE organizations since 1999 with the aim of securing high standards of care, safeguarding patients against poor professional performance and reducing variations between providers. Each hospital, community trust and GP service has to institute measures to monitor and continuously improve clinical care, implement the standards and service frameworks developed by the National Institute for Clinical Excellence (NICE) and identify and manage poor performance. Progress is scrutinized by annual self-assessments and by the Commission for Health Improvement. (MM)

Cohabitation

Living together as a couple not legally married. In 2000 estimates are that there are about 1.5 million cohabiting heterosexual couples in Great Britain. This is mainly pre- or post-marriage, not usually instead of marriage. A key policy issue concerns the inconsistent treatment of cohabitation in family law, tax and SOCIAL SECURITY. (JM)

Cole, George Douglas Howard (1899–1959)

A SOCIALIST theoretician and activist, Cole joined the FABIAN Society in 1908, but resigned, temporarily as it transpired, in 1915 as a result of Labour's fraternization with the Liberals. He joined the Fabian Research Department (which was eventually renamed the Labour Research Department) in 1913 and worked there until 1928. He established the New Fabian Research Bureau in 1931 and was chair of the FABIAN Society from 1939 to 1946 and from 1948 to 1950. He was a tutor for the Workers' Education Association and a London university lecturer from 1921–4 before taking up a readership at Oxford, where he went on to become a Professor of Social and Political Theory (1944–57). His publications include *The World of Labour* (1913), *Guild Socialism Restated* (1920) and *The Condition of Britain* (with Margaret Cole, 1937). Cole helped to shift Labour opinion towards greater use of state intervention in the economy to achieve social objectives. He is best known for his advocacy of GUILD SOCIALISM – a variant of SYNDICALISM based on the medieval guild system. Guild SOCIALISTS disliked the BUREAUCRATIC nationalization of industry, arguing instead for workers' control through the trade unions. Cole was a leading supporter of the

National Guilds League, which was formed in 1915 by erstwhile members of the FABIAN Society. The league was disbanded in 1925 following an unsuccessful foray into housing construction. (RMP)

Commissioning

A process introduced in the early 1990s, whereby health service agencies and LOCAL AUTHORITY SOCIAL SERVICE DEPARTMENTS profile local NEEDS, assess these against available public and independent provision, prepare annual plans and develop and purchase services through contracts and SERVICE AGREEMENTS. While originally intended to encourage competition, it increasingly involves a consultative, PARTNERSHIP approach. (MM)

Commodification

The process of increasing marketization of production and distribution in society. In pre-capitalist societies social reproduction was only partly dependent on the labour contract – that is the commodity form of labour was incomplete. With capitalism becoming the dominant form of production, markets became the principal location for exchanging goods as well as labour. As a result, labour became a commodity in the sense that workers' survival became contingent on the successful sale of their labour power, while social reproduction outside the labour contract became increasingly difficult and precarious. See also DECOMMODIFICATION. (JC)

Communitarianism

This is the notion that collective interests and collective action are best developed at the level of local COMMUNITIES. Communitarian approaches can exist alongside public provision of welfare services, but strong adherents to the communitarian approach argue that COMMUNITY activity is always preferable to state provision. (DWS)

Community

Social relationships and social identities which may be characterized by relative closeness, familiarity, shared interests or significance. Communities may be spatial (or geographic) – a local neighbourhood of a few streets – or social – a network of friends or members of an interest community or a wider identity grouping defined, for example, by ethnicity or sexuality. Closeness, familiarity and significance can be exclusive as well as inclusive, and communities may in practice act to exclude stigmatized individuals or groups. (DWS)

Community action

The development by local COMMUNITIES of campaigning activity to respond to specific local problems, such as housing or environmental conditions, crime and vandalism, or the availability and quality of play facilities. COMMUNITY action is usually focused on particular issues and is therefore generally of a temporary nature. (DWS)

Community association

Local groups of people with common purposes of a non-profit distributing kind; they frequently express these in more or less formal rules. Typical examples are village halls; a section of a church or school; common activities involve pre-school playgroups, youth clubs, luncheon clubs for older people and other leisure and educational pursuits. (DWS)

Community capacity building

See COMMUNITY DEVELOPMENT

Community care

A set of policy objectives and the arrangements for implementing them, first developed in the late 1950s in response to concerns over traditional institutional forms of care for people with MENTAL HEALTH problems and LEARNING DIFFICULTIES. Initially the primary aim was to replace the huge hospitals built by the Victorians on out-of-town country estates with small, 'homely' units in the COMMUNITY, a process facilitated by the rapid development of drug therapy, especially tranquillizers, which meant that long-term custodial care was no longer thought necessary.

From the 1960s, particularly the 1970s, this policy, enshrined in the 1959 Mental Health Act, was extended to elder care and in the process took on a different meaning. This became manifest with the publication in 1978 of a consultative document called, significantly, *A Happier Old Age*, which argued that elderly people would be happier if they were able to remain in their own homes, cared for 'by' the COMMUNITY. Thus the meaning of the term 'community care' slipped, in the 1970s, from meaning care 'in' the COMMUNITY to care 'by' the COMMUNITY. The intention was that public funds would be switched from RESIDENTIAL to DOMICILIARY CARE and that INFORMAL CARE would play a major part in provision for the elderly and others with special and long-term NEEDS.

The policy to close the vast mental hospitals was very slow to get off the ground, but took off in the 1990s, partially as a result of the property boom which made their large, semi-rural sites attractive to developers. As far as the elderly were concerned, the policy was a complete failure. Although many LOCAL AUTHORITY RESIDENTIAL CARE homes closed, between 1980 and 1990 the number of elderly people living in RESIDENTIAL CARE increased by 52 per cent and exceeded the growth in population aged over 75. This was due to a very rapid expansion of PRIVATE SECTOR RESIDENTIAL CARE funded by SOCIAL SECURITY arrangements that meant that those with low incomes were able to enter care without bearing the costs. It was also clear that elderly people, especially those aged over 85 and with the resources to do so (whether from the SOCIAL SECURITY system, their own income and wealth, or the support of their kin CARERS), were opting to enter RESIDENTIAL CARE in very large numbers. In 1991, 23.7 per cent of people aged 85 and over were in RESIDENTIAL CARE.

A strong FEMINIST critique of the policy for community care began as soon as its implementation took off in the 1970s. This was partially an accident of timing. Just as the rhetoric of 'community care' was finding its place high on the SOCIAL POLICY agenda, so the British women's movement with its particular focus on the family and the oppressions contained within it, and a FEMINIST critique of the way in which the WELFARE STATE exploited women, also began to develop. The particular FEMINIST criticisms of policies for 'community care' were based on the assumption of the availability of women's unpaid labour within the home: as the first piece of FEMINIST criticism published in 1980 put it: 'care by the community equals care by the family equals care by women'.

Since then the FEMINIST critique has developed to take account of the fact that, according to quantitative national sample surveys, there are almost as many men as women who are CARERS and that there are other significant divisions between class, 'race' and ethnicity, residence and co-residence, when it comes to care for people that is unpaid. It is also the case that FEMINISTS were addressing one fraction of the whole of 'community care', namely the part of care that is delivered by CARERS who have a long biography with the person they care for, and who are not being paid or employed to care. This essentially unpaid part of 'community care' is now named as INFORMAL CARE.

Community care is also a set of arrangements laid down in the National Health Service and Community Care Act, 1990. This legislation, and the codes of guidance accompanying it, changed the way in which LOCAL AUTHORITIES are funded, so that there are now very strong INCENTIVES on them to develop DOMICILIARY CARE to ensure that people with special NEEDS can remain in their own homes rather than enter RESIDENTIAL CARE. The original funding came partially from the SOCIAL SECURITY budget that paid for the RESIDENTIAL CARE fees of very poor elderly people. This SUBSIDY has now been stopped.

At the same time, with the aim of promoting a MIXED ECONOMY OF WELFARE, the LOCAL AUTHORITY's role was changed from that of service provider to an ENABLER, charged with COMMISSIONING and contracting services from competing PRIVATE SECTOR and VOLUNTARY organizations and fostering INFORMAL CARE. To support this shift, separate purchasing and provider units (the PURCHASER/PROVIDER SPLIT) have been introduced along with the new occupation of care manager. USERS with the highest NEEDS are TARGETED and pay MEANS-TESTED CHARGES. Those with lower NEEDS are advised as to what services are available and pay for them privately. One of the objectives of the community care legislation is the EMPOWERMENT of USERS. But there is considerable controversy as to whether this has been effected. Some contend that USERS are no more empowered than under the old system since they receive very similar services for which they pay a contribution, and many have been DISEMPOWERED as the result of TARGETING services on only those in the highest NEED category. The variability of CHARGING and provision more generally between authorities and the overall standard and quality of care provided by both statutory and non-statutory agencies have also been criticized.

Supported home-based care remains a central plank of UK government policy and a new regulatory framework, supported by a raft of standard setting, AUDIT, INSPECTION and QUALITY ASSURANCE measures to overcome these concerns, is now in place. LOCAL AUTHORITIES are also increasingly expected to work in PARTNERSHIP with potential service providers rather than on a competitive contractual basis and opt for forms of provision, which offer BEST VALUE. Whether, without a substantial injection of funds, these arrangements will enhance provision or EMPOWER USERS is, however, unclear. (CU)

Community Care Plans

As with CHILDREN'S SERVICES, SOCIAL SERVICES DEPARTMENTS in the UK are obliged by law to produce and review COMMUNITY CARE Plans at fixed intervals. Other statutory and voluntary services are expected to contribute to the plan, which includes information about local need, services provided and planned, and relevant finances. (PA/MH)

Community Charge

The system of local RATES was replaced in Scotland in 1989 by the Community Charge, commonly referred to as the POLL TAX. Similar reform in England and Wales followed in the next year. It involved a charge on each individual adult member of a household. Problems were experienced in collecting the charge from all individuals. It was replaced by COUNCIL TAX in 1993. (AM)

Community development

Support and encouragement provided for local COMMUNITY ACTION, often as part of publicly funded projects aimed at NEIGHBOURHOOD RENEWAL, in which the active involvement of local people is being promoted. Community development aims to improve the capacity of local CITIZENS to join local VOLUNTARY organizations and participate in public democratic processes. It is sometimes referred to as community capacity building. (DWS)

Community orders

Penalties that may be imposed by the courts as an alternative to imprisonment for moderately serious criminal offences. They include probation orders, community service orders, curfew orders (enforced by electronic tagging), supervision orders (for under-18 year olds) and attendance centre orders. (HD)

Community safety

Emerged during the 1990s in the context of debates about crime prevention. The idea of community safety as a policy objective is to broaden the approach to crime prevention beyond the situational aspects of crime and the role of the police, so as also to encompass the social aspects of crime and the role of the COMMUNITY. It is intended as a response not only to crime, but also to evidence that the fear of crime can have a disproportionate and corrosive effect on local COMMUNITIES. The concept of community safety was given legislative form in England and Wales through the Crime and Disorder Act 1998. Central to the concept is a multi-agency approach, involving locally based PARTNERSHIPS that bring together the LOCAL AUTHORITY, the police service, other statutory agencies and the VOLUNTARY SECTOR. These PARTNERSHIPS are required to conduct local crime AUDITS, to consult with local agencies and to draw up and publish a local community safety strategy, specifying targets and time-scales for the reduction of crime and disorder. (HD)

Community sector

A generic term for the activity of small associations and groups operating at local COMMUNITY level and generally mainly dependent upon voluntary support from local CITIZENS. Examples include pre-school playgroups, day centres for older people or youth organizations. (DWS)

Community sentences

COMMUNITY ORDERS that are available to the courts in cases where neither a financial nor a custodial punishment is appropriate. They represent a cheaper and, some have argued, more effective form of punishment than imprisonment. (HD)

Community work

Developing a COMMUNITY's own resources to provide local support for individuals and families. Once closely linked with SOCIAL WORK and popular in the 1960s and 1970s, it is enjoying a renaissance within REGENERATION activity supported by the new resources available under AREA BASED INITIATIVES. (SB)

Compacts

Formal agreements about the principles that should govern relationships (PARTNERSHIPS) between government and the PRIVATE, VOLUNTARY or COMMUNITY SECTORS. The development of a concordat or compact between national government and VOLUNTARY SECTOR organizations in order to improve joint planning arrangements was proposed by the Deakin Commission on the future of the sector in 1996, and since then LOCAL GOVERNMENT has also sought to develop compacts to facilitate local joint working. (DWS)

Compensatory education

The idea that education could – and should – compensate for the disadvantages of home and neighbourhood, which received its principal expression in the UK in the 1967 Plowden Report, *Children and their Primary Schools*. Influenced by the contemporaneous Operation Headstart and the War on Poverty in the USA, it attributed educational underachievement to the social and economic conditions characteristic of deprived localities. To ensure effective EQUALITY of educational opportunity, it advocated a policy of POSITIVE DISCRIMINATION to channel extra resources into such areas to counter the lack of parental and COMMUNITY support. Under the ensuing programme, schools in designated EDUCATIONAL PRIORITY AREAS were to receive extra funding to limit class size to thirty, provide extra pay for teachers and teachers' aides, improve buildings and expand NURSERY provision. In practice, however, few additional resources were made available and there was considerable criticism of compensatory education both in terms of its 'deficit' view of working-class homes and neighbourhoods and the measures for securing POSITIVE DISCRIMINATION. By the mid-1970s political and professional faith in what could be achieved by this strategy had evaporated and the scheme was phased out. Aspects of this approach can, however, be traced in more recent AREA BASED INITIATIVES such as Education ACTION ZONES. (DEG)

Competitive tendering

The processes whereby service suppliers bid for contracts with the expectation that the offer closest to the purchaser's requirements is accepted. Traditionally such arrangements characterized technical, equipment and building rather than welfare or human maintenance services. From the 1980s as part of the government's attempt to reduce public spending, extend CHOICE and develop market-based forms of provision, national and local state agencies were increasingly expected to out-source services to external contractors and subject in-house providers to competition from commercial and VOLUNTARY organizations. Some, mainly ANCILLARY services were subject to compulsory competitive tendering (CCT). Elsewhere, as in health and social care, contracting was engineered through the creation of INTERNAL and QUASI-MARKETS reinforced by fiscal measures. The extent to which this encouraged innovation or enhanced consumer CHOICE is disputed, but CCT in particular was criticized for prioritizing cost savings rather than quality improvements. Although it has been replaced by BEST VALUE and recent policy emphasizes a PARTNERSHIP-based approach, tendering remains a key instrument in securing appropriate service provision. (MM)

Complaints

A means of REDRESS by which an individual may challenge the way she or he has been treated in relation to the provision of a service, but not amounting to a legal APPEAL. New RIGHTS of complaint and statutory complaints procedures have recently been introduced, for example for LOCAL AUTHORITY social services provision and the NATIONAL HEALTH SERVICE. (HD)

Complementary medicine

See ALTERNATIVE MEDICINE

Comprehensive education

The provision of a common system of state schools for children of SECONDARY school age with the aim of increasing EQUALITY of opportunity and ensuring all children received similar provision. Though there were earlier antecedents, it effectively began with a Labour government circular (10/65) requesting LOCAL EDUCATION AUTHORITIES (LEAs) to dismantle the existing TRIPARTITE SYSTEM and abolish selective testing at age 11. Though all but a few subsequently adopted this policy, the continuance of selective state and INDEPENDENT SCHOOLS undermined the implementation of the 'comprehensive ideal', while more recent policy has favoured the provision of specialist SECONDARY schools. (DEG)

Comprehensive schools

See COMPREHENSIVE EDUCATION

Comprehensive Spending Review

The new term used to refer to the review of all PUBLIC EXPENDITURE plans and commitments conducted regularly by central government, which TARGETS spending for the following three years. (PA)

Conditionality

The extent to which ELIGIBILITY for BENEFITS or services is subject, for example, to tests of means or income, participation in job-seeking/training, NATIONAL INSURANCE contribution record, parenthood, age, DISABILITY or CITIZENSHIP. Though BENEFITS are never in practice entirely unconditional, conditionality is the conceptual opposite of UNIVERSALISM. (HD)

Conservatism

A somewhat disparate political philosophy, originating in the late eighteenth century as a reaction to the rationalism of the Enlightenment and the radicalism of the French Revolution. It was based on the defence of established authority and the importance of tradition – the present's debt to the past and its duty to the future. This allegiance to the status quo is tempered, however, with an acceptance of change as long as it is in harmony with the individuals in society and their traditions. Conservatism thus espouses slow, natural, evolutionary change rather than any radical break with the past. Its defence of tradition and commitment to gradual change come together in the principle of political scepticism. This sets Conservatives apart from those who believe it is possible to engineer the good society and makes them sceptical about the role of government intervention. There is, however, diversity within

Conservatism between PATERNALISTS and LIBERTARIANS, for example, and also between the principles of Conservatism and the actions – past and present – of the Conservatives as a political party. (DEG)

Consumerism

Economists refer to consumers as those who buy services at a market price. They are depicted as drivers of the market. Firms respond to their preferences and this produces an efficient result. In practice there are sometimes monopolies (one provider) and a small number of big firms can shape consumers' preferences. However, international competition and changing technology have made markets for goods and services more responsive than ever to changing consumer demand. This has affected SOCIAL POLICY. Consumers have come to expect prompt and EFFECTIVE services in the private market and the same from public services. Consumers are better educated than in the past. They do not hold professionals in the awe they once did. Social services USERS too have become more consumer conscious and demanding. SOCIAL POLICY reforms have sought to give consumers more CHOICE of schools and PERSONAL SOCIAL SERVICE providers. (HG)

Contingent benefits

ELIGIBILITY to benefit dependent upon the occurrence of an event (a contingency). The term is closely related to the idea of a risk in INSURANCE. Contingencies often covered in SOCIAL INSURANCE systems include SICKNESS (see SICK PAY), MATERNITY, UNEMPLOYMENT and RETIREMENT. (DM)

Contract culture

An umbrella term encompassing the changes experienced by VOLUNTARY organizations following shifts in their funding and the concerns these generated. Traditionally they could apply to central or LOCAL GOVERNMENT for grant aid to support their activities. This was typically awarded with few conditions and could be used to fund services, campaigning or general administration. From the 1980s it was increasingly replaced by contracts, which were held to offer a more cost-effective, accountable way of dispensing public money, forcing competition between providers and enabling purchasing authorities to specify their requirements and monitor outcomes. For VOLUNTARY agencies they potentially offered greater security and clearer responsibilities, but they were also extensively criticized. Larger organizations were better placed than small, COMMUNITY or minority-based groups to compete against commercial and statutory providers and carry the high TRANSACTION COSTS. Contracts were budget- rather than quality-driven, geared to provision rather than wider campaigning or advocacy, the use of paid rather than VOLUNTARY workers and a commercial, MANAGERIALIST approach. Moreover, tight specifications and monitoring appeared to threaten agencies' independence and the broader VOLUNTARY ethos. Recent policy has attempted to address these concerns, emphasizing a PARTNERSHIP approach based on clear COMPACTS between national and LOCAL GOVERNMENT and the VOLUNTARY and COMMUNITY SECTORS. (MM)

Contracting out

Where participation in a state SOCIAL SECURITY scheme is compulsory unless there is equivalent private insurance or PENSION provision, the purchase of private cover is referred to as contracting out. In the 1980s the government promoted contracting out as a method of privatizing the STATE EARNINGS RELATED PENSION SCHEME (SERPS). (DM)

Contributory benefits

Limited to those who have paid NATIONAL or SOCIAL INSURANCE contributions (and, sometimes, to their dependants). Contributions may be credited for periods spent raising children, studying, or while unemployed, in order to improve the coverage of the INSURANCE system. (DM)

Contributory principle

The application of the norms of RECIPROCITY and exchange to the SOCIAL SECURITY system. ELIGIBILITY for contributory BENEFITS is confined to those who have paid in, and this is said to create a stronger, semi-contractual ENTITLEMENT to the BENEFIT or PENSION. (DM)

Convergence thesis

According to this thesis differences between WELFARE STATES and societies more broadly will gradually diminish due to international pressures and developments which affect countries in similar ways. Functionalist–structuralist theorists have argued that the origins and expansion of WELFARE STATES have to be regarded largely as a response to economic and DEMOGRAPHIC CHANGES in society. Accordingly, with countries becoming more similar in the long run in terms of industrial development and demographic composition, their welfare strategies will converge. A more recent version of the convergence theory is implicit in the notion of GLOBALIZATION as a force, which will diminish cross-national differences in terms of level and form of welfare provision. (JC)

Co-operative

A union of individuals formally organized in a common worker or consumer enterprise. There is no separate group of investor-owners, and capital is remunerated not with a share in the surpluses but with fixed and limited interest. Surpluses are distributed by agreement of the members, either to a 'social dividend' that benefits members collectively, or to individual members on the basis of their use of the co-op. Consumer co-ops operate in fields such as food retailing, housing, health and social care, banking and insurance. Worker co-ops tend to operate in labour- rather than capital-intensive fields, except where they achieve a high density or are backed by a co-operative bank. (DWS)

Corporatism

A pattern of state-controlled interest mediation and decision making, usually involving top-level representatives from employer organizations, trade unions and state officials. Corporatist arrangements for negotiating and co-ordinating economic and social affairs were prevalent in the 1970s and early 1980s. They are more common in Scandinavia, the Netherlands and some other continental European countries than in English-speaking nations. The rise of UNEMPLOYMENT in the 1970s, plus changes in the economy and labour markets since then, have all contributed to a relative decline of corporatism. However, corporatist negotiations have remained crucial for labour market improvements in some countries, such as the Netherlands and Denmark where UNEMPLOYMENT declined considerably in the mid-1990s. (JC)

Cost benefit analysis

A form of economic analysis dating from the late 1950s which measures the full resource costs associated with a PUBLIC POLICY or programme and sets them against the economic benefits of that policy. (HG)

Council housing

Housing within the ownership of LOCAL AUTHORITIES and rented out to local tenants. In the majority of cases these are properties purpose-built by the LOCAL AUTHORITY, but some may have been acquired by it. The term may also refer to housing that was once in the ownership of LOCAL AUTHORITIES or was built by LOCAL AUTHORITIES although it is currently no longer in the council housing sector. (AM)

Council Tax

The system of local taxation which replaced the COMMUNITY CHARGE in 1993. It involves a rate of tax linked to a banding of domestic properties by value – business properties are subject to separate national RATES. LOCAL AUTHORITIES then set Council Tax rates (subject to capping) for each of the eight bands (A–H) involved, with the highest tax levied on the highest value property band. (AM)

Council tenants

See COUNCIL HOUSING

Cream skimming

The strategies insurance companies or any service provider may adopt to exclude potentially expensive USERS from ACCESS to the service (see also ADVERSE SELECTION). Health service providers may exclude those who are likely to have prior histories leading to greater risk of illness, or put up premiums for such groups so as to exclude them. One way to counter such perverse effects is to pay different amounts to providers for more costly users. Children with SPECIAL EDUCATIONAL NEEDS are already treated in this way. However, many differences are not easy to define in ways that can attract additional funds. (HG)

Credit unions

Small-scale CO-OPERATIVE banking agencies that operate on the principle of a 'common bond' between members (e.g. a workplace, church group or geographical COMMUNITY). Individuals wishing to borrow have first to become members and save a minimum amount. Interest rates on savings and borrowings are kept low. Credit unions are strong in many countries, notably the USA, Ireland and Canada, and are growing in the UK. (DWS)

Criminal responsibility

Our capacity to understand when the acts we commit are morally wrong. There is a presumption that, in certain circumstances, children and people with LEARNING DIFFICULTIES or mental illnesses may be incapable of or have diminished responsibility for any crimes they commit. (HD)

Crosland, Charles Anthony Raven (1918–1977)

After securing a first-class honours degree in PPE at Oxford in 1946 Crosland became a lecturer then Fellow in Economics from 1947 to 1950. He was Labour MP for South Gloucestershire from 1950 to 1955 and for Grimsby from 1959 to 1977. He held various ministerial posts, including Secretary of State for Education and Science (1965–7) where he presided over the decisive shift towards COMPREHENSIVE EDUCATION. He was also Secretary of State for Local Government and Regional Planning (1969–70), Secretary of State for the Environment (1974–6) and Foreign Secretary (1976–7). His book on *The Future of Socialism* (1956) is credited with shifting Labour Party thinking away from its concern with public ownership towards a new egalitarian political strategy in which the beneficial aspects of market activity could, in conjunction with REDISTRIBUTIVE social policies, be harnessed to serve the public interest.

While Crosland was committed to EQUALITY of opportunity, not least in the area of education, he also recognized the importance of a more equal distribution of income and wealth. For Crosland, inequalities of income could only be justified on grounds of service to the wider community, not on the basis of privilege or endowment. (RMP)

Crossman, Richard Howard Stafford (1907–1974)

Educated at Winchester and Oxford, Crossman became a fellow and tutor at New College Oxford from 1931 to 1937. He was active in the Workers' Education Association. He was a journalist on both *The Spectator* and *New Statesman*, acting as editor of the latter from 1970 to 1972 after leaving the government. He was MP for Coventry East from 1945 to 1970. He was heavily involved with both the BEVANITE 'Keep Left' group and the FABIAN Society in the immediate postwar period and edited an influential collection of New Fabian Essays in 1952. Although usually regarded as on the left of the party, Crossman had something of a maverick reputation, not least because of his willingness to take issue with conventional viewpoints. He held a variety of ministerial positions in the 1964–70 Labour government (Minister of Housing and Local Government 1964–6; Lord President of the Council and Leader of the House of Commons 1966–8; Secretary of State for Social Services 1968–70). He wrote a number of books, including *Government and the Governed* (1939) and *Planning for Freedom* (1965). He is best remembered for his diaries *(The Diaries of a Cabinet Minister*, 3 vols, 1975–6), which provided an insight into the workings of the 1964–70 Labour government. (RMP)

Cultural capital

The bundle of culturally specific information, knowledge and skills that is possessed and passed on within a particular social class or group and that enables its individual members to access resources, opportunities and institutions. The concept is sometimes applied in explanations of the differential experiences and LIFE CHANCES available to members of different classes or groups. On the one hand, it is argued that stakes in the dominant culture of a society tend to be unevenly distributed; on the other, that the failure of the working class or of oppressed groups within a society to thrive relates not to any deficiency in their cultural attributes, but to the systematic way in which the dominant class imposes its culture upon others and devalues the cultural capital of others. It is the cultural capital of the British middle classes that explains the in-built advantages their children enjoy within the education system, the labour-market opportunities that are open to them and even, for example, the more EFFECTIVE use they make of professionally delivered healthcare. By contrast, the cultural capital of oppressed or marginalized groups may give their members access to resources within their own COMMUNITIES but not beyond. (HD)

Culture of contentment

Coined by the American academic J. K. Galbraith to describe the consequences of the democratic process in many advanced industrial countries. Because a majority of people in such societies can achieve financial contentment they have no INCENTIVE to support policy measures designed to assist the poor minority, especially where these will be paid for by the better-off majority. (PA)

Culture of poverty

Initially coined by the American academic Oscar Lewis to describe the social circumstances he discovered in research carried out in poor Puerto Rican communities. He found that a large proportion of the people were poor and unemployed. In order to cope with the deprivation and depression that this produced, members of the COMMUNITY developed shared expectations of low material and social advancement – a culture of poverty. However, such a culture could have a mutually reinforcing effect, reducing future expectations and reproducing poverty and DEPRIVATION. This was taken up by other writers who suggested that such cultures could themselves become 'causes' of the poverty experienced in poor neighbourhoods, leading to CYCLES OF DEPRIVATION operating across succeeding generations and creating an UNDERCLASS of workless and hopeless CITIZENS in these areas. Lewis's work did not attribute such causation to the culture of poverty, and the notion that such cultures can cause material deprivation has been criticized by some as creating a pathological model of poverty, which 'blames' the poor for their plight. See also POVERTY. (PA)

Cycle of deprivation

The process of the transfer of DEPRIVATION across generations within poor communities, also sometimes referred to as TRANSMITTED DEPRIVATION. The concept was adapted from Lewis's notion of the CULTURE OF POVERTY. It was popularized in the UK in the 1980s by the Conservative politician KEITH JOSEPH. He argued that the high levels of deprivation found in some local communities in the country were caused, in large part, by the low expectations and aspirations which children in these areas acquired from their unemployed and socially excluded parents. Thus deprivation was reproducing in a cyclical fashion over time. See also POVERTY and CULTURE OF POVERTY. (PA)

D

Dataset

Information, usually in numerical form, presented or grouped in such a way that it can be readily analysed and inferences drawn. (TM)

Day centres

Centres where people with special needs may spend the day. Services such as occupational therapy and physiotherapy will often be available, plus various leisure activities and personal services like hairdressing and bathing. They are provided by commercial agencies and, more commonly, by large VOLUNTARY organizations, both of which offer places under contractual arrangements with LOCAL AUTHORITIES but may also provide places directly to self-funding individuals. (CU)

Decency threshold

Contained in the SOCIAL CHARTER adopted by the Council of Europe, it is the standard set for a national MINIMUM WAGE. (JC)

Decentralization

Policies or processes by which political power and decision-making are dispersed to lower tiers of government and/or COMMUNITY level bodies. Formal processes of decentralization entail DEVOLUTION and, for example, the creation of new elected regional bodies or assemblies or the extension of the powers of existing LOCAL AUTHORITIES. The term has also been applied to a variety of initiatives intended to democratize the provision of welfare, or to delegate day-to-day management to the local level. Examples of the former have included the creation at a sub-LOCAL GOVERNMENT level of informal neighbourhood councils and neighbourhood fora or PARTNERSHIP initiatives involving LOCAL GOVERNMENT and the introduction of new consultation processes, such as CITIZENS' JURIES. Examples of the latter have included the introduction of neighbourhood management in public housing and social services provision, of local financial management in schools, of budget-holding GENERAL PRACTITIONERS or, more recently, primary healthcare trusts. The general trend towards WELFARE PLURALISM has acted as a force for the decentralization of social welfare provision, since the GOVERNANCE of welfare has become more diffuse, but this has not always increased its ACCOUNTABILITY. See also CENTRALIZATION. (HD)

Decommodification

Originally applied by Polanyi but later taken up by Esping-Andersen in his theory of WELFARE REGIMES. The concept thus captures the degree to which WELFARE STATES diminish the cash nexus by granting ENTI-TLEMENTS to resources independently of participation in labour markets, thus weakening the status of labour as a commodity. Measuring the relative level of decommodification associated with major BENEFIT programmes is a central indicator for the classification of WELFARE STATES. See also COMMODIFICATION. (JC)

Defined benefit

A PENSION scheme that promises to pay a predetermined BENEFIT, often expressed in relation to the salary and years of service of the beneficiary. The scheme must have a guarantor, often the employer, who will make up any difference between the funds available and the defined BENEFITS promised. (DM)

Defined contribution

A PENSION scheme in which the BENEFITS payable depend on the amount contributed and the rate of return earned on contributions. Unlike a DEFINED BENEFIT scheme, there is no need for a guarantor, as low returns on the fund simply lead to lower pensions. (DM)

Democratic deficit

Circumstances in which decision-making is insulated or remote from public scrutiny and electoral ACCOUNTABILITY. It has been used to describe the constitutional arrangements of the European Union, under which unelected European Commissioners are not fully answerable to the elected European Parliament. (HD)

Democratic socialism

A political ideology traditionally promoting the idea of a universal WELFARE STATE as an important mechanism for counteracting the effects of capitalism and creating a more egalitarian and SOLIDARISTIC society. Despite different traditions and schools of thought, democratic socialists have broadly agreed on the ends and means of changing capitalism. They aspire to abolish POVERTY, reduce class inequalities and improve living conditions with the help of WELFARE STATES. The means to achieve those aims included, traditionally, the nationalization of key industries, utilities and services, FULL EMPLOYMENT, UNIVERSAL social services and PROGRESSIVE TAXATION. (JC)

Demographic change

The study of population statistics, in particular births, deaths and MIGRATION, which are the basic variables for understanding population growth and change. There is a strong policy interest in demographic change, since different population structures create different demands for social provision – schools, for example, or health and social care for elderly people. The population of Britain increased rapidly after 1750, mainly due to steep falls in mortality in all age groups, associated with rising standards. The main factor driving demographic change in Britain throughout the twentieth century was the FERTILITY RATE which, apart from 'baby boom' fluctuations, has been generally falling. Fertility has been below replacement level since about 1973. Changing family formation patterns – delayed child bearing and restricted family size – are key factors in this. MIGRATION makes little difference to the overall demographic picture for the UK, since inward and outward migrations are more or less in balance. It is difficult to make accurate projections of future population size and structure, since relatively small changes can have quite substantial short-term effects. But some further ageing of the population structure is expected, including increases in the number of very elderly people. (JM)

Denominational schools

A term originally denoting grant-aided schools managed in the nineteenth century by the Church of England National Society and the Nonconformist British and Foreign Schools Society, but now applied to grant-aided schools managed by religious bodies. See also FAITH SCHOOLS. (DEG)

Dependency

The state individuals are in when they need the support of others, usually over a long period of time. Thus young children are in a state of dependency in relation to the adults who care for them. Within the SOCIAL POLICY literature the term tends to be used in two contexts to describe the way in which individuals are apparently dependent on the WELFARE STATE for their support (in particular cash support) and people with special needs who rely on the support of those who care for them. In the first context, it is often used as part of the term 'welfare dependency'. This indicates that individuals are reliant on state BENEFITS to satisfy their material needs, rather than wages from their own paid labour. In the second context, dependency is assumed to exist if there are CARERS present – the people they care for are their dependants.

Both uses of the term are profoundly controversial. First, in general, dependency is not regarded as a satisfactory state to be in: it is highly stigmatized, while independence is widely regarded as an appropriate goal for everyone. The term 'welfare dependency' reflects the fact that dependency is regarded as intrinsically undesirable and is commonly used by right-wing commentators to suggest that provision of state BENEFITS saps recipients' will to support themselves through paid work. It thus encourages a CULTURE OF POVERTY, sometimes known as a DEPENDENCY CULTURE. Left-wing commentators eschew the term 'welfare dependency', preferring to use the term CLAIMANTS to describe those who rely on SOCIAL SECURITY BENEFITS, in order to point up that such individuals and families are claiming a RIGHT to BENEFIT, and that they are acting with agency.

Similarly, the way in which the notion of dependency is used in relation to people with special NEEDS is highly controversial, although not along right-wing/left-wing fault lines. The fault line, in this instance, is much more between people with DISABILITIES on the one hand and FEM-INISTS who write about INFORMAL CARE on the other. Here the argument is about whether there is a clear dichotomy between those who care and those who receive it, such that one (the CARER) acts with agency and the other (the care recipient) is passive. The argument made by disabled people is that this is a travesty of the RECIPROCITIES embedded in the care relationship and is deeply demeaning. Moreover, there are many disabled people who are caring parents and grandparents, and thus those who receive care can also be CARERS. A further objective of many disabled individuals is to achieve INDEPENDENT LIVING whereby they neither live in RESIDENTIAL CARE nor are supported by INFORMAL CARERS, but rather employ their own personal assistants.

Given the controversies surrounding the use of the term 'dependency' it is not surprising that there are difficulties in operationalizing it, let alone measuring it. Nevertheless, in the context of care provision by the state, there is a need to measure relative dependency in order to judge who should receive TARGETED and rationed support services and to evaluate how far these services are being allocated EFFICIENTLY and with EQUITY. One conventional way of gauging these relativities is to use a measure known as the 'activities of daily living' index. These activities refer to both personal self-care – such as the ability to bath or wash oneself, dress, feed oneself, use the WC and get out of bed or a chair unsupported – and also to instrumental activities like shopping, cooking and handling personal affairs. Within the literature on care, dependency can therefore be treated on occasion as a simple matter of technical mea-surement. Contingent on how many 'activities of daily living' are 'failed', individuals can be classified as having 'low', 'moderate' or 'high' dependency, and the extent of such measured dependency, which grows with age, can be predicted for any demographic structure.

Such methodologies to assess dependency are useful, but they do not refer at all to relations of dependency. Nor do they indicate how all humans live within societies where dependencies of many different kinds exist, and where interdependence is the common feature of everyday life. An alternative strand within the care literature, which has close links to political and psychological theory informed by FEMINISM, does refer to these questions of relationship and interdependence. The argument is that there is, and should be, an ethic of care whereby we value both the givers and the receivers of care, since through their actions and their relationships, societies are transformable. Those who are depend-ent will no longer be construed as burdens. Those who give care will no longer be stigmatized and marginalized. See also FEMINISM and HOUSEHOLD MEANS TEST. (CU)

Dependency culture

A term used pejoratively to describe those wholly or partially reliant upon (especially MEANS-TESTED) BENEFITS, who have supposedly accepted too willingly their status as welfare recipients. See DEPENDENCY. (PA)

Dependency ratio

The ratio of people of RETIREMENT age or below the age of employment in relation to the number of people of working age in a given population. The term assumes that all people over retirement age are DEPENDENT, usually for their PENSIONS and care, on all those of working age. (CU)

Deprivation

See POVERTY

Deregulation

See REGULATION

Desert

An approach to the ALLOCATION of resources based primarily upon a moral or ideological judgement rather than upon an *a priori* principle such as NEED or EQUITY. See also DESERVING/UNDESERVING and SOCIAL JUSTICE. (AE)

Deserving

Underlying much SOCIAL POLICY has been the belief that BENEFIT payment should not be made to everyone in a particular situation, such as UNEMPLOYMENT or RETIREMENT, but rather should depend upon whether those likely to receive the BENEFITS are deserving or undeserving of help from the public purse. There is a long tradition in SOCIAL

POLICY of only helping the deserving and ignoring the undeserving. The POOR LAW categorized those seeking assistance (PAUPERS) into different groups according to their DESERT. This separation continues today. For example, in public debate pensioners or disabled people are usually seen as deserving, because they are portrayed as passive and unable to help themselves, whereas the unemployed are seen as undeserving – they can get a job. Groups such as ASYLUM SEEKERS are also portrayed as undeserving, not because of passivity, but because they are portrayed as not being the responsibility of the state in which they seek ASYLUM – they do not deserve help from the taxpayers. This separation between the deserving and the undeserving involves a moral evaluation reflecting powerful moral codes. (AE)

Deviance

Behaviour that infringes established legal rules or social norms is described as deviant. There is, however, widespread disagreement concerning the explanation of deviant behaviour and of what constitutes deviance. Classical theorists see deviance as the outcome of rational choices by wicked people. Positivist scientists see it as the outcome of individual biological or psychological defects. Sociologists have tended to focus either on functionalist explanations that regard deviance as the outcome of failures in society (such as POVERTY, COMMUNITY breakdown or deviant sub-cultures) or upon a variety of critical explanations that regard deviance as a socially constructed phenomenon. Among the critical sociological accounts are MARXIST theories which argue that deviance is defined by those who hold power in society; interactionist theories which argue that deviance results from LABELLING processes; and poststructuralist theories which argue that deviance is the discursive creation of power relations within a disciplinary society. Different understandings of deviance are reflected in quite different policies for countering or correcting it. For example, policies of ZERO-TOLERANCE have been associated with a renaissance of classical thinking, while COMMUNITY SAFETY policy might be associated more with functionalist thinking. (HD)

Devolution

The process by which national government delegates or transfers components of its power to a lower tier of government. Britain's tradition of parliamentary sovereignty has resulted in a highly centralized form of government dominated, many argue, by English interests. Recent debates about devolution have focused on demands for self-government. Britain became the 'United Kingdom' as a result of historical settlements by which Wales, Scotland and Ireland were brought under the constitutional GOVERNANCE of the Westminster parliament. When the Republic of Ireland was subsequently created, Northern Ireland remained under British rule with a form of devolved government, though this was suspended in 1972. Since 1998 a Scottish Parliament, Welsh Assembly, Northern Ireland Assembly, Greater London Assembly and London mayor have been established. The range of powers devolved to these bodies is different in each case. (HD)

Direct grant schools

SECONDARY schools which from 1919 opted to receive funding direct from central government and in return offered a proportion of free places. Their abolition by the Labour government in 1975 paradoxically had the effect of enlarging the PRIVATE SECTOR, as many chose to become INDEPENDENT SCHOOLS. (DEG)

Direct payments

A scheme whereby LOCAL AUTHORITIES can give individuals in receipt of DOMICILIARY CARE the option of receiving cash to spend on employing personal assistants themselves, instead of relying on services contracted on their behalf. Originally confined to younger people with DISABILITIES, since 2000 they have been available to those over 65. (CU)

Direct taxation

Levied on the incomes of individuals or companies, including INCOME TAX or SOCIAL SECURITY contributions. Most tax systems excuse payment of tax on the first part of an individual's income, and may reduce tax for CHILD CARE costs or for other reasons (see FISCAL WELFARE). Direct taxes may be proportional to income (flat tax), or rise with income (PROGRESSIVE TAX), or they may be levied on the profits of firms. (HG)

Disability

Traditionally a term grounded in medical models of particular forms of IMPAIRMENT or ill-health, which still underpin much social legislation. However, as a result of activism by disabled people and their organizations, it is now more frequently used in a politicized way, to refer to forms of DISCRIMINATION experienced by people with perceived impairments. This social model is now common in EQUAL OPPORTUNITIES POLICIES, anti-discriminatory legislation and debates on CIVIL RIGHTS. From this perspective, disability is viewed as the result of disabling barriers and attitudes in society, rather than the necessary result of impairment within the individual. The simultaneous use of these two models within recent policy has led to many debates and some confusion of terminology. See MEDICALIZATION. (MP)

Disability benefits

A generic term referring to the special cash payments, SUBSIDIES and allowances available to those who fulfil certain ELIGIBILITY criteria, usually defined in terms of IMPAIRMENT and physical functioning or INCAPACITY. Such assistance is usually in addition to general SOCIAL SECURITY BENEFITS. They comprise specific CONTRIBUTORY and NON-CONTRIBUTORY BENEFITS, TAX RELIEFS and discretionary assistance from LOCAL AUTHORITIES, including special equipment and home adaptations, HOME HELPS, laundry services, local bus and train fares, holidays, special housing, day NURSERIES or playgroups, DAY CENTRES, residential accommodation, and advice from SOCIAL WORKERS. In addition those registered as disabled may get help with travelling to work and assistance in the workplace. (MP)

Disaggregation

This refers to the treatment of the resources of individual family and household members as belonging to them as separate individuals, rather than the AGGREGATION of these into one family pot. Incomes are disaggregated for tax and NATIONAL INSURANCE purposes; and some (particularly FEMINIST) campaigners have argued for disaggregation of resources and provision of individual RIGHTS and obligations in all circumstances, in order to avoid the imposed DEPENDENCY of adult family members on their partners. (PA)

Discretion

The process of policy delivery that leaves considerable power and influence over the nature of services or BENEFITS provided to the front-line service providers or STREET-LEVEL BUREAUCRATS. Thus social workers may have discretion over what support to provide to clients, or BENEFIT administrators may have discretion over what levels of BENEFIT to pay, and to whom. It is often contrasted with RIGHTS to welfare, where specific levels of BENEFIT or support are laid down in regulations; and where failure to provide these can then be subject to legal challenge or APPEAL by CLAIMANTS or USERS. (PA)

Discrimination

Actions, practices and processes which deny the equal treatment of, or disadvantage, members of a social group or category. It may occur on the grounds of, for example, gender, 'race', age, sexual orientation, religion, DISABILITY or health status and reflects stereotypical beliefs about differences between social groups. It may be direct (e.g. abuse, harassment or attempts to segregate a social group) or indirect (where a condition or requirement is applied equally but has unequal implications or outcomes for a social group) and structured by both formal and informal processes. Thus it may be difficult to measure.

Though discrimination is often associated with prejudice the two terms should be distinguished. It is possible for individuals to engage in discriminatory actions even if they do not hold prejudicial views, while those who hold prejudices against others do not necessarily adopt discriminatory behaviour. Discrimination may be for or against a social group and can extend to POSITIVE DISCRIMINATION, whereby categories of people are actively sought, for example to apply for employment or promotion. (SP)

Disempowerment

Individuals and groups in society are disempowered where they are denied the power to ENABLE them to exercise control over their own lives, for instance due to inability to communicate effectively, feelings of social isolation or STIGMA, or lack of social networks. Disempowerment is socially structured, rather than inherent in individuals, and is compounded by poor health or education and low income, absence of enforceable CITIZENS' RIGHTS, or lack of information about RIGHTS that do exist. (MEH)

Disincentive

A tax or BENEFIT rule may prevent or inhibit someone from following some desired action, such as taking a job. High levels of INCOME TAX or loss of MEANS-TESTED BENEFITS may reduce the number of hours someone may wish to work. The way an organization or a professional is paid may be a disincentive to taking more clients or difficult clients. (HG)

Diswelfare

The classic SOCIAL DEMOCRATIC defence of the WELFARE STATE was that it would serve to ameliorate the diswelfare that is inherent in a free-market economy. In particular, it provided the working class with an element of protection against exploitation. More generally, however, diswelfare is a term that may also be applied to any circumstance warranting welfare intervention: BEVERIDGE's five giants – disease, idleness, ignorance, squalor and want – were intended to symbolize the principal manifestations of diswelfare. To that list we might add, for example, such diverse diswelfares as SOCIAL EXCLUSION, DISCRIMINATION, DISABILITY, HOMELESSNESS, criminal victimization, industrial pollution, road traffic congestion, etc. (HD)

Dole

'Being on the dole' is a colloquial expression for being unemployed and receiving SOCIAL SECURITY support in the UK. It probably derives from the medieval monastic practice of 'doling out', i.e. distributing cash or other forms of support to the poor. The equivalent in Scotland would be 'being on the brew'. It is associated particularly with the interwar years when BENEFIT CLAIMANTS had to register with a local LABOUR EXCHANGE (an early form of JOBCENTRE) in order to be eligible for BENEFITS. (JC)

Domiciliary care

Personal care or practical help delivered to people with special NEEDS who are living in their own or their CARERS' home (in Latin, *domus*).

The term is usually used to refer to non-medical care, where those who deliver the service are not medical practitioners. The services include home care, meals on wheels, community nursing and chiropody.

Domiciliary care workers, sometimes referred to as home helps, may be employed by statutory or non-statutory agencies, paid directly by USERS (or their families) or, especially in the case of MEALS ON WHEELS, they may be VOLUNTEERS. Generally, the recipients of domiciliary care are frail older people. LOCAL AUTHORITY funded provision is TARGETED and subject to MEANS-TESTED CHARGES. CARE MANAGERS, who are also responsible for provision, determine ELIGIBILITY based on local criteria. Typically this includes a mixture of various services and providers with occasional RESPITE CARE for any INFORMAL CARERS. Domiciliary care and RESIDENTIAL CARE, taken together, to distinguish them from informal care, are often referred to as 'formal care'. (CU)

E

Earnings-related benefits

A situation where the amount of BENEFIT payable is based upon the beneficiary's previous earnings. SOCIAL INSURANCE systems generally require workers to contribute a proportion of their income to the scheme, subject to upper and lower limits, and earnings-related BENEFITS can be designed to achieve a degree of proportionality between contributions and BENEFITS. (DM)

Eco-feminism

There are two main strands to the incorporation of FEMINIST concerns into green political theory. The 'essentialist' position regards the traditional feminine attributes of nurturing, caring and compassion as identifying women closely with nature. Masculine characteristics of toughness, aggression and ambition are associated with environmental damage, while women are potential champions of environmental protection. This position is criticized for reinforcing gender stereotypes.

The 'materialist' position argues that women's identification with nature arises from a perception that the exploitation of women by men is analogous to the exploitation of nature by mankind. Environmental degradation and the oppression of women by men both result from the power structures dominating capitalist society. This argument does not account for cases where non-capitalist societies have inflicted severe environmental damage or where patriarchal societies have protected their environments. (MEH)

Eco-socialism

Environmental concerns have entered debates in all major traditions of Western political thought. SOCIALISM sees environmental problems as stemming from the effects of capitalism, the CONSUMERIST ethos and the persistence of POVERTY. Green political thought roots the problems in economic growth, expanding means of production, technological development and materialist values. Eco-socialism attempts to imbue SOCIALIST ideology with green political ideas, although there is no consensus on this. However, both Greens and SOCIALISTS are turning to NEW SOCIAL MOVEMENTS as agents for change. Green principles of participatory democracy and SOCIAL JUSTICE are finding resonance in SOCIALIST concerns about equitable resource distribution and natural limits to economic expansion are gaining recognition among SOCIALISTS. (MEH)

Education vouchers

A proposal whereby the state provides parents with tokens to enable them to 'purchase' the schooling they consider most appropriate for their children, topping it up with their own funds if necessary. They are associated particularly with the political right and strategies to maximize PARENTAL CHOICE. (DEG)

Education Welfare Service

Advice and support provided by LOCAL EDUCATION AUTHORITIES in liaison with parents and schools for pupils with school-based problems such as TRUANCY, bullying or disruptive behaviour. It also operates where it is believed that home circumstances may be having an adverse effect on educational attainment. (DEG)

Educational Priority Areas

Areas of multiple DEPRIVATION designated under the 1967 Plowden Report, which were to be allocated extra resources to enable schools to provide COMPENSATORY EDUCATION to counter the disadvantages of home and neighbourhood. (DEG)

Effectiveness

For economists, one policy is more effective than another if it involves the use of fewer resources but achieves the same policy result. Alternatively the policy may use the same resources but achieve more. No question is raised here about its good or bad effects. Thus we can measure the effectiveness of a MEALS ON WHEELS service by taking some measure of the quality of the service – whether the food was nutritious, liked by the USER and arrived hot and on time. Then we can look at the cost and see how costly it was to provide an effective service on these measures. Two providers of service can be compared to see who provides the most effective service. See also EFFICIENCY. (HG)

Efficiency

In economics, a broader term than EFFECTIVENESS. An economist concerned with efficiency questions would want to ask, for example, if a MEALS ON WHEELS service is the best way of ensuring that an old person gets adequately fed. ALLOCATIVE efficiency means that a policy will contribute to the overall WELFARE of a society. Resources are ALLOCATED between activities – industries and individuals – in a way that maximizes the WELFARE of the whole. Where no further ALLOCATION can be made which would increase the welfare of individuals then that ALLOCATION is perfectly efficient. Classical economists believe that such conditions only apply where there is a perfect free market. Trade will take place to exchange goods until that perfect state is reached because it will be in the interests of some individual or firm to make such an exchange. However, modern economists accept that there are many reasons for MARKET FAILURE and there are monopolies or other imperfections in the market. Overall efficiency may demand that governments or other agencies provide PUBLIC GOODS or take other corrective action. (HG)

Egalitarianism

The belief in or advocacy of a society based upon the principle of EQUALITY between people, in particular the pursuit of EQUALITY of outcome. (AE)

Eleven plus

An examination introduced in 1944 to assess a pupil's aptitude at age 11 for selective state SECONDARY EDUCATION: GRAMMAR, secondary TECHNICAL and SECONDARY MODERN SCHOOLS. It was much criticized for its bias towards the children of middle-class parents, who generally did better in the examination, and was largely phased out with the introduction of COMPREHENSIVE EDUCATION. (DEG)

Eligibility

An individual or a family will be eligible for a BENEFIT or service if they comply with the rules set by the appropriate agency. The rule may be that the individual has a specified number of contributions or particular needs, lives within a certain area (a catchment area or ACTION ZONE) or undertakes to meet pre-set conditions, such as seeking work or retraining. (HG)

Empiricism

An approach to investigation based upon the collection of observable data and the analysis of such data to generate facts about the social world. Empiricism assumes that facts generate theories, rather than the other way round. British SOCIAL POLICY has been influenced by empiricism, as exemplified in the work of Booth and ROWNTREE in their studies of POVERTY at the turn of the twentieth century. (AE)

Employment office

See JOBCENTRE

Employment policies

A term often used interchangeably with LABOUR-MARKET POLICIES, yet the former is a broader term than the latter, including any form of public intervention aimed to maintain a high and stable level of employment. Thus policies might be primarily directed towards stimulating labour demand, such as providing SUBSIDIES for particular industries, improving infrastructure, granting tax SUBSIDIES for attracting employment-generating investment in particular regions. More conventional LABOUR MARKET POLICIES, such as job creation and temporary work opportunities, can also be subsumed under this category. Regulatory policies can also be aimed at employment generation, i.e. limiting overtime work or legislating on part-time or job-share work. Other employment policies focus more on the supply of labour, such as training and retraining pro-grammes or work experience schemes. Another form of employment policy is facilitating job-search activities and matching labour demand with labour supply. (JC)

Employment protection

RIGHTS for workers that can be legally enforced, generally contained in legislation, including restrictions on working hours or protection against REDUNDANCY, loss of income, or downgrading of type of job. For individual workers the degree of protection often depends on seniority. (JC)

Empowerment

The process through which people gain power and authority over their own affairs. It can mean individual CITIZENS taking responsibility for their own well-being and that of their families and consequently reducing their demands on state provision, or the use of collective action to empower previously DISEMPOWERED groups. In welfare provision this often involves a shift of power from service providers to service USERS. Conditions conducive to empowerment exist where CITIZENS have access to information; where education or training is available; where organizational structures support CITIZEN PARTICIPATION; and where CITIZENS are able to influence decisions in policy making. (MEH)

Enabling

Enabling means EMPOWERING rather than caring. Enabling an individual to achieve independence and CHOICE involves support, training and resources. DIRECT PAYMENTS are a good example of this. An 'enabling authority' purchases quality services for USERS from independent providers as well as empowering individuals and communities through developing participatory democracy. (SB)

Enterprise culture

A term used by the NEW RIGHT to describe the competitive, initiative-taking behavioural patterns into which it would seek to inculcate society. It is contrasted with the DEPENDENCY CULTURE that is allegedly fostered by an overweening WELFARE STATE. (HD)

Entitlement

The RIGHT by which certain people, in particular circumstances, may receive specific BENEFITS or services, or the principle by which it may be held that such receipt is justified. The term is characteristically used to denote a RIGHT defined by rules and is therefore conceived as the conceptual opposite of DISCRETION. Entitlement in this sense is something that is legally enforceable: it provides the calculable basis upon which welfare can be justly and consistently provided and, to supporters of this view, 'a discretionary entitlement' is a contradiction in terms. However, entitlement is a contested concept and there is also a view that it should be based on DESERT as much as justice; it may be morally as well as legally defined. Under this definition, entitlement arises when BENEFITS or services are needed and/or deserved and determining a person's entitlement may require the creative exercise of administrative or professional judgement. Even when entitlement is defined by legally prescribed rules, interpreting those rules and applying them often entails the exercise of some element of DISCRETION. (HD)

Environmentalism

Concern about the environmental degradation caused by human activities. Its adherents range from eco-centric 'dark' greens who link environmental protection with radical structural social change, to more reformist 'light' greens who see the value of the environment as residing only in its utility to human beings and regard environmental protection as compatible with economic growth. (MEH)

Equal opportunity policies

Generally derive from measures that outlaw DISCRIMINATION on the grounds of gender, 'race' and DISABILITY. This legislation means that both private and public organizations should ensure EQUALITY for all, in areas such as employment, training, education, the provision of goods, services and facilities, and the disposal and management of premises. As examples, employers should have fair and open recruitment procedures, schools must ensure that both girls and boys have equal ACCESS to all subject areas in the curriculum, and landlords cannot exclude certain groups from renting their property.

This legislation is based on the concept of equal opportunity, generally interpreted as equal treatment except in a few specific areas (see EQUALITY and EQUITY). Importantly, different treatment is embedded in the legislation for women around the issues of pregnancy, for example maternity leave and time off for ante-natal classes, and for disabled people, for example in terms of access to buildings and transport.

As well as national legislation, the European Union has also had an important impact on equal opportunity policies, particularly in the area of gender. All member states have to comply with directives on equal pay, equal treatment in employment, and EQUALITY in SOCIAL SECURITY for women and men. More recently, the European Commission has brought forward directives aimed at helping parents to combine their paid work with their domestic and caring responsibilities – FAMILY FRIENDLY provisions and family and work reconciliation. These have included RIGHTS to minimum maternity leave, PATERNITY LEAVE and PARENTAL LEAVE when children are ill and in need of care. EQUALITY between women and men has also been enforced through the European Court of Justice, for example the UK case on pension ages for women and men. In the areas of 'race' and DISABILITY the European Commission has been less active, relying on non-directive recommendations.

Equal opportunity policies within organizations must be constructed and implemented to comply with the law. However, some organizations, particularly in the PUBLIC SECTOR, have policies that go further than their requirements under the law to attempt to ensure equal opportunity. For example, this may involve including other potential targets of DISCRIMINATION within the jurisdiction of their policies, such as gay men and lesbians and older people, or providing more generous conditions for maternity or PATERNITY LEAVE than those dictated by the legislation.

Organizational approaches to equal opportunity policies can be classified on a continuum from minimalist at one end, through liberal, to radical at the other. The minimalist approach is most commonly encountered in private industry and is favoured by those on the political right. It is assumed that market forces will maximize fairness and only individual irrationality and prejudice introduce distortions. Therefore, only policies that strictly comply with the legislation are enacted.

The liberal perspective is strongly committed to the equal-treatment approach, assuming that a 'level playing field' will ensure equal opportunity. Despite recognizing that organizational DISCRIMINATION may exist in the form of unfair procedures and practices, equal opportunity is seen as possible by the elimination of barriers to free competition between individuals. The development of fair, bureaucratic and formal procedures and rules is emphasized.

The radical approach takes equal opportunity on to another plain by adopting an EQUALITY of outcome approach (see EQUALITY for a discussion of this concept). This is most often encountered in the PUBLIC SECTOR, and is favoured more by those on the political left. The policies may use different and preferential treatment of certain groups to ensure equal opportunity, for example the use of positive action in favour of women entering HIGHER EDUCATION in offering them access courses to disciplines where they are under-represented, such as engineering and science.

Many organizational equal opportunity policies are a mixture of the different approaches outlined above, and cannot necessarily be neatly classified. However, many organizations have given primacy to equal opportunity policies aimed at employment rather than service delivery. This is true even of organizations responsible for welfare provision, such as SOCIAL SERVICES DEPARTMENTS and the NATIONAL HEALTH SERVICE. Also, the vast majority of organizations, both in the PRIVATE and PUBLIC SECTORS, have concentrated on the less difficult side of equal opportunity policies, ensuring non-discriminatory structures in terms of changing formal regulations, procedures and practices. Very few organizations have also tackled the very difficult area of attempting to change their informal culture, which can maintain a climate not conducive to equal opportunity, or even hostile to it.

It is increasingly recognized that both organizational structures and cultures need to be challenged and changed by equal opportunity policies. There is a need to change both behaviours and attitudes within organizations, in other words to tackle institutionalized DISCRIMINATION. Institutionalized DISCRIMINATION can be seen as the collective failure of an organization to provide EQUALITY of opportunity in employment and service delivery, through processes, attitudes and behaviour which are affected by prejudice, ignorance, thoughtlessness and stereotyping. The definition of institutionalized DISCRIMINATION demonstrates the difficulties and complexities that equal opportunity policies have to tackle. (BB)

Equality

A NORMATIVE concept – about values or ideals – which plays an important role as a principle against which social policies are judged. It is also a highly contested concept, the position on which has traditionally been treated as a litmus test, distinguishing left and right approaches in SOCIAL POLICY. More recently it has been one of the most controversial aspects of Labour's political and social philosophy. These debates can best be understood by distinguishing between a number of different meanings of equality.

In its most basic form, equality refers to equal worth. This is a moral principle, deriving from our common humanity. As human beings, we should be treated as having equal worth, regardless of gender, 'race', social class, sexuality or other distinctions. It is possible to distinguish 'thin' and 'thick' versions of the principle of equal worth. In its 'thin' minimalist form the principle of equal worth is about equal treatment before the law, that is treatment without bias or prejudice. This is often called 'formal equality'. Even those on the political right, who would argue fiercely against the principle of economic equality, normally support the principle of equality before the law as fundamental to a free society.

The 'thin' version of the principle of equal worth underpins other forms of equality. The 'thick' version has been variously called 'social equality', 'equality of status' or 'equality of regard'. It is about the recognition of the fundamental equality of each human being in social relationships. It is, thus, a principle that opposes social hierarchy and privilege.

The principle of equal worth is a moral rather than a distributional principle – it does not imply any particular distribution of resources. However, some argue that the more unequal the distribution of income and wealth, the less likely a society is to be able to apply the thick principle of equal worth. If there are substantial differences in the rewards that different groups in society receive and a big gap between those at the top and the bottom, it is difficult to maintain that people are being treated as of equal worth in any meaningful sense.

This leads to a more substantive, distributional form of equality, which concerns ACCESS to material resources. The principle of distributional equality has implications for a range of SOCIAL POLICIES that are concerned with the allocation of BENEFITS and services between different groups and individuals. There are two main approaches commonly called 'equality of opportunity' and 'equality of outcome'.

Equality of opportunity is the principle that everyone should have the same opportunity to succeed, regardless of factors such as social class, gender or 'race'. Ability and effort, not social background, should determine how far any individual succeeds in life and the rewards that they receive. The principle is often illustrated using the metaphor of a level playing field. Education is the key policy instrument for promoting equality of opportunity in this broad sense (see also EQUAL OPPORTUNITY POLICIES for policies focused specifically on inequalities of gender, 'race' and DISABILITY). New Labour emphasizes that its vision of equality of opportunity is not about a single chance to climb the ladder while young, but about life-long equality of opportunity. This puts a duty on government to promote opportunities through education and employment throughout people's lives. Critics have argued that, even if successful, this approach simply leads to a MERITOCRACY. Moreover, in today's global economy, we face a 'winners take all' society, where a minority, with talents or skills that are highly valued, can command huge rewards. This raises questions about the rewards for talents and jobs; for instance, should a successful footballer be worth so much more than a nurse or care-worker? Some, following TAWNEY, also characterize equality of opportunity as an equal opportunity to become unequal, which then legitimizes that inequality and the privileges associated with it. The successful can then pass on those privileges to their children, thereby undermining the principle of equality of opportunity. They would argue that genuine equality of opportunity is not possible without greater equality of outcomes.

Equality of outcome is generally regarded as a more radical approach to equality. It shifts the concern from starting points to end results, from opportunities to rewards. In its most extreme form, it would mean everyone ending up with the same level of resources, or at least an equitable level of resources that reflected different levels of need such as family size. However, very few indeed argue for equality of outcome in this absolute sense, even though opponents of equality of outcome sometimes caricature them as doing so. Most EGALITARIANS, who subscribe to the equality of outcome position, instead argue for greater equality in the distribution of resources than that which currently exists in a highly unequal society. They thus tend to make the case for policies of REDISTRIBUTION from the better off to the worse off. Against those who maintain that equality of outcome would spell dreary uniformity, they counter, following TAWNEY, that it is inequalities that stifle human diversity and potential and the flowering of the human spirit.

Official figures show that economic inequality in the UK is high by both international and historical standards. The debate about which principles of equality should underpin SOCIAL and FISCAL POLICY can thus be seen as critical to the future well-being of society. (RL)

Equity

A distributional principle applied to the allocation of services and BENEFITS in order to achieve what is considered a fair division. It is a two-part principle. The first part, which is reasonably straightforward, is about treating like cases alike. So, for example, if two people have no resources and are assessed as having the same level of need, they should receive the same amount of any INCOME-RELATED SOCIAL SECURITY BENEFIT. The second part of the principle is based on a recognition that people are different in various ways and that a more equal and just set of outcomes is not always best achieved by treating everybody in the same way. Thus, for example, it is generally seen as fair or equitable to provide higher SOCIAL SECURITY payments to disabled people to help meet the costs associated with DISABILITY. Thus the application of the principle of equity relies also on an ASSESSMENT of NEEDS. (RL)

Equivalence scale

Scales used in equivalization of income and other data such as that compiled by the HOUSEHOLDS BELOW AVERAGE INCOME, FAMILY EXPENDITURE SURVEY and other statistical series. Through the equivalization process, the data (e.g. household income) is adjusted to account for differences in household sizes and composition (number of adults and number and ages of dependants). An overall value is calculated for each household by aggregating the appropriate scale values for each member of the household. Equivalized household income is then calculated by dividing household income by the household's equivalence value. The scales are used to reflect the notion that the larger the household composition, the higher the income required to maintain a comparable standard of living. There are a large number of such scales, each having their own weaknesses; hence there is no general consensus about the best method of equivalization. However, to enhance comparability in the UK, many government and other agencies use the McClements scale. (TM)

Espace sociale

A French initiative in the early 1980s taken up by Jacques Delors, the former President of the European Commission. It refers to the attempt, at the time, to give more prominence to aspects of social policy within the process of increasing integration between the member states of the then European Community. (JC)

Ethical socialism

Seminal thinkers on welfare like TAWNEY are characterized as ethical SOCIALISTS, because their commitment to socialism and the pursuit of social EQUALITY was based not on belief in class struggle, but a notion of social morality. It is often contended that the social reformism of the early Labour Party was informed as much by Nonconformist Christianity as by MARXIAN ideas, and by a deep conviction that social inequality was morally offensive. Later thinkers have brought a somewhat different perspective to the concept of ethical socialism – one rooted less in radical Christian values and more in admiration for the supposed virtues of the traditional working class. Adherents of the latter view distinguish between the egoistical socialism of LIBERTARIAN middle-class intellectuals and an ethical socialism that embraces the CONSERVATIVE values of family life, hard work and self-responsibility. This strand of ethical socialism is able to share some common ground with the NEW RIGHT. (HD)

Eugenics

A term coined by Francis Galton in 1883 from the Greek word meaning 'good in birth' to signify social improvement through the use of genetic policies. In the late nineteenth and early twentieth centuries eugenicists argued for enhancing the quality of the population by measures such as ameliorative social reform, selective breeding and sterilization of the unfit. (DEG)

Eurostat

The statistical office of the European Union consolidates data provided by European countries, processes data and makes it comparable at

European level. It is an important source for all types of social, economic, demographic and political data for the European Union and countries intending to join the European Union. (JC)

Euthanasia

Putting individuals painlessly to death when they are suffering from terminal illnesses. There is controversy about 'informed consent' in relation to this and about the roles doctors and nurses may play. In practice much hinges on the extent of use of painkillers that may shorten life. (MJH)

Evaluation

Research may be applied to asking questions about the EFFECTIVENESS or EFFICIENCY of social programmes or individual projects. Evaluation has become an increasingly common element in social action since the 1960s and is today frequently linked to attempts to measure performance through the use of indicators, to assess BEST VALUE or to inform policy making. Evaluations may be summative (seeking at the end of a programme or piece of social action to assess whether or not it was successful) or formative (designed to inform policy as it develops). The latter is sometimes referred to as action research. (AE)

Evidence-based practice

An approach to service provision development centred on ensuring that USERS are given the most effective and appropriate provision as indicated by currently available research findings. Initially promoted in the 1990s as a means of disseminating best practice within health care, it is a key feature of recent UK social policy, though most developed in medicine where the National Institute of Clinical Excellence (NICE) produces clinical practice guidelines based on the most up-to-date scientific knowledge. (MJH)

Exit

Coined by A. Hirschmann to refer to the sanction a purchaser of a product or USER of a service could exert on a provider by threatening to, or actually, taking away their custom. This brings home to the supplier that it is not doing a good job and that it must change if it is to sustain its income. Exit is often contrasted with VOICE. (HG)

Externalities

Economists refer to the side effects (good or bad) of a market process as an externality. These effects are not reflected in the price we pay for the product. Driving a car produces fumes that affect children's health – a bad thing. Immunization of children improves their health and reduces the risk of infectious disease in others – a good thing. (HG)

F

Fabianism

H. G. Wells, George Bernard Shaw and BEATRICE and SIDNEY WEBB all joined the Fabian Society at around the time of its foundation in 1884. The Fabians believed that the free-market system was grossly inefficient and unable to resolve such problems as POVERTY and inequality. Such problems could only be resolved, they believed, by a scientific form of collectivism based on social ownership, economic planning and active government. Rejecting the revolutionary strategy of MARXISM as inappropriate, the Fabians believed that persuasion and argument could achieve social reform. Unlike Marxists they also believed that the existing state machinery at both local and national level could be used for the pursuit of collectivist goals. At first the Fabians sought to persuade existing political parties to adopt their ideas through a process of permeation. However, they gradually established much closer ties with the fledgling Labour Party.

Eventually the Fabians acted as the Labour Party's research body and SIDNEY WEBB drafted the party's constitution in 1918. Fabian ideas have been influential in Labour circles not least in the development of SOCIAL POLICY from 1945 to the early 1970s. However, its top-down approach has found less favour in more recent decades, not least because of growing public scepticism about expert-led policy making. After an era in which NEO-LIBERAL ideas have been in the ascendancy, Fabianism is enjoying something of a renaissance as it seeks to develop a modernized DEMOCRATIC SOCIALIST strategy. (RMP)

Fair rents

The system introduced in 1964 to regulate rents in the PRIVATE RENTED SECTOR. It was designed to prevent households from being charged inflated rents associated with shortages of accommodation, and so was based on a calculation which sought to identify the rent which would be payable in a market where scarcity did not exist. (AM)

Faith schools

Schools managed by religious bodies which may be supported by grant-aid, but operate on a voluntary basis providing specialist schooling outside normal school hours. See DENOMINATIONAL SCHOOLS. (MM)

Familism/Familialism

The way in which the interests and needs of individuals – men, women and children – are subsumed within the family as a whole, and how this is constructed by state welfare provisions. Also used to refer to the ideological dominance accorded to the 'family' as a form of social relations. (JM)

Family Allowances

Introduced in the UK at the end of the Second World War as a UNIVERSAL BENEFIT payment intended to cover some of the costs of caring for children, and paid to parents with more than one child. In 1978 they were replaced by CHILD BENEFIT, which was paid to the parents of all children. (PA)

Family Expenditure Survey

A continuous survey of expenditure and income started in 1957 to provide information for the Retail Price Index. Data are collected from around 7,000 private households in Great Britain (response rate about 60 per cent), including a household questionnaire and two-week expenditure diaries for all aged 16 and above. Results are published annually in *Family Spending*. (JM)

Family-friendly policies

Measure initially developed to enable parents, especially mothers, to combine employment with child care, but increasingly used to include provisions for other employees with caring responsibilities. They range from arrangements for support during particular contingencies such as maternity, paternity, adoptive parents, parental, carers or emergency leave, to financial assistance and advice or (rarely) on-site facilities. More controversially, the term may also be extended to incorporate the use of flexible forms of employment. Apart from maternity leave, caring-related leave was, until recently, offered on a voluntary basis by some employers. But in line with European Union Directives various forms of leave are increasingly becoming statutory rights in the UK. The notion of 'family-friendly' employment practices is also giving way to the broader concept of 'work–life balance' and attempts to enable all employees to reconcile their work and other commitments. Whether these developments are likely to increase organizational productivity generally or reduce gender divisions in paid and unpaid employment, however, remains unclear. (MM)

Family planning

The birth control movement in Britain dates back to the mid-nineteenth century but came to prominence following the trial in 1877 of Bradlaugh and Besant, who were prosecuted for obscenity for publishing a pamphlet describing and recommending contraceptive methods. The case was eventually decided in their favour and soon after the first MALTHUSIAN League was founded, with the aim of promoting family limitation through contraceptive techniques as well as through abstinence and marriage postponement. In the early years of the twentieth century various other organizations also began campaigning for wider access to birth control, and family planning clinics were established to offer information and advice on a voluntary basis. The National Birth Control Association was established in 1930 and by 1939 was running 66 family planning clinics. These were intended for married couples and not for unmarried persons, the aim being to help such couples control the timing and spacing of their children. Family planning clinics continued mainly as voluntary bodies until the 1970s, when contraceptive advice was made available, again to married persons only, on the NATIONAL HEALTH SERVICE. See also REPRODUCTION POLICIES. (JM)

Family policy

Until recently the term 'family policy' was very little used in either research or policy discussions. However, over the past twenty to twenty-five years it has increasingly taken centre stage, not least as a reaction to the radical transformations in family structures and patterns over the past two or three decades. This is true both nationally and internationally. For example, the European Commission established an Observatory on National Family Policies in 1989 and the United Nations declared 1994 the Year of the Family. However, an agreed definition of family policy remains elusive. Some seek to identify the field or the boundaries of family policy. These range from maximalist definitions, which include everything that affects families whether intended or not, to much more minimalist approaches, which include only those policies directly targeted on families and which aim to affect family behaviour in some way. Most authors would include the following three main areas of policy:

- The legal regulation of family behaviour: laws relating to marriage and divorce, sexual behaviour, contraception and ABORTION, parental RIGHTS and duties, CHILD PROTECTION.
- Policies to support family income: tax allowances, family and CHILD BENEFITS, PARENTAL LEAVE and BENEFITS, enforcement of CHILD SUPPORT.
- The provision of services for families: CHILD CARE provisions, SUB-SIDIZED housing, social services, COMMUNITY CARE.

Other analyses of family policy focus much more upon the objectives of policy, and the extent to which these are, for example, pro-natalist, or aim to promote gender EQUALITY or support 'traditional' family structures. However, such policy objectives are not necessarily overt or explicit. The extent to which governments are willing to intervene (or to be seen to intervene) in family behaviour may be constrained by the ideological importance accorded to family privacy. The concept of SUB-SIDIARITY is sometimes evoked to argue that families should be left alone and governments should only intervene in times of crisis or to protect vulnerable family members, in particular children. There is a growing literature that compares the range and objectives of family policy in different countries and which points to the cultural, as well as economic and demographic, differences across different family policy models. One contrast often made is between the family-centred southern European countries, where extended families play an important role in welfare and support of family members, and the more individualistic Scandinavian countries, where family relationships are not generally accorded special treatment and where gender EQUALITY is given a higher priority in policy.

The phrase 'family policy' tends to imply a co-ordinated and coherent set of policies with clear objectives and delivered through established institutions, but in practice family policy tends to be much more fragmented, inconsistent and without designated institutional support. Again, of course, this varies across countries, with some having specific government departments to deal with family policy and including family goals in constitutional and other government statements, while other countries do not make family policy a specific area of government. The UK has for many years been a country without a strong family policy – no government department, no senior ministers with responsibility for family policy, and no clear statements of policy goals and intentions. Family policy in the UK has been described as 'reluctant', focused on problem families and on providing TARGETED support to those in NEED, rather than offering general support for all families.

However, the Labour government elected in 1997 not only increased the level and range of support offered to families but also proved to be more willing to make explicit its family policy objectives and orientations. The discussion document *Supporting Families* published in 1998 by the Home Office and the (new) Ministerial Group on the Family set out principles for policy and proposed the establishment of various new bodies to help support and advise families. The three principles were that children should come first, that children need stability, and that families raise children and should be supported, but not superseded, by government in this. The five main areas for intervention were: access to support and advice; family incomes and prosperity; the balance between work and family life; strengthening families and reducing family breakdown; and tackling problems of abuse, violence and neglect. The document received a mixed reception, reflecting the fact that family issues are deeply ideological and achieving consensus can be very difficult – a reason, perhaps, for not making policy too explicit in this area.

The 1980s CHILD SUPPORT legislation, which sought to enforce a particular definition of the financial obligations of separated parents, illustrated some of the difficulties that policy intervention can create. The legitimacy of this policy was seriously called into question and many protests, including public demonstrations, forced later revisions and amendments. Policies that step outside of NORMATIVE views about what family members can and should do for each other are likely to be very difficult to enforce. Politicians are fond of claiming to be in the 'party of the family' but at a time when family patterns are increasingly complex and diverse, family policy can become a dangerous political battleground. (JM)

Family Resources Survey

A continuous survey started in 1992 for the Department of Social Security to provide data on incomes, BENEFIT receipt and TAKE-UP rates. Data are collected from around 24,000 private households in Great Britain (response rate about 66 per cent). Results are published annually in *Family Resources Survey*. (JM)

Feminism(s)

A feminist analysis of SOCIAL POLICY emerged during the 1970s and 1980s, although a number of its insights can be found in the writings of early and mid-twentieth century feminist campaigners such as ELEANOR RATHBONE. Initially feminist analyses tended to focus on a critique of existing SOCIAL POLICIES and mainstream SOCIAL POLICY writing. Women and their concerns were marginalized despite the importance of WELFARE to women's lives and of women to WELFARE, as paid and unpaid providers.

While sharing these common concerns, different strands of feminism have approached social policy in diverse ways. Thus liberal feminism tended to emphasize equal RIGHTS and opportunities, with a focus on how the individual is treated in the law, education and the labour market. Radical feminism has been more concerned with male power at both a systemic and individual level and with how it is exercised in the domestic 'private' sphere through, for instance, domestic violence. It has also helped to put issues such as reproductive technology (see REPRODUCTION POLICIES) and sexuality on the SOCIAL POLICY agenda. SOCIALIST feminism focused more on the systems of production and reproduction under capitalism and the intersection between gender and social class. It has highlighted, in particular, the importance of women's domestic labour to SOCIAL POLICY.

More recently black feminism has challenged these feminist positions' claims to speak for all women, ignoring the different perspectives of black women and the centrality of RACISM to their lives. The black feminist critique has been part of a broader challenge to the very category of 'woman', which has been taken up by other groups such as disabled feminists. This broader challenge also reflects a suspicion of such categories under POSTMODERNITY. Nevertheless, most feminist analysis continues to deploy the category 'woman', varying in the extent to which it acknowledges differences between women.

Feminism has developed a gendered analysis of the institutions, relations and discourses that constitute SOCIAL POLICY, examining how these reflect and shape relationships between women and men and their different implications for both. More NORMATIVE feminist analysis represents an attempt to 'regender' these institutions, relations and discourses so that they better reflect the varied perspectives and NEEDS of women. In many ways feminism has posed a fundamental challenge to the discipline, causing it to rethink both its focus and some of its most basic concepts.

Feminist analysis has also drawn attention to the family as a key site of welfare and to the importance of the gendered interactions between the family and the other main sources of welfare: the state, labour market and VOLUNTARY and PRIVATE SECTORS. This reflects a broader reconceptualization of the relationship between the domestic private sphere (traditionally associated with women) and the public sphere of the labour market, state and polity (associated with men). This has had three main implications:

- the translation of a number of issues deemed private into legitimate concerns of PUBLIC POLICY, examples being CHILD CARE and domestic violence;
- the demonstration of the importance of the impact of social policies on relations within the private sphere;
- the illumination of the ways in which gender relations in the private sphere differentially shape the access of women and men to the public sphere. Thus, for example, women's main responsibility for care and housework makes it easier for men to participate in the labour market and politics and harder for women to do so.

Feminism has analysed the family as a gendered site of the production and consumption of WELFARE and of the distribution of material resources. It has also deconstructed the family at the level of ideology or discourse, showing the ways in which traditional family forms have been privileged over other ways of living.

Initially feminist analysis of the state tended to cast it as either a tool of capitalism (SOCIALIST feminist) or of PATRIARCHY (radical feminist), or accept it as a neutral instrument to which women can appeal (liberal). Subsequent analysis has tended to be subtler in its recognition of

- the ways in which the state can be simultaneously supportive and oppressive of women;
- variations between and within states, so that, for instance, some have described the Scandinavian welfare states as 'women-friendly';
- the diversity of the relationship to the state of different groups of women as USERS, providers and, to a lesser extent, shapers of welfare.

What remains is an understanding of the ways in which the state, as a gendered institution, regulates the family and the labour market and the relationship between the two, with differing implications for women and men. In the same way, feminist analysis of women's employment patterns tends to emphasize how women's position is a product of both labour-market practices and institutions and of their position in the family and their treatment by the state. Feminist analyses also involve a rethinking of some key SOCIAL POLICY concepts:

- Work, which is seen to embrace unpaid care and domestic work, and not just paid work.
- Care, which is revealed to involve work (often very hard work) as well as a set of relationships and values.
- DEPENDENCY, which is analysed as a relationship in which women are often economically dependent upon men to a greater or lesser extent, while men are dependent upon women for care and servicing.
- CITIZENSHIP, which has been exposed as initially excluding women in both theory and practice and then including them on different terms to men.

Feminism is above all a politics which has fought to improve the position of women. Within that politics there has long been a tension between couching demands in the name of women's EQUALITY with men, on the one hand, and women's difference from men, deriving from their caring responsibilities, on the other. This tension raises again the issue of how far women (and men) can be treated as monolithic groups. (RL)

Feminization of poverty

First coined in the US to denote women's greater vulnerability to POVERTY compared to that of men. This greater vulnerability reflects women's position in the family as well as the labour market. The true extent of women's POVERTY tends to be hidden in official statistics, which generally measure individual POVERTY on the basis of family income rather than that of individuals within families. Yet research indicates that resources are often not shared fairly within families, so that a woman can be poorer than her male partner. It also indicates that women tend to take the main responsibility for and the strain of managing POVERTY, often putting the NEEDS of their children and partners before their own. This can have implications for their physical and MENTAL HEALTH. The term can be used misleadingly to suggest that women's greater exposure to POVERTY is a new development. In fact it is a very old phenomenon which has become more visible in recent years. This is due, in part, to the increase in the number of female-headed households, who are particularly vulnerable to POVERTY, but also to the work of FEMINIST researchers. (RL)

Fertility rate

Birth rates are number of births per 1,000 women, usually grouped by age. Total period fertility rates are the average number of children that would be born if women experienced the age-specific fertility rates of the period in question throughout their child-bearing years. (JM)

Financial exclusion

The consequence of unequal access to modern financial services such as banking, automatic credit and insurance. Some, often poorer, people do not in practice have access to these services and as a result are excluded from financial security and protection, and from some forms of purchasing and investment. (PA)

Fiscal crisis

Refers to the tendency of capitalist economies to move towards instability and eventual collapse because they depend on growing levels of

PUBLIC EXPENDITURE to survive, yet they cannot induce voters to pay for them. Capitalist economies, it has been argued, need government to invest in roads and other basic services which markets do not do to an adequate level. Individual workers need to be educated, but the firm has no INCENTIVE to pay for their education. Since most people will not be in a position to invest adequately in their HUMAN CAPITAL, the taxpayer must do so. The costs of these measures will increase over time, but the public's capacity and willingness to pay the needed taxes will not keep pace. This could lead to social instability, conflict and eventual revolution. (HG)

Fiscal policies

Policies that governments pursue in relation to tax have to address three main questions:

- how much to tax – the overall balance between taxation and the whole economy;
- what to tax – for example, the distribution of that taxation between INDIRECT and DIRECT TAX;
- how much to tax which income groups – how PROGRESSIVE to make taxes.

Since 1997 the UK government has sought to keep to a 'golden rule' that it will not borrow more over an economic cycle than it spends on current account (on items other than on buildings). Taxes may be used to foster particular spending or saving patterns (e.g. spending on HOME OWNERSHIP) or they may be used to inhibit certain kinds of spending (e.g. high taxes on tobacco). Tax policies may also be used to help particular groups, such as families with children or married couples, by providing allowances (TAX RELIEFS) against income for such groups. This use of the tax system has been called FISCAL WELFARE. (HG)

Fiscal welfare

The use of FISCAL POLICY to benefit families or individuals with particular NEEDS, such as encouragement of a preferred type of housing (HOME OWNERSHIP) or PENSION contributions. In the past, exempting taxpayers from tax on a part of their income if, for instance, they had children or MORTGAGE interest payments had this aim. This benefited the highest income groups most. It did not benefit non-taxpayers at all. More recently government has used refundable TAX CREDITS which do not suffer from this problem. It also encompasses TAX RELIEF to employers providing various occupational benefits, a process which has similarly been criticized for being of greatest benefit to higher income earners. See OCCUPATIONAL WELFARE. (HG)

Flat-rate benefits

A beneficiary receives a fixed level of BENEFIT on occurrence of a specified contingency or from membership of a category, i.e. the BENEFIT is neither EARNINGS-RELATED on the one hand, nor INCOME-RELATED or MEANS-TESTED on the other. (DM)

Fordism

Initially coined to characterize a transition within the organization of manufacturing industry from large-scale factory-based production of goods (epitomized by the sort of production-line process once pioneered by the Ford motor company) to the dispersed and flexible small-scale operational production of diversified goods and services for niche markets. Regardless of the extent to which the existence of this trend is empirically observable, the terms 'Fordism' and 'post-Fordism' have been widely adopted as a 'shorthand' means by which to capture one of the essences of several intersecting processes. These include economic GLOBALIZATION, the arrival of late capitalism's 'electronic/information age' and/or the emergence of POSTMODERNITY. The term has been influential in explanations of labour-market trends and in particular the tendency to increased polarization between 'core' and 'peripheral' jobs. It has also been used to explain the trends towards WELFARE PLURALISM and DECENTRALIZATION, and the transition from the UNIVERSALIST and monolithic (Fordist) WELFARE STATE of the post-Second World War era to the selectivist and MANAGERIALIST (post-Fordist) WELFARE STATE of the present era. (HD)

Foster care

Care for children living full-time with a family other than their birth family, on a temporary, long-term or permanent basis. Although private fostering occurs, LOCAL AUTHORITIES arrange most foster placements in the UK. Normally legal responsibilities for the child rest with the birth parents or LOCAL AUTHORITY. (MH)

Fraud

In its legal sense fraud is an act of criminal deception by which the perpetrator obtains a material advantage – for example welfare services or BENEFITS – to which she or he is not entitled. However, the term is sometimes also used to refer to practices or alleged 'abuses' which are not strictly fraudulent. (HD)

Free rider

An economic expression referring to someone who gains from a service without paying for it. If I pay to have a street light put up in a dark street my neighbours benefit too. It is a reason why markets may fail – everyone may leave essential tasks to others. But if everyone agrees to co-operate and pay all will benefit. (HG)

Freedom

Perhaps best conceptualized as the human individual's capacity for and right to self-determination. What has been called the 'negative' view of freedom looks upon it as no more and no less than the absence of coercion. However, there is also a 'positive' view of freedom that looks upon it as the power to choose. Finally, freedom can also be understood in an ontological (or, some would say, psychological) sense: personal AUTONOMY or 'consciousness in itself', it has been argued, is a defining NEED of human beings and may be attainable sometimes in spite of, yet sometimes because of, external intervention by others. Critics from different parts of the ideological spectrum have claimed that the WELFARE STATE is coercive and/or PATERNALISTIC. It therefore violates the freedom of those that it taxes and of those that it purports to assist or protect (while MARXISTS would say that under capitalism freedom could in any event be no more than an illusion). Defenders of state welfare have argued that it can serve to guarantee or even enhance freedom, including particularly the freedom of the more vulnerable members of society. (HD)

Frictional unemployment

See FULL EMPLOYMENT

Friendly Society

First developed in the seventeenth century as collective responses to the need for health insurance and burial costs, these expanded with the growth of industrial towns in the nineteenth century. Many had a strong social element, which subsequently declined as the emphasis on MUTUAL AID and INSURANCE increased. Men from the respectable working class dominated Friendly Societies; the poor, unskilled working class never figured prominently. Formalization and specialization in the late nineteenth century were followed by legislation at the beginning of the twentieth, which both confirmed the role of friendly societies and paved the way for greater state INSURANCE schemes, which eventually took over many of their roles. There are still around seventy friendly societies in Britain providing small-scale savings and personal insurance. Government still provides TAX RELIEFS for some financial products, and some societies are based on occupational groups, so that in a restricted range of products they have a marginal advantage over conventional companies. The Registrar of Friendly Societies, soon to become part of a broader Financial Services Authority, regulates them. (DWS)

Fringe benefits

A popular term for OCCUPATIONAL WELFARE, often also referred to as 'perks', particularly the financial support provided by employers in addition to employees' basic remuneration. (MM)

Full employment

Full employment is the basic aim of LABOUR-MARKET POLICY and refers to a labour market in which everybody who wants a job can find one, although sometimes taken to mean MALE BREADWINNERS only. This can mean that there are more vacancies than job seekers but not zero UNEMPLOYMENT, since some individuals are between jobs or expect to be working in the near future (frictional unemployment). It is sometimes argued by economists that the NATURAL RATE OF UNEMPLOYMENT (or

NAIRU) has risen over time, which means that any attempt to reduce unemployment below NAIRU would result in accelerating inflation. (JC)

Fundholding

A system that, during the 1990s, enabled GENERAL PRACTITIONERS to apply for a budget enabling them to purchase hospital services for their patients, but which has been replaced by arrangements for PRIMARY CARE Trusts. (MJH)

Further education

Post-school, non-compulsory education and training delivered either in the workplace or a variety of public and private establishments, including sixth-form colleges where academic courses predominate, tertiary colleges and colleges of further education which provide a wider range of vocational and academic courses. (DEG)

G

Gaitskell, Hugh Todd Naylor (1906–1963)

Educated at Winchester and Oxford, he pursued an academic career as a lecturer then reader in Political Economy at University College London. He became Labour MP for South Leeds in 1945, having failed to win Chatham in 1935. He was brought into government as parliamentary secretary at Fuel and Power in 1946, becoming Minister in the same department in 1947. He became Minister of State for Economic Affairs at the Treasury in 1950, becoming Chancellor of the Exchequer in October of the same year. His cautious budget of 1951 (in which CHARGES for dentures and spectacles were introduced) was seen as a factor in Labour's electoral defeat later in the year. He defeated Morrison and BEVAN to become leader of the party in 1955. After the 1959 general election defeat, Gaitskell attempted to modernize the party and widen its appeal by shifting its emphasis towards the goals of SOCIAL JUSTICE and EQUALITY rather than nationalization. He would probably have led Labour back into government but for his untimely death in 1963. (RMP)

Gatekeeping

A rationing device restricting ACCESS to services. It may be managed by professional or front-line staff, e.g. a GENERAL PRACTITIONER's receptionist or a duty social worker, or through ELIGIBILITY criteria and CHARGES. It may be seen as central to SOCIAL WORK and other professions, but also criticized as the result of inadequate resources. (SB)

General Household Survey

A multi-purpose survey started in 1971 to collect data on a range of topics, such as housing, employment, education, health, and family information. Data are collected from around 9,000 private households in Great Britain (response rate of around 72 per cent). Results published annually as *Living in Britain*. (JM)

General Practitioners (GPs)

The commonly used short form for PRIMARY CARE doctors in the UK. (MJH)

Generational contract

A term used to denote the relationship between the 'old' and the 'young' implicit within the SOCIAL SECURITY system and related arrangements in all WELFARE STATES, whereby the employed 'support' their non-working elders through taxation and INSURANCE contributions. DEMO-GRAPHIC CHANGE and rising RETIREMENT rates have led to concerns over this contract and suggestions that older people were extracting more than their fair shares of welfare expenditure to the detriment of younger age groups. The resultant debate over generational EQUITY has cen-tred particularly on state retirement PENSIONS whose funding is based upon future as well as current public spending and contributed to the promotion of occupational and PERSONAL PENSIONS. However, survey analysis across the European Union consistently demonstrates full support for the 'contract' and for continued funding of welfare BENE-FITS, in particular pensions, by taxes or contributions from younger gen-erations of workers. (TM)

Genetic screening

Processes which enable identification of RISKS of the transmission of dis-eases to offspring. While important in reducing serious health risks, its implications for INSURANCE cover and genetic controls are highly con-troversial. (MJH)

Gerontology

The study of later life and the ageing process. Its sub-field, social geron-tology, is the study of the social, behavioural and psychological aspects of the ageing process, societal attitudes to older people and the place of older people in society. (TM)

Ghettos

First popularized in the 1930s to describe urban areas inhabited by the most underprivileged and disadvantaged sections of a society and characterized by great POVERTY, a deteriorating housing stock and poor welfare support. (KA)

Gift economy

See ALTRUISM

Gift relationship

See ALTRUISM

Gini coefficient

A measure of the level of inequality within an INCOME DISTRIBUTION. Maximum inequality is given a value of 1 (one person has all the income in a society) and perfect EQUALITY is measured as 0. In practice inequalities range between these limits. (HG)

Globalization

A characteristic of POSTMODERN society has been identified as the 'shrinking of the world', resulting in similar social, economic, technical and political developments across the globe. Globalization is accompanied by localization – the articulation of the local in the global, for example in the growth of ethnic conflicts that assert the specificity of particular groups in a globalizing world. Proponents of the globalization thesis tend to account for globalization in terms of the development of new information technologies which increase global communication and the adoption of free-trade regimes across the world which encourage the creation of a world market for goods and production. Globalization can be both a prescriptive and descriptive theory, suggesting not just that this process is happening but that it is a process that should be encouraged and strengthened. Opponents of the globalization thesis point to the globalizing tendencies of capitalism that can be seen as having been developed since the nineteenth century and to globalization as a political project founded in NEO-LIBERAL economic and political thinking. They stress the practical limits of globalization, e.g. the majority of the world's population do not have access to clean water or electricity in their homes. Also there is considerable evidence that national states are able to pursue policies apparently at odds with the dictates of global economic forces. Globalization may thus be no more than a political project of a group of the minority world's intellectuals and politicians. (AE)

Governance

Refers to the process of governing, to the manner and mechanisms by which political power is exercised. The term extends, therefore, to encompass the functioning of non-governmental bodies, including, for example, QUANGOS and the range of commercial and VOLUNTARY organizations that administer public functions or implement public policies. (HD)

Government overload

Used by neo-CONSERVATIVES in the 1970s, and also left-ecological groups, criticizing governments for adopting an increasing and unnecessary role of regulator and provider, thereby stifling a more effective self-regulation and direct provision of social welfare by CITIZENS and COMMUNITIES. (JC)

Grammar schools

Selective secondary schools taking only children of high academic ability as measured by their performance in the ELEVEN PLUS examination and providing a specifically academic curriculum. Most LOCAL AUTHORITIES phased them out following the introduction of COMPREHENSIVE EDUCATION in the mid-1960s, though they remain in some areas. (DEG)

Grant maintained schools

Self-governing schools which, after a ballot of parents, have opted to leave LOCAL AUTHORITY control and receive their funding directly from central government. Introduced by the Conservative government in 1988, they were opposed by those who feared they would dilute the COMPREHENSIVE EDUCATION system and introduce a selective pupil intake. (DEG)

Grant related expenditure

The expenditure undertaken by LOCAL AUTHORITIES which is eligible for support by an annual grant from central government. (AM)

Green belt

A key element in planning provisions to control land use changes and development around the largest conurbations in Britain is the designation of areas of land where there are restrictions on development. Their intention is to restrict urban sprawl and to preserve the quality of rural environments on the edge of cities for recreational and other uses. (AM)

Green Paper

A UK government consultative document, now published electronically as well as on paper, which outlines a government's preliminary policy proposals with a view to eliciting public reactions. It is usually followed by a WHITE PAPER outlining proposed legislation. (MJH)

Guaranteed minimum income

See BASIC INCOME

Guardianship

The status of adults other than a child's parents who in law have parental responsibilities for the child. Parents themselves may nominate a guardian to act in the event of their deaths. Courts may also appoint a guardian for orphans or children with no parent able to be responsible for them. (MH)

Guild socialists

Those in the early twentieth century who rejected the then dominant themes of British socialism, political action and state control of the means of production as the route to a SOCIALIST society, in favour of economic action and the democratic control of industry by workers' groups. (DEG)

H

Harmonization

Under Article 117 of the 1957 Treaty of Rome that established the Common Market, the precursor to the European Union, member states agreed to work towards the harmonization of their systems of SOCIAL PROTECTION. The intention was to allow for the movement of labour between countries not being discouraged by the effects of different SOCIAL SECURITY systems. It did not imply an intention to create one SOCIAL SECURITY system across Europe. (AE)

Hayek, Frederick August von (1899–1992)

Born into an academic family in Vienna, Hayek's early work was in the area of theoretical economics where he was a strong opponent of KEYNESIANISM. He became a Professor at the LSE in 1931. He moved into the area of social philosophy in the 1940s, setting out the case for a classical form of LIBERALISM. In his best-known book, *The Road to Serfdom* (1944), he sets out the case against increasing government intervention in both economic and social life. Hayek moved to the USA in 1949 and was Professor at the University of Chicago from 1950 to 1962. He published *The Constitution of Liberty* in 1960 and a trilogy entitled *Law, Legislation and Liberty* in the 1970s. He was awarded the Nobel Prize for Economics (jointly with Gunnar MYRDAL) in 1974. Hayek returned to prominence in the 1970s and 1980s when NEW RIGHT thinkers and organizations in both the USA and Britain used his ideas to promote the cause of liberty and the free market. Both KEITH JOSEPH and Margaret Thatcher were among his admirers. (RMP)

Health and safety

A general expression that is also used to refer to specific regulations and services appertaining to the maintenance of a healthy and safe environment in workplaces developed by the UK government and the EU. (MJH)

Health gain

The notion that improving people's health is contingent on a broad range of interventions rather than specific medical services and that health policy should focus on those that have been shown to have an impact on overall health with the aim not only of prolonging life but enhancing its quality. These include the ASSESSMENT of health NEEDS and outcomes, developing EVIDENCE-BASED MEDICAL PRACTICE and HEALTH AND SAFETY, HEALTH PROMOTION, PREVENTATIVE MEDICINE and PUBLIC HEALTH programmes and, more broadly, the reduction of POVERTY, poor housing and UNEMPLOYMENT. (MJH)

Health Maintenance Organizations (HMOs)

A system of controlling patient demand developed by insurance companies in the United States where there is no NATIONAL HEALTH SERVICE. The HMO manages ACCESS to medical services for those paying a fixed annual premium. The idea influenced the introduction of FUNDHOLDING in the UK. (MJH)

Health management

The management of health services is complex. Governments are inevitably concerned to maximize the EFFICIENCY of an activity that consumes much public money, while the crucial decision makers are professional employees whose work requires considerable AUTONOMY. This is particularly true of doctors. Historically they had considerable FREEDOM within the NATIONAL HEALTH SERVICE and were able to use their collective power to maintain both their AUTONOMY and income. Recent decades, however, have seen successive attempts to restructure the management of the NATIONAL HEALTH SERVICE and delimit the role of the medical profession, particularly within hospitals. Initially the service was organized on broadly collegial, professional–bureaucratic lines and professional staff were represented in the administrative structure along with representatives of the public. The 1980s saw a shift to new MANAGERIALISM, and the introduction of a system overseen by chief executives supported by small appointed executive bodies. Doctors were represented in this management scheme. More recent policy has focused on increasing the public ACCOUNTABIL-ITY of doctors and involving them more fully in managerial and moni-toring arrangements rather than simply imposing hierarchical controls. Crucial to this are processes of CLINICAL GOVERNANCE and EVIDENCE-BASED PRACTICE. (MJH)

Health promotion

An aspect of health policy often neglected by the NATIONAL HEALTH SERVICE, which historically focused on treating illness rather than the advancement and protection of good health. Health promotion embraces three related activities: health education, PREVENTATIVE MED-ICINE and health protection or PUBLIC HEALTH. In an effort to contain costs and improve the quality of people's lives as well as their LIFE CHANCES, recent governments have attempted to involve GPs and other care practitioners in this area, offering financial inducements for pro-viding services such as HEALTH SCREENING and counselling. But it can also be an activity in which many others can participate. VOLUNTARY organizations have come to play an important part in campaigns drawing attention to the steps that may be taken by individuals, orga-nizations and the government to foster better health. Employers, schools and other agencies are also encouraged to organize their activities so as to increase health awareness, while the producers of goods and services are increasingly expected to minimize the ill-effects of their products upon health. (MJH)

Health screening

The use of diagnostic tests to identify impending illness. This can lead to preventative measures and early treatment of conditions, and may save lives. There may however be reservations about it on cost grounds when the techniques are of limited accuracy or few benefit and more broadly when it involves GENETIC SCREENING. (MJH)

Higher education

Increasingly used as an umbrella term for institutions offering advanced certificate, diploma, professional and degree and postgraduate qualifications, but traditionally confined to degree-awarding establishments. Currently in the UK these include UNIVERSITIES and university colleges who can award their own degrees, and colleges of higher or FURTHER EDUCATION that must have their degrees validated by a university. For much of the last century universities provided predominantly academic courses aimed particularly at the minority of young people who continued their studies beyond the school-leaving age and based on their exam performance, initially at matriculation and from the 1960s at 'A' level. Alongside them a variety of LOCAL AUTHORITY institutions offered more vocationally oriented courses to an increasingly diverse body of students. After a slow but steady increase earlier in the century, student numbers rose after the war, gaining momentum from the 1960s as both universities and LOCAL AUTHORITIES were encouraged to expand provision, the latter often merging colleges into POLYTECHNICS whose degrees were validated by the Council for National Academic Awards. This binary system was abolished in 1992 when POLYTECHNICS and Scottish Central Institutions received university status. Recent decades have witnessed a bi-partisan political commitment to fostering mass higher education, with institutions being expected to invest in a wider range of full- and part-time courses, taught through more diverse modes, accessed by a variety of pre-entry qualifications leading to both degrees and other awards. They thus face the prospect of teaching and accrediting larger numbers of students while at the same time their AUTONOMY is being challenged by greater ACCOUNTABILITY. (DEG)

Hill, Octavia (1838–1912)

A leading authority on VOLUNTARY action in the nineteenth century, best remembered for her pioneering work in housing management in London which rested on a redefinition of the roles of landlord and tenant. Both, she believed, were responsible for the existence of slum conditions: landlords by setting rent levels too high (to compensate for bad debts) and by failing to carry out repairs; tenants, by their drunken and feckless character which made them content to live in squalid conditions. In an ever-growing succession of properties in London she introduced her new principles: prompt and regular payment of rent by tenants matched by repair and improvement to the house carried out by the landlord. Her work as a landlord, however, went beyond a concern for bricks and mortar. Through her own involvement and that of middle-class women visitors, she made housing management a form of SOCIAL WORK, in which the moral improvement of the residents was paramount. (DEG)

Holistic government

An approach to service planning and delivery associated with New Labour. It emphasizes the multi-faceted nature of individual and COMMU-NITY NEEDS, the limitations of traditional functional, departmentalized responses and the benefits of 'joined-up' multi-agency and cross-agency working and PARTNERSHIP interventions at national and sub-national levels based on consultation with USERS and CITIZENS. (MM)

Home helps

See DOMICILIARY CARE

Home ownership

The legal status of occupation of housing where the individual occupying the dwelling is also the owner of it – also called owner-occupation. It is distinguished from the other major tenures in the British housing system (PRIVATE RENTING, COUNCIL HOUSING and HOUSING ASSOCIA-TIONS or REGISTERED SOCIAL LANDLORDS). Home ownership itself is highly diverse, both in terms of house condition and value and household status. It includes households which own properties outright as well as those at different stages in the process of owning where another organization (usually a financial institution) has rights associated with the property (such as under a MORTGAGE). The home ownership sector now caters for some 70 per cent of all households in the UK. (AM)

Homelessness

The term generally used to refer to the condition of lacking adequate housing. At one extreme this may refer to rooflessness or ROUGH SLEEP-ING, but its more general usage is to refer to a range of different circumstances which mean that people lack adequate and secure accommodation. It is also widely used in relation to the provisions of housing legislation, which define homeless persons and establish the rights for different groups of homeless persons. Statistics related to homelessness tend to refer to the numbers of households who have been accepted as homeless under this legislation and those which have been provided with accommodation because of their ENTITLEMENTS under the legislation. These statistics thus refer to households that are no longer homeless but have been homeless in the past and have been rehoused. Responsibilities in relation to homelessness under legislation fall upon LOCAL AUTHORITIES, but a range of VOLUNTARY organizations also provide services for homeless people. (AM)

Horizontal transfers

See TRANSFERS

Hospice

A residential home for terminally ill people, pioneered in the UK by VOL-UNTARY organizations but increasingly also supported by NATIONAL HEALTH SERVICE funding. (MJH)

Household means-test

When an individual makes a claim for a MEANS-TESTED BENEFIT the authorities may assess not only the individual's income and assets but also the resources of other members of the household. This practice may reflect social conventions about the duty of cohabiting family members to support each other. However, the translation of social convention into administrative practice can be criticized as perpetuating relation-ships of DEPENDENCY within families, as well as raising issues when the authorities infer duties between unmarried couples, adult siblings, or others who may be living together without expecting to take on duties of support. (DM)

Households Below Average Income (HBAI)

Snapshot estimates of the current income of the lower half of the INCOME DISTRIBUTION based on data collected for the FAMILY EXPEN-

DITURE SURVEY and the FAMILY RESOURCES SURVEY. The DATASET excludes people in residential accommodation and the HOMELESS (those living rough and/or in bed and breakfast accommodation). The tabulations present income both before and after housing costs. (TM)

Housing Action Trusts (HATs)

HATs were established under legislation passed in 1986. They receive substantial additional funding from government to take over the management and hence transform large LOCAL AUTHORITY housing estates. Examples can be found in Birmingham, Liverpool, Waltham Forest and Hull. (AM)

Housing associations

There are over 2,000 housing associations in Britain covering a wide range of different organizations operating on a charitable or not-for-profit basis and providing housing and housing services. Many are very small organizations (such as almshouse trusts) or dormant organizations no longer actively building properties or adding to their housing stock. There are a number of large active housing associations operating nationally or locally and involved in the full range of activities associated with the building and provision of housing. Their dominant activity relates to the provision of housing for rent TARGETED at social NEED groups including the HOMELESS. However, housing associations are widely involved in the provision of shared ownership and housing for sale, again TARGETED at groups in identified social NEED, including older people and people in need of supported housing. Housing associations are also involved in a wider range of social and COMMUNITY activities. Active housing associations can receive SUBSIDY or funding from the government if they are REGISTERED SOCIAL LANDLORDS. (AM)

Housing Benefit

A SOCIAL SECURITY payment directly related to rent, available to households living in rented accommodation, in the social rented sector or the PRIVATE RENTED SECTOR. It is a MEANS-TESTED BENEFIT where ENTITLEMENT relates to income, to household composition, and to the level of rent paid. For households in receipt of INCOME SUPPORT, the BENEFIT ENTITLEMENT is 100 per cent. As incomes rise there is a steep withdrawal of ENTITLEMENT, and this has been strongly associated with the operation of the POVERTY TRAP. (AM)

Housing finance

The financing of housing production and consumption. Capital finance refers to finance for activities associated with land and property acquisition, house building and major repairs; and revenue finance relates to the running costs associated with housing provision, including the management and maintenance of housing. Systems of housing finance differ between tenures. For HOME OWNERS capital finance is strongly associated with loans from financial institutions, banks and BUILDING SOCIETIES, while management and maintenance costs are absorbed in current household expenditure. For the social rented sector (see SOCIAL HOUSING) SUBSIDIES are provided to landlords to reduce building costs. These are restricted through the system of PUBLIC EXPENDITURE controls. Housing SUBSIDIES continue to exist although at a lower level than in the past and the financing of management and maintenance relates to these subsidies and gross rent payments. For individual tenants assistance with rent payment is available through HOUSING BENEFIT. (AM)

Housing standards

The physical standards associated with housing relate to building REGULATIONS, planning requirements and, in the social rented sector, good practice standards. For older dwellings housing standards reflect the period and circumstances in which they were built as well as standards of maintenance and repair and any subsequent work carried out. In some cases older housing stock may have house condition problems or disrepair problems which fall within the terms of environmental health legislation. (AM)

Human capital

An economic term that refers to the fact that individuals can increase their future earnings or their value to society by undertaking training or education. It is like an investment in the person because it produces a future return in the form of higher earnings to the individual, as well as more output for the economy. (HG)

Hypothecated taxation

Tax devoted exclusively to a particular purpose. NATIONAL INSURANCE contributions are such a tax, and some have advocated a health tax to fund the NATIONAL HEALTH SERVICE. (HG)

I

Immigration policies

Policies and procedures that define and/or determine flows of migrants from one country into another and which specify immigrants' RIGHTS of entry, CITIZENSHIP status, residence or settlement and other ENTITLEMENTS. In the UK over the last half-century such measures have become progressively tighter and more restrictive. The reasons for this have caused much debate and controversy. Some commentators have linked increasing immigration control to changing economic needs and priorities; others to concerns over the social pressures associated with large numbers of immigrants, political agitation following immigration from certain areas and the need to maintain 'British culture'. However, a consistent theme in recent legislation has been a distinction between those who were thought of as 'white' and those who were not and the way in which successive measures have closed the door to certain groups while opening it to others. The Immigration Acts of 1962, 1968 and 1971, for example, restricted primary MIGRATION from the New Commonwealth, and retained the right of entry for many Old Commonwealth CITIZENS. Entry requirements were tightened further during the 1980s and 1990s and controls over visa requirements for visitors to the UK extended along with those over ASYLUM SEEKERS and REFUGEES, a process increasingly affected by membership of the European Union. (SP)

Impairment

A generic term referring to any absence, lack of, or damage to an organ or function of the body (when compared against normal functioning). Within a medical model, impairment has been used to define DISABILITY and ENTITLEMENT to DISABILITY BENEFITS. (MP)

Incapacity

Denotes the perceived inability of people with particular kinds of IMPAIRMENTS or health conditions to work, and therefore their ELIGI-BILITY for various DISABILITY BENEFITS. (MP)

Incentives

An inducement to affect behaviour, such as high pay for some professions. It may be in a desired direction or in a way that is not wanted – a PERVERSE INCENTIVE. (HG)

Income distribution

There are a variety of ways in which income is spread between different social groups. The most frequent analysis is of the numbers of families or individuals who are rich and poor. One common analysis is to rank all individuals or households from the richest to the poorest and to divide them into the richest tenth, next richest tenth and so on to the poorest tenth. These tenths are called deciles. The split may be into five groups called quintiles. The average of each group's income and distributions across different countries may be compared. There are more complex methods that try to capture the measure of inequality in a single number. The best known is the GINI COEFFICIENT. (HG)

Income maintenance

The role of SOCIAL SECURITY BENEFITS in providing an income for CLAIMANTS at times when their previous income, for example earnings from employment, is interrupted or lost. BENEFITS may be related to previous earnings received in employment. (PA)

Income protection

A particular form of INCOME MAINTENANCE, where the BENEFITS received by individuals or families aim to secure for them an income similar to that received in employment. Income protection can be provided by the state or by private insurance cover. (PA)

Income support

A generic term referring to INCOME MAINTENANCE or INCOME PROTEC-
TION, but more commonly used to refer to the MEANS-TESTED BENEFITS
paid to individuals and families outside the labour market under the UK
SOCIAL ASSISTANCE scheme. This form of income support replaced SUP-
PLEMENTARY BENEFITS in 1988. (PA)

Income tax

A DIRECT TAX levied, for example, on earned income, self-employed
income or on rent from a house. The first part of income earned is
usually exempt – a tax allowance. Allowances are granted on spending,
such as contributions to a private PENSION scheme (see FISCAL
WELFARE). Income tax in the UK is progressive, ranging from 10 per
cent on the first band of taxable income to 40 per cent on higher bands.
(HG)

Income-related benefits

Where the maximum BENEFIT is payable if the CLAIMANT has no other
income, and the amount payable falls as other income rises. Because the
practice of MEANS-TESTING has acquired pejorative overtones, governments may prefer to describe BENEFITS operating in this way as income-
related. Strictly speaking, a MEANS-TEST covers both income and assets,
whereas an income-related BENEFIT ignores assets. (DM)

Incrementalism

In the United Kingdom in the twentieth century social policies tended
to be developed step by step, building upon the past and avoiding radical
or revolutionary changes. This incremental approach to policy making
makes the understanding of the historical roots of policy important in
the analysis of current policies. (AE)

Independent living

A term denoting disabled people's objectives of living in their own
homes rather than in RESIDENTIAL CARE, assisted if necessary by directly

employed personal assistants, and participating fully in society. DIRECT PAYMENTS are a direct consequence of the Movement for Independent Living. (CU)

Independent schools

Fee-charging, privately managed schools, which are independent of central or LOCAL GOVERNMENT control. Often known paradoxically as PUBLIC SCHOOLS, many benefit from CHARITABLE status. Approximately 7 per cent of the UK school-age population currently attend such schools. See PRIVATE SCHOOLING. (DEG)

Indexing of benefits

The process of linking the money amount of a BENEFIT to an index that tracks the cost of living (prices) or the living standards of the non-beneficiary population (wages). Generally BENEFITS are uprated (the money amount is changed in line with the index) once or twice a year. (DM)

Indirect taxation

Levied on the purchases people make through VALUE ADDED TAX or excise duties on specific goods like tobacco and alcohol, they may have a regressive effect because the poor typically spend all their income while the rich save more of theirs. See also DIRECT TAXATION. (HG)

Individual learning accounts

A component of the 1997 Labour government's commitment to life-long learning designed to produce a fiscal INCENTIVE for individuals to undertake ongoing training. Public money augmented by 'top ups' from employers and workers is paid into an account, which can then be used to 'buy' credit-bearing education and training programmes. See LIFE-LONG LEARNING. (DEG)

Individualism

This is an essential component of LIBERALISM, but in its own right it represents an ideology that is committed to the pursuit of individual as opposed to collective interests. It holds that societies are no more than the sum of the individuals that compose them and that there can therefore be no such thing as a 'public interest' and certainly none that may take precedence over individual interests. It has many forms, depending on how optimistic a view of human nature is taken, but at its most extreme it is a plea for selfishness. It has been argued that 'possessive individualism' characterizes the essential nature of capitalism and the outlook and motivation of people in capitalist societies is inherently individualistic. There are, however, more CONSERVATIVE or moralistic strands of individualism that are concerned to promote individual SELF-HELP or self-responsibility. (HD)

Industrial achievement model

TITMUSS distinguished three models of SOCIAL POLICY. In his industrial achievement–performance model the main purpose of SOCIAL POLICY is to be a handmaiden or adjunct of the economy, with social NEEDS to be met on the basis of merit, work performance and productivity. (JC)

Industrial injuries

Growing industrialization led to demands for compulsory employer-based or publicly funded health care and sickness BENEFITS in industries that had a particularly high risk of occupational injury and accidents. Even though the coverage of health and sickness insurance has since expanded to include other occupations and eventually entire populations, many countries continue to run separate funds, collecting earmarked contributions often from employers only (Germany) in order to provide health care and income security following work-related injuries and diseases. (JC)

Informal care

The provision of unpaid care to those with LONG-TERM special NEEDS by CARERS who feel some emotional and/or obligatory bond with the person they are caring for. Such individuals are commonly the partners/spouses or the kin of the person in NEED, and they co-reside or live close to the people they care for. Less usually, they are friends or neighbours. Unlike VOLUNTEERS, who also provide unpaid care, informal CARERS are likely to have known the person they care for over a long period of time, during which a sense of obligation and emotional bonding has been established. In contrast, VOLUNTEERS will have met the person or people they look after through an agency such as a VOLUNTARY organization, and although they may become attached to the people they care for, their relationship does not arise out of kinship, marriage, friendship or neighbouring.

The number and characteristics of people defined as informal CARERS depends, however, on the definition of 'care'. In the UK data from three GENERAL HOUSEHOLD SURVEY questionnaires (1985, 1990, 1995) has been used to estimate the number of CARERS, their gender and the role of relationship and residential factors in determining who cares, and the services provided. They established that there are approximately 6 million people who claim they are CARERS and that surprisingly similar proportions of men (11 per cent) and of women (14 per cent) make that claim. Three per cent of men and 4 per cent of women said they were caring for at least twenty hours a week. Neither the aggregate number, nor the proportions of men and women who say they care, changed very much over the three surveys. Secondary data analysis has subsequently devised a typology of care tasks, distinguishing between 'personal' and 'practical' help. The former ranges from the most intimate forms of human service, such as bathing and toileting, to helping someone in and out of bed or a chair. Practical tasks range from helping with housework and cooking, looking after their financial affairs to simply 'keeping an eye out for' or taking someone to the shops for their weekly shopping. If care is defined within the narrower bounds of those tasks that are the most urgent, the most messy and the most time consuming (those which conform to the demands of caring, for instance, for someone with senile dementia), then it is estimated that there are currently about 1.2 million CARERS in the UK.

COMMUNITY CARE policies have meant that informal care is now treated as one of the assumed sources of LONG-TERM CARE, alongside RESIDENTIAL CARE, DOMICILIARY CARE and hospital care for the chronically ill. Recognition of its importance does not, however, rid the concept of controversy or debate. A long-standing discussion has drawn on FEMINISM to highlight the way in which informal care assumes the availability of family members, particularly women, to care. Other debates concern the best means to support CARERS to prevent the breakdown of care and whether or not CARERS should have the right to support services, such as RESPITE CARE. Many disabled people prefer not to use the term 'care' at all, since it has the implication of DEPENDENCY and it may be that alternative terms, such as 'assistance', are likely to develop in popularity and perhaps eventually replace 'care'.

There are increasing anxieties about the availability of informal caring labour within the context of an ageing population and the increasing emphasis on the responsibility of CITIZENS to participate in paid work. Concern over what has been termed the 'care deficit' is reflected in increasing debates about ways of securing informal labour and, for example, ensuring that care in the home does not necessarily involve loss of income on the part of CARERS, particularly those of working age. Such debates tend to look to ways in which material support for CARERS is developing in continental Europe and Scandinavian countries where working-age CARERS acquire rights to paid care leave through their participation in the labour market. Other models of financial support in Europe and the USA include developing systems of DIRECT PAYMENTS whereby USERS can pay their relatives to care for them, or building on the SOCIAL SECURITY system which in the UK (as in Ireland) currently provides CARERS with small subsistence-level incomes.

Thus informal care may be at the point of losing one of its defining characteristics – that it is unpaid. There is little doubt, however, that care *per se*, whether it is informally or formally delivered, will remain very low paid, largely because so many care tasks are assumed to be intuitively and experientially based, particularly for women. Nevertheless, so long as there remains a division between the private world of the home and the public world of paid work, the distinction between informal care delivered by kin (long-term intimates) and formal care delivered by paid workers (intimate strangers) will remain a crucial one, and the term 'informal care' will continue to have meaning. (CU)

Informal sector

See INFORMAL CARE

Inheritance tax

The tax levied on estates following death, in practice in most cases linked to the ownership of property. It has generally been designed to be charged only on larger estates. Periodically, the size of estate that is liable to taxation tends to be adjusted upwards. (AM)

In-kind benefits

Provided in the form of goods or services rather than cash. The effect is that the recipient only obtains the benefit by consuming the designated good or service. Examples are free school meals and concessions to pensioners using public transport. (DM)

Insertion

A multi-policy programme aimed at SOCIAL INTEGRATION and ENABLING CITIZENS to regain their independence and participation in society, most prominently linked with French SOCIAL POLICY. Against the background of high and stable UNEMPLOYMENT, particularly among young and immigrant workers, insertion policies started in the early 1980s. They involve an integration into employment via training or employment contracts, housing allowances, SOCIAL WORK services for those not entitled to SOCIAL SECURITY BENEFITS and the provision of RMI (*revenue minimum d'insertion*) as a central INCOME MAINTE-NANCE element. The latter rests on a contractual relationship between CLAIMANTS and welfare organizations and requires willingness on the part of recipients to participate in specific social reintegration pro-grammes. (JC)

Inspection

A means for ensuring that legislation regarding employment and the production, supply and delivery of goods and services is observed, that national and local standards are met, REGULATIONS complied with and public funding used appropriately. It is based on a system of regular visits (pre-planned and unannounced) and reports. It originated in the nineteenth century when central government departments became responsible for scrutinizing service provision across the country and LOCAL AUTHORITIES developed similar schemes to check their own ser-vices. Traditionally those charged with inspecting adopted a devel-opmental, advisory role, favouring the use of informal pressure and guidance material rather than the use of sanctions against poor per-formers and the process itself attracted little public attention.

Since the 1980s central inspectorates have been revamped (often under new titles such as OFSTED for education), their powers and responsibilities increased and new agencies instituted, many supplanting previous local systems. They have taken a more proactive, high-profile, evaluative role, not only monitoring but developing PERFOR-MANCE INDICATORS, directly enforcing standards and pinpointing poor performers. Their remit has broadened to include both ensuring value for money and continuous service improvement. Procedures have become more extensive, detailed and user-centred. Increasingly this involves working in tandem with other standard-setting and regulatory agencies.

While these developments have contributed to improved provision, the burden on providers and staff has been widely questioned and concerns raised about the mechanisms for assessing the work of the many agencies themselves – who inspects the inspectors? Recently, some services have seen a 'lighter touch' approach, although a strong, performance-centred inspectorate remains central to government commitment to securing national service standards and regulating the UK's welfare mix. See also REGULATION. (MM)

Institutional care

An umbrella term that denotes all forms of care delivered in settings where the care USERS are not living in their own homes or those of their CARERS. It thus encompasses RESIDENTIAL CARE, NURSING HOME care and hospital care, but not FOSTER CARE. Many of these institutions will be called 'rest homes' or 'old people's homes', but they are unlike domestic households in that they provide services on the spot for a number of residents who are not related to each other. Such establishments cater for a wide range of people with special NEEDS, including LOOKED-AFTER CHILDREN and the mentally ill. It is not a term that is used a great deal currently since it contains within it a sense of STIGMA deriving from the nineteenth-century WORKHOUSE origins of much of the institutional provision of the twentieth century. It is also a term that has connotations of the TOTAL INSTITUTION and hence has an implication of regimes of management and of service delivery that DISEMPOWER the residents. (CU)

Institutional racism

Taken-for-granted assumptions embedded in organizational cultures, policies and practices which lead to racially discriminatory processes or outcomes irrespective of the motives or values of individuals working in these environments. (KA)

Institutional welfare

A term which refers to welfare services and BENEFITS which are embedded in and an integral aspect of society, rather than a residual form of support for the poor only. TITMUSS distinguished between RESIDUAL and institutional WELFARE STATES. Institutional welfare is underpinned by a comprehensive and encompassing notion of SOCIAL POLICY. It includes the entire population in the financing and receipt of welfare and favours UNIVERSALISM. It extends RIGHTS to welfare to all areas vital to well-being and has a strong institutionalized commitment to public SOCIAL POLICY, with private and VOLUNTARY forms of provision being marginalized. (JC)

Insurance principle

Sometimes used interchangeably with CONTRIBUTORY PRINCIPLE, but may have the narrower meaning that contributions (premiums) are determined by the expected loss rate for the insured category. Private insurance companies calculate premiums in this way. (DM)

Intergenerational transfers

See TRANSFERS

Intermediary agencies

Act as a link between local and national VOLUNTARY organizations and between them and other sectors, particularly the state. Two main types exist: those with a general co-ordinating role, such as Councils of Voluntary Service (CVS) in urban areas or Rural Community Councils, and specialist agencies that link particular fields of activity, such as health (Community Health Councils) or race relations (Community Relations Councils). (DWS)

Internal market

The simulation of market conditions within state services. These are different from QUASI-MARKETS, which involve public agencies competing with commercial and VOLUNTARY organizations as well as each other.

But, like QUASI-MARKETS, they involve the separation of purchasing from providing of services, aiming to extend consumer CHOICE. (MM)

Inverse care law

Postulates that those most at risk of ill-health tend to experience the least satisfactory ACCESS to medical services. This is a consequence of an amalgam of factors related to social inequalities, including the geographical distribution of services, the way services are provided and USERS' awareness of them. (MJH)

Invisible hand

See SMITH, ADAM

In-work benefits

Many types of SOCIAL SECURITY BENEFITS are reserved for people out of work (e.g. INCOME SUPPORT). Yet in order to encourage employment, some BENEFITS are provided for those who accept lower-paid jobs or part-time work. In effect, those in-work BENEFITS function as a wage SUBSIDY and are increasingly provided as a TAX CREDIT rather than a cash TRANSFER, for instance Working Families Tax Credit. (JC)

J

Jobcentres

The modern version of labour exchanges or EMPLOYMENT OFFICES. They have a dual role: allocating SOCIAL SECURITY support for the unemployed and assessing BENEFIT ELIGIBILITY, and facilitating (and controlling) job-search activities. (JC)

Jobseekers Allowance (JSA)

In the past, BENEFITS for unemployed persons were either paid as CONTRIBUTORY UNEMPLOYMENT BENEFIT for up to twelve months, or as MEANS-TESTED INCOME SUPPORT. Since 1996 the JSA has superseded and integrated both. Depending on ELIGIBILITY, up to six months' contribution-based JSA may be paid. Thereafter, or in other cases, ELIGIBILITY is dependent on a MEANS TEST. (JC)

Johnson, Lyndon Baines (1908–1973)

Acceded to the presidency of the United States following the assassination of John F. Kennedy in 1963. Although Johnson's name is most closely associated with the war in Vietnam, he should also be remembered as one of the great reforming American presidents. His vision of the Great Society and his War on Poverty took forward Kennedy's New Frontier programme. His astute understanding of congressional politics enabled him to push forward some notable reforms in areas such as CIVIL RIGHTS, health care (Medicare) and education (Head Start). (RMP)

Joseph, Keith Sinjohn (1918–1994)

In the first part of his political career Joseph was known as a One-Nation Tory and a high-spending Minister at the Department of Health and Social Security. Subsequently he is credited with providing the intellectual backbone of THATCHERISM. Following the defeat of the Heath government in 1974, Joseph played a leading role in the creation of the Centre for Policy Studies, which promoted the free-market ideas of HAYEK and Friedman. (RMP)

Juvenile delinquency

DEVIANT behaviour by young people. In current policy discourse it is more often referred to as youth offending. Juvenile delinquency has been the focus of an enduring policy debate between advocates of welfare approaches favouring corrective treatment and support and justice approaches favouring swift and effective punishment. (HD)

K

Keynes, John Maynard (1883–1946)

Educated at Eton and Cambridge, he served at the India Office (1906–8) before becoming a fellow at Kings College Cambridge in 1909. He served in the Treasury in both the First and Second World Wars. In his first influential publication, *The Economic Consequences of the Peace* (1919), Keynes outlined his objections to the Versailles treaty of 1918. He believed that the punitive sanctions imposed on Germany would damage international trade. In his most influential work, *The General Theory of Employment, Interest and Money* (1936), Keynes demonstrated how, contrary to the received wisdom of the time, an unregulated capitalist economy could operate at less than FULL EMPLOYMENT. This insight paved the way for more interventionist forms of economic policy.

Keynes was always keen to ensure that his ideas had a practical influence. He participated in the Liberal general election campaign of 1929 and negotiated the postwar Lend-Lease agreement between the USA and Britain. He also played a leading role in the Bretton Woods conference of 1944, out of which emerged two important postwar institutions for regulating exchange rates and lending: the International Monetary Fund and the International Bank for Reconstruction and Development. Keynes had a broad range of cultural interests and was a member of the Bloomsbury group of intellectuals and artists. Plagued by heart trouble since 1937, Keynes's death in 1946 was linked to his punishing work schedule during the preceding years. (RMP)

Keynesian Welfare State

The term used to describe the economic and SOCIAL POLICIES pursued by a number of SOCIAL DEMOCRATIC governments in the period from

1945 to the mid-1970s. A combination of Keynesian economic policy and increased spending on the WELFARE STATE was seen as a way of countering the inequalities associated with the market economy. In essence, the aim was not to abolish capitalism but rather to control the market by a combination of fiscal and monetary means in order to ensure that demand and growth remained buoyant and that FULL EMPLOYMENT was maintained. Income TRANSFERS and social service provision complemented this economic strategy, which were intended to rectify the remaining DISWELFARES created by market activity. This approach came under sustained pressure in the 1970s when growing welfare expenditure became associated with faltering economic performance. (RMP)

L

Labelling

A term coined to describe the process by which people may be socially 'marked' as DEVIANT. It has been used to refer both to the way that popular and media-inspired 'moral panics' can stigmatize particular behaviours and the tendency for offenders to assume a criminalized identity. (HD)

Labour exchange

See JOBCENTRES

Labour Force Survey

A national quarterly survey produced by the UK government since the early 1970s. It provides individual- and household-based data about the labour market in general, as well as disaggregated information on employment and UNEMPLOYMENT, e.g. distribution of occupations, location, gender, age, etc. (JC)

Labour-market policies

Rather than merely focusing on entry to employment, labour-market policies might be regarded as public programmes aimed at facilitating labour-market transitions; that is, transitions from UNEMPLOYMENT to employment, from school to work, from unpaid to paid work, or from paid work to early RETIREMENT and other forms of labour-market exit. This includes providing income TRANSFERS to unemployed people, to placement services, PARENTAL LEAVE schemes, training and work experience programmes, job creation and WELFARE TO WORK schemes, wage SUBSIDIES and many more. Some are TARGETED at particular groups, such as LONG-TERM UNEMPLOYED people or school leavers. There are disputes over the EFFECTIVENESS of labour-market programmes, and there are measurement problems since effectiveness can be defined in different ways and from different perspectives, e.g. the perspective of individual job seekers or a macro-economic perspective. (JC)

Laissez-faire

A term describing minimal government intervention in matters of defence or public order and opposition to state action in all other spheres, especially the economic. Based on the French phrase meaning 'leave alone'. (DEG)

League tables

Compilations of official data relating to their performance which LOCAL AUTHORITIES, schools, UNIVERSITIES, health trusts and other public service agencies are required to provide and which are based on indicators set by government. They range from, for example, pupil tests scores, hospital waiting lists and housing arrears to achievement in meeting national or locally set targets. When this information is published the media can draw up tabulations of relative performance. This may lead to invidious comparisons between service providers, particularly when performance is affected by factors outside their control. (MJH)

Learning difficulties

A term which has replaced the earlier one of MENTAL HANDICAP and which has been claimed directly by people with the label of learning difficulties through their SELF-ADVOCACY organizations. However, policy makers and practitioners often use the variation learning DISABILITIES as an equivalent term. (DG)

Legal aid

Britain's first national legal aid scheme was instituted as part of the post-Second World War welfare settlement, by creating a mechanism for disbursing public funds to meet private lawyers' fees in cases where they acted for clients of insufficient means. Schemes developed to encompass provision for representation in civil and criminal cases and for advice and assistance in other matters. ELIGIBILITY was subject to a MEANS TEST and the merits of the case. In the 1980s and 1990s the scope of legal aid was restricted, the income levels at which people could qualify for aid were reduced, a system of franchising was introduced to regulate the numbers and the performance of the practitioners who could provide aid. In addition, for certain kinds of litigation, aid was withdrawn in favour of 'no win–no fee' arrangements. In 2000 the system was replaced by the Community Legal Service, through which funding is available for a range of 'quality marked' legal service providers (including private solicitors' firms, law centres, Citizens' Advice Bureaux and certain other ADVICE CENTRES) to take on a set number of cases. (HD)

Legitimation crisis

Neo-MARXIST writers in particular stressed that advanced WELFARE STATES in the 1970s were faced by a legitimation crisis due to interrelated problems. Lower economic growth and rising UNEMPLOYMENT led to fiscal problems, since tax receipts dwindled at a time when pressure for more social spending increased. In addition, an overblown bureaucratic welfare apparatus was deemed to have become unaccountable and too distant from the needs of CITIZENS. Under these circumstances state intervention was regarded as particularistic and acting to preserve market-generated inequalities and power structures rather than bringing about social change and greater EQUALITY. As a result, the WELFARE STATE was thought to be losing legitimacy, authority and mass support. (JC)

Less eligibility

A concept formulated by JEREMY BENTHAM. It became an integral feature of the New POOR LAW under which relief was to be made conditional on entry to a WORKHOUSE where conditions were to be worse (or less eligible) than those experienced by the lowest classes of independent labourers earning their own living. The notion still influences SOCIAL SECURITY policy and other welfare arrangements. (DEG)

Liberalism

This dominant ideology of global capitalism is a doctrine containing several potentially contradictory facets, including elements of

INDIVIDUALISM, LIBERTARIANISM, MERITOCRACY, pluralism and human-itarianism. Liberalism sets the interests of individuals before those of the social collectivity. It is essentially permissive and values FREEDOM of individual CHOICE. It promotes not substantive EQUALITY, but EQUAL-ITY of opportunity and competition on equal terms. It favours pluralist representative democracy and government by consensus. It recognizes that because necessitous people cannot be free there is a role for state welfare. At the heart of liberalism lies the idea of a social contract, a notional agreement by which individual CITIZENS forfeit to the state elements of their individual sovereignty in return for the protection of their vital FREEDOMS. While the 'classical' liberalism of the nineteenth century was closely associated with LAISSEZ-FAIRE economics, the 'social' liberalism of the twentieth century was associated with certain key developments in the WELFARE STATE. Confusingly, therefore, the term 'liberalism' may be applied to denote 'right-wing' as opposed to SOCIALIST economic policies or 'left-wing' as opposed to CONSERVATIVE SOCIAL POLICIES. Similarly, nineteenth-century UTILITARIANISM and twentieth-century NEO-LIBERALISM, though radically different, each have their roots in liberalism. (HD)

Libertarianism

An anti-state ideology that regards the liberty of the individual as para-mount and which has an important influence within LIBERALISM. Lib-ertarianism in its unfettered form can find expression within both right-wing and left-wing versions of anarchist thinking. (HD)

Life chances

An umbrella term denoting people's likely LIFE EXPECTANCY or MOR-TALITY RATE and experience of MORBIDITY and the extent to which their social origins influence their education and employment patterns. (MJH)

Life course

A term employed in the study of the development of an individual, cohort or group throughout a lifetime in order to augment and enhance the understanding of various socio-economic, behavioural and political interactions. (TM)

Life expectancy

The expected duration of life of an individual in a population estimated by the mean age of death given stated age-specific MORTALITY RATES. It is conventionally measured from birth (E_0) or from any other age, for example 65 years (E_{65}). In most societies female life expectancy exceeds that of the male, so that later life has become increasingly feminized. During the twentieth century life expectancy at birth almost doubled, rising from 45 years for men and 49 for women in 1901 to 75 and 80 years respectively by the beginning of the twenty-first century. It is estimated that this trend will continue, leading – in combination with declining birth rates and rising RETIREMENT – to a general ageing of the population and a continued increase in the number of retirees. (TM)

Lifecycle transfers

A form of REDISTRIBUTING resources through state intervention either from one generation to another (INTERGENERATIONAL TRANSFERS) or between members of a single generation (intragenerational). It usually involves expenditure on SOCIAL SECURITY but can include also health, education, housing and similar assets. Determining the effects upon individuals and generational cohorts is usually achieved using econometric modelling or simulations, such as PHYLIS (Pensions and Hypothetical Lifetime Income Simulation Model). While these cannot produce representations of real outcomes, they can help SOCIAL POLICY analysts and policy makers to consider the effects of particular policies upon individuals and cohorts across the LIFE COURSE, and also the impact of the GENERATIONAL CONTRACT. (TM)

Lifelong learning

A concept that has gained increasing currency over the last two decades and which highlights the extent to which learning is ongoing and not confined to formal educational settings or particular stages in the life cycle. Its promoters emphasize both economic and social objectives. In economic terms, a lifelong programme of education, training and skill acquisition creates a better equipped labour force more capable of competing in an increasingly globalized economy and attractive to international investors. In social terms it not only enables individuals to maintain their employability through investing in continuous personal or professional development, but represents a political concern with improving the LIFE CHANCES and opportunities of those who have hitherto had no formal education or training beyond the compulsory school leaving age. Strategies designed to facilitate lifelong learning include INDIVIDUAL LEARNING ACCOUNTS, Skills Councils and the University for Industry established in the 1990s, as well as the ongoing expansion of FURTHER and HIGHER EDUCATION and work-based training. (DEG)

Llewellyn Smith, Hubert (1864–1945)

Regarded as one of the greatest civil servants of his generation, Llewellyn-Smith became Permanent Secretary at the Board of Trade in 1907. He was instrumental in setting up the new system of UNEMPLOYMENT INSURANCE as well as the LABOUR EXCHANGES. Following his retirement from the civil service in 1927, he became Director of the New Survey of London Life and Labour, which was a sequel to Charles Booth's earlier work. (RMP)

Lloyd George, David (1863–1945)

Regarded by many as 'the true founder of the British WELFARE STATE', he was born in Manchester and spent his formative years in Nonconformist North Wales. He became Liberal MP for Caernarvon Boroughs following a by-election victory in 1890. After lengthy service as a backbencher he was appointed President of the Board of Trade in 1905 and then Chancellor of the Exchequer in 1908. In this latter role his commitment to social reform was demonstrated in three main ways. First, he initiated a highly popular NON-CONTRIBUTORY old-age PENSION in 1908 for those aged 70 or over who had limited means. Second, he introduced a 'people's budget' in 1909 which sought to meet the costs of social reform by increasing the level of DIRECT TAX on higher earners, including a super tax on the rich. Third, he introduced the National Insurance Act of 1911 which provided protection against the twin threats of UNEMPLOYMENT (for those in vulnerable industries) and ill-health (for those of modest means). Subsequently, as Minister of Munitions (1915–16), he improved the working conditions in factories and as Prime Minister he extended ELIGIBILITY for unemployment INSURANCE to all and established the Ministry of Health in 1919. (RMP)

Local authority

See LOCAL GOVERNMENT

Local education authority (LEA)

The term used to refer to LOCAL AUTHORITIES, or their departments, when carrying out their statutory responsibility for the provision of public education. (PA)

Local exchange trading scheme (LETS)

Local not-for-profit COMMUNITY enterprises whose members (usually small in number) list their offers of, and requests for, work in a directory and exchanges then take place with reference to local units of 'currency' (e.g. exchanging engineering for gardening, computer lessons for cooking). By the 1990s the number of listed groups was over 400. (DWS)

Local government

The system of local administration in Britain, based on local democracy under which regular local elections are held to elect councillors as representatives of local neighbourhoods or wards. LOCAL AUTHORITIES are established by parliament under statute. They are independent and AUTONOMOUS organizations operating within the law. They are not agents of central government, nor are they QUANGOS. However, they are subject to a variety of pressures from central government limiting their DISCRETION and they are required to operate within the boundaries of laws that restrict their activities to things which statute explicitly empowers them to do. (AM)

Local management of schools

A system introduced by the 1988 Education Reform Act giving schools and their governing bodies control of their own budgets, including responsibility for the recruitment and remuneration of teaching and non-teaching staff. It was one of the measures designed to reduce the role of LOCAL EDUCATION AUTHORITIES. (DEG)

Local strategic partnership (LSP)

Local planning bodies comprising representatives from major PUBLIC, PRIVATE and VOLUNTARY SECTOR agencies, whose role is the co-ordination of the development and delivery of AREA-BASED INITIATIVES in a LOCAL AUTHORITY area. (PA)

Loch, Charles Stewart (1849–1923)

The leading light of the CHARITY ORGANIZATION SOCIETY in which he acted as secretary from 1875 to 1914. Influenced by the work of THOMAS CHALMERS, Loch was a firm advocate of SELF-HELP and was highly critical of the rise of STATE WELFARE, which he believed would demoralize the poor, bankrupt the nation and 'sterilize the productive power of the COMMUNITY'. He served on the Royal Commission on the POOR LAWS (1905–9) and was a major contributor to the majority report. (RMP)

Lone parents

The standard UK definition of a lone-parent family is that adopted by the Finer Commission on One-Parent Families in 1974: 'a mother or father living without a spouse (and not cohabiting) with his or her never-married child or children aged either under 16 or from 16 to under 19 and undertaking full-time education'. In the 1990s there were about 1.6 million lone-parent families, with 2.7 million children. Nine in ten lone parents are women, mostly ex-married or ex-cohabitants. The UK has a high rate of lone parenthood compared with other countries, but such families have been increasing in number in most countries. Lone parents in the UK are at a very high risk of POVERTY, due to relatively low levels of employment and relatively high levels of dependence on BENEFITS. Lone parenthood has been a significant political and policy issue in the UK over the past 20–30 years and SOCIAL POLICY towards lone parents is an area of considerable and continuing controversy. Key debates concern whether or not government policy should seek to discourage lone parenthood, the RIGHTS and obligations (especially financial) of separated parents, and the responsibilities of lone parents to support themselves through employment. (JM)

Long-term care

An umbrella term denoting all types of provision for individuals with continuing care NEEDS. It encompasses RESIDENTIAL and NURSING

HOME CARE, DOMICILIARY CARE and INFORMAL CARE, but not hospital care, which is intended for the acutely ill. It is commonly used with reference to the care of frail elderly people. However, there is no reason why it should be used with reference to one demographic group only and it can equally be used to refer to the care of everyone with chronic DISABILITIES. Since long-term care does not include hospitalization, which is free under the NATIONAL HEALTH SERVICE, and usually involves services for which there are CHARGES, there is a major issue as to whether individuals should be expected to pay for their care, particularly in residential settings. This is compounded by uncertainties as to whether an individual has acute or long-term problems, and whether they are more appropriately a patient in a hospital, where they could be 'cured' (and pay nothing), or a care home resident (paying some or all of the costs). This debate has been compounded by the emergence of different funding regimes in Scotland and the rest of the UK. (CU)

Long-term unemployment

Now internationally and conventionally regarded as indicating twelve months or more of enforced absence from paid work. In the past, people looking for a job for longer than six months were regarded as long-term unemployed in the UK, and in Sweden this is still the case. Long-term unemployment tends to be expressed as a proportion of total unemployment. Yet this is somewhat misleading, since a decline in the latter will lead to a rise in the former, even if total long-term unemployment is stable or declining at a lower rate. A preferable expression is long-term unemployment as a proportion of employment. Counting unemployment at a particular day in the year (rather than over a longer period) tends to understate UNEMPLOYMENT of shorter spells and overstate long-term unemployment. On the other hand, there is 'hidden' long-term unemployment, since even short interruptions of unemployment spells (due to brief periods of work or illness) will lead to a new unemployment spell. See also UNEMPLOYMENT. (JC)

Looked-after children

'Looked after' was the phrase introduced into England and Wales by the Children Act 1989 to replace the expression 'in care', which was thought to be stigmatizing although it has remained in use there and elsewhere. Children become looked after by a LOCAL AUTHORITY when they are 'accommodated' with parental agreement or made subject to a CARE ORDER. Most are placed in FOSTER or RESIDENTIAL CARE. In Scotland the concept is broader and includes children placed on home supervision. LOCAL AUTHORITIES have several legal duties with respect to looked-after children. These include safeguarding and promoting the child's welfare; taking into consideration the wishes of the child and parents; taking account of the child's religious persuasion, racial origin and cultural and linguistic background; devising and reviewing care plans. Most looked-after children have a background of POVERTY and family instability. Research has shown that many looked-after children experience frequent moves and perform poorly at school. A system of records known as the Looking After Children materials is now used by most LOCAL AUTHORITIES in Great Britain to help promote the monitoring and promotion of children's development on seven dimensions: health, education, relationships, emotional/behavioural development, identity, self-esteem and self-care. (MH)

Loyalty

Describes one means by which individuals can affect the policy of an organization, through loyalty to it. It is contrasted with VOICE (being critical in meetings) and EXIT (shifting to another provider). Loyalty may have perverse effects by putting less pressure on agencies to change. (HG)

Luxembourg Income Study (LIS)

An international co-operative project that collects household data from participating countries and stores it electronically in order to make it comparable and available online to interested researchers. It has facilitated new comparative work on POVERTY, INCOME DISTRIBUTION and the impact of BENEFITS on household resources. (JC)

M

Maastricht Treaty

See SOCIAL CHAPTER

Macmillan, Maurice Harold (1894–1986)

Became Conservative MP for Stockton-on-Tees in 1924. He was highly critical of his party's adherence to LAISSEZ-FAIRE policies at that time, arguing for the introduction of an employer-led form of planned capitalism. Subsequently, in his book entitled *The Middle Way* (1938), he outlined a more radical economic and social philosophy based on a MIXED ECONOMY and a social minimum. Macmillan's reputation as a ONE-NATION reformer grew in the post-1945 era, not least because he was able to meet his party's ambitious house-building target of 300,000 homes per year during his tenure as Minister at the Department of Housing and Local Government (1951–4). He succeeded Eden as party leader in 1957 and won the 1959 general election, during which he reminded voters that they had 'never had it so good'. Although Macmillan served as Prime Minister until 1963, he was unable to secure a permanent shift within the party for his brand of progressive Toryism. Indeed, his approach was explicitly repudiated after Thatcher was elected as leader of the party in 1975 on a NEO-LIBERAL platform. In his later years Macmillan became a critic of the THATCHERITE version of CONSERVATISM, famously equating her PRIVATIZATION policy with the selling of the family silver. See also MIDDLE WAY. (RMP)

Mainstreaming

Used first to refer to the process of seeking to alter the procedures and practices of major providers of welfare services, in particular in the

PUBLIC SECTOR. The aim is that specific new initiatives to develop additional provision or promote alternative forms of delivery are gradually incorporated into mainstream services by the existing providers. It is also used to refer to attempts to ensure that EQUAL OPPORTUNITIES policies are treated as integral to and embedded in the decision-making processes, procedures and practices of government and other organizations. (PA)

Male breadwinner model

A family structure in which the husband goes out to work and earns a wage to support the family as a whole, while the wife stays at home and cares for the family. Used as an analytical tool to examine the gendered assumptions underlying state welfare provision. (JM)

Malthus, Thomas (1766–1834)

A Church of England clergyman and political economist, best known for his *Essay on the Principles of Population* (1798). He believed population was likely to increase more rapidly than the available means of subsistence unless checked by 'misery' (war, famine, disease), 'vice' (ABORTION, infanticide, birth control) or 'moral restraint' (later marriage and sexual continence before marriage). This pessimistic vision had clear implications for the Old POOR LAW, particularly as administered under the SPEENHAMLAND system. To Malthus this not only encouraged improvident marriages but unsupportable population growth and he became one of the leading advocates of the abolition of the POOR LAW. For him, the only real remedy for distress lay with the poor themselves and their exercise of moral restraint, supplemented by carefully guided charity. Contemporary and subsequent critics have challenged Malthus both for advocating restraint only to the poor and for failing to emphasize the possibility of and encouragement of increased production to relieve the pressure on subsistence. (DEG)

Managerialism

Used to describe both the spread of NEW PUBLIC MANAGEMENT and an ideology upholding the superiority of a particular way of co-ordinating the delivery of BENEFITS and services and effective resource ALLOCA-

TION. It embodies a body of knowledge and techniques and a set of pre-scriptions about the most EFFECTIVE and EFFICIENT ways to run state services. Both hinge on a particular representation of the dynamic, consumer-driven, decision-making processes generated by competitive markets and assumed to characterize business enterprises, often con-trasted with depictions of BUREAU-PROFESSIONALISM as inert, unre-sponsive, union dominated and governed by producer interests.

Some commentators suggest such views have led to the large-scale importation of commercially derived practices and terminology into public services, the displacement of traditional administrative mecha-nisms and a shift in the power and nature of professional work. Others contend that, though business-based approaches and personnel have become dominant, they have not supplanted traditional decision-making processes, but have led to complex forms of accommodation. In any event, managerialization was not a unitary development; rather it encompassed different strands of thinking, ranging from versions of Taylorism to more recent notions of employee EMPOWERMENT and cultural management, and was often applied differentially to different groups of staff.

For many public service workers it has negative connotations asso-ciated with the loss of past securities and an intensification of work demands. The implicit valorization of business has also been questioned by those emphasizing the distinctive nature of public provision and the need to balance the often conflicting interests of politicians, providers, CITIZEN-taxpayers and USERS (some of whom may be receiving services under duress rather than from CHOICE). (MM)

Manpower Services Commission (MSC)

Established in 1973 as a tripartite agency with strong trade-union involvement and the brief of co-ordinating policy in the training and employment area, it was based on CORPORATISM and continued to operate for most of the 1980s, but was finally abolished in 1988. (JC)

Marginal tax rate

INCOME TAXES are charged on bands of a person's income. An individ-ual may pay no tax on the first proportion of income, then 10 per cent on the next band, 22 per cent on the next and so on. These percentages are marginal tax rates as they apply only to the income in those bands.

The average tax rate is the total sum paid in tax divided by the individual's total income. However, the marginal rate is likely to be higher than this, and it is this rate which may act as a (dis)INCENTIVE to increase earnings. Loss of MEANS-TESTED BENEFITS can also contribute to a higher marginal tax rate. See POVERTY TRAP. (HG)

Marginalization

The process whereby social groups or individuals are pushed to the edges of society. Within many democratic societies the political processes may ignore the interests and views of minority groups. Capitalist societies may also marginalize the needs of those who cannot afford to purchase goods in the market-place. For example, it is difficult to find houses on the private market which will accommodate wheelchair USERS because wheelchair users are a minority group whose needs are marginal to architects and house builders. (AE)

Market failure

Classical economists take as their starting point that in a perfectly free market with no monopolies or other restrictions on trade, markets produce an EFFICIENT allocation of resources. This rests on the explicit assumptions that:

- goods can be purchased and the benefits consumed exclusively by the individuals who bought them;
- there is perfect information shared by seller and buyer.

This holds for many goods but by no means all, and thus the founding assumptions of the EFFICIENCY of free markets do not always hold. Everyone in a society or a local area can consume some goods – for example, police services or defence: these are called PUBLIC GOODS. Individuals can buy other services but the benefits spread wider than the buyer (see EXTERNALITIES). Buyers and sellers do not equally share information: these are called information failures. (HG)

Markets in welfare

A market is a way of allocating resources, formed when individuals voluntarily engage in the exchange of goods or services at openly advertised prices which adjust over time to balance supply and demand. For its advocates the unrestricted free market is the most EFFECTIVE and EFFICIENT mechanism for harnessing a society's wealth, generating growth and innovation, maximizing the range and quality of products available, distributing them according to people's expressed preferences and responding to unmet NEEDS. It thus secures non-discriminatory outcomes and broader individual FREEDOMS. These collectively beneficial outcomes are held to arise automatically from individuals' pursuit of their own self-interest and the primacy given to consumers. Competition and the free flow of information ensures that provision is geared to their NEEDS, and that suppliers, having to respond to their signals, offer both quality and value for money or else lose custom.

In practice few markets conform to this ideal model, but their benefits were widely promoted in the 1980s and 1990s as a more EFFECTIVE way of delivering welfare than that proffered by monopolist public services. In a bid to cut state expenditure and promote individual CHOICE and responsibility, welfare services were exposed to market forces, directly through PRIVATIZATION or indirectly through internal and QUASI-MARKETS. The prevalence of the last and more recent policy emphases on REGULATION and PARTNERSHIP rather than competition, however, points to a continuing debate over the applicability of free-market processes to welfare BENEFITS and services. This partly reflects different concepts and measurements of EFFICIENCY, but it also reflects concerns over asymmetries of information between USERS and providers and the limits to consumer sovereignty in many welfare transactions. More fundamentally critics of market-based welfare point to the divisive, inequitable and often exclusionary outcomes of unfettered market forces. Ultimately, however, judgements about the place of markets in welfare depend on the extent to which it is viewed as a tradeable commodity or has characteristics that are incompatible with the application of conventional commercial yardsticks. (MM)

Marshall, Thomas Humphrey (1893–1981)

Following a fellowship in history at Trinity College, Cambridge, T. H. Marshall moved to the Social Science Department at the LSE in 1925, where he acted as a tutor in SOCIAL WORK before joining Morris Ginsberg's Department of Sociology in 1929, becoming a reader in 1930. Subsequently he became Professor of Social Institutions (1944) and then Professor of Sociology (1954). Marshall was an elegant essayist, publishing *Citizenship and Social Class and Other Essays* in 1950, which was later reprinted with some additional material as *Sociology at the Crossroads* in 1963. In his work on CITIZENSHIP Marshall explored how the development of social RIGHTS in the twentieth century had (following the emergence of civil and political RIGHTS in previous centuries) served to create an EQUALITY of status. These would ensure that the material inequalities thrown up by capitalism would not engender social unrest.

Following his retirement in 1960 Marshall's work focused more directly on SOCIAL POLICY issues. He published *Social Policy in the Twentieth Century* in 1967 and *The Right to Welfare* in 1981. (RMP)

Marx, Karl (1818–1883)

Born in Trier, Germany, Marx became one of the most prominent SOCIALIST thinkers and activists, whose influence lived on long after his death. After studying at the universities of Bonn and Berlin he became editor of the *Rheinische Zeitung* in 1842, which was subsequently closed by the Prussian authorities because of its trenchant criticisms of prevailing economic and social conditions. Marx moved to Paris in 1843, where he was expelled because of his revolutionary activities, and then to Brussels (1845) where he developed his materialist conception of history, set out in *The German Ideology* (1846). He also established the Communist League, whose guiding principles were published in *The Communist Manifesto*, which he co-wrote with Engels in 1847. The revolutions in France and Germany in 1848 led to Marx's banishment from Belgium in the same year. Subsequently, he was banished from Germany and France. He sought refuge in London in 1849, where he lived until his death in 1883. Despite severe financial difficulties, Marx was able to produce his major three-volume treatise on *Capital* (two volumes of which were published posthumously) as well as a number of influential pamphlets, including *The 18th Brumaire of Louis Bonaparte* (1852) and *The Civil War in France* (1871). Following the dissolution of the Communist League in 1852, Marx helped to forge a new revolutionary grouping and played a major role in establishing the First International in London in 1864, where he was elected to its General Council. (RMP)

Marxism

One key insight provided by Marxism concerns the way in which the owners of the means of production are able under capitalism to maximize their own welfare by extracting surplus value from an exploited and subservient working class through a supposedly free market. Classical Marxists do not believe that it is possible for this exploitative, conflictual relationship to be ameliorated by state action. This is because the state, like other aspects of social and political life, reflects this underlying economic relationship. Accordingly, the state will be unable to act in ways that undermine the interests of the ruling class in a given period. In contrast to FABIANS and SOCIAL DEMOCRATS, Marxists do not believe that those state institutions operating under capitalism can function in more progressive ways as a result of the election of reform-minded politicians. Indeed, the transformation of capitalism is seen as necessitating revolutionary social change in which the workers seize control of the state machine as a prelude to the establishment of a communist society.

Given that classical Marxists believe that capitalism is unable to sustain itself through crises of increasing intensity its collapse is seen as historically inevitable, though the timing and circumstances of this occurrence remain imprecise. The resilience of capitalism has led to reappraisals about the relevance of MARX's class analysis for the study of modern society. The possibility of the state having a greater degree of AUTONOMY under advanced capitalism has also been raised.

MARX's support for extensions of the franchise and some aspects of social reform was based on the belief that such developments could sharpen class conflict and pave the way for revolutionary change. Accordingly, he had little interest in the minutiae of SOCIAL POLICY or indeed in preparing blueprints for a post-revolutionary society. This has made it difficult to relate Marxist ideas to the subject of SOCIAL POLICY or the development of the WELFARE STATE. Nevertheless in the last forty years or so various Marxist and neo-Marxist accounts of the WELFARE STATE have begun to emerge. Scholars such as Saville and Miliband have used the insights of Marxism to contest SOCIAL DEMOCRATIC ideas about the progressive potential of state welfare. For example, the introduction of increased health and education provision was seen as serving the accumulation needs of capitalists for a fit and healthy workforce rather than as a triumph for the working class. In addition, others have drawn attention to the way in which the WELFARE STATE operates in an oppressive, anti-democratic, bureaucratic fashion. Marxists have criticized state welfare for redistributing resources across the life cycle rather than from the rich to the poor and drawn attention to the various ways in which welfare professionals attempt to control the behaviour of the working class.

Recent commentators such as O'Connor, Offe and Gough have also explored the contradictions within the WELFARE STATE. For example, in *The Fiscal Crisis of the State* (1973) O'Connor argues that the state is expected to perform two functions that are likely to come into conflict. First, the state needs to ensure that conditions favourable to capital accumulation are maintained. Second, it must ensure that there is social harmony within society. Sufficient resources need to be devoted to this latter purpose if exploitative market conditions are to prevail. However, if the costs of legitimation increase sharply this will begin to undermine capital accumulation. According to O'Connor a FISCAL CRISIS of this kind occurred in the USA in the early 1970s.

Gough has drawn attention to the way in which the WELFARE STATE has both positive and negative features for both capital and labour. In *The Political Economy of the Welfare State* (1979) Gough attempts to demonstrate the limitations of functionalist approaches to state welfare. He explores the way in which a dynamic WELFARE STATE can promote the interests of capital by sustaining accumulation and reproducing class relations and labour power, while simultaneously undermining it by providing working people with the capacity to resist employer attempts to reduce wages or increase productivity.

For Claus Offe, the WELFARE STATE represents an attempt to contain the crisis-prone nature of capitalism. In *The Contradictions of the Welfare State* (1984) Offe acknowledges that although the WELFARE STATE has had some initial success in crisis management it is itself prone to crisis because of growing costs, limited EFFECTIVENESS and a lack of legitimacy.

In terms of the practical application of Marxist principles attention is often focused, some neo-Marxists would say inappropriately, on the situation prevailing in the former Soviet Union and Eastern Bloc countries. Although these regimes have been criticized for their economic failures and suppression of INDIVIDUALISM there were undoubted achievements in terms of meeting CITIZENS' welfare NEEDS. The diversion of substantial economic resources for military and defence purposes during the Cold War era raises the interesting question of whether state intervention in the economy and social life might have achieved greater success if global circumstances had been rather different. (RMP)

Maternal deprivation

Associated in particular with the work of John Bowlby in the 1940s, the theory of maternal deprivation stated that young children suffered adverse mental consequences if they did not receive continuous full-time care from their mothers. In his report to the United Nations, published in the early 1950s and based on the experiences of children evacuated and made HOMELESS during the war, Bowlby wrote that 'mother-love' is as important for MENTAL HEALTH as vitamins and protein are for physical health. Lack of such love and care would have long-term consequences for psychological development and could lead to future delinquency and anti-social behaviour. This theory had a major impact on FAMILY POLICIES in the postwar period. Women were encouraged to stay at home rather than go out into employment, there was little development of NURSERY provision, and fostering rather than INSTITUTIONAL CARE became the preferred way of looking after children in the care of LOCAL AUTHORITIES. The theory was effectively challenged in the 1960s by other research. In the 1970s especially, feminists increasingly saw it as primarily ideological in function. The concept of maternal deprivation had a profound and long-lasting impact on policies and on women's own attitudes to mothering and paid employment. (JM)

Maternity benefits

BENEFITS paid to women who are pregnant or have recently given birth. These can be in the form of lump-sum payments (to contribute to the additional costs that arise with the birth) or regular payments (to replace lost earnings during maternity leave). (JM)

Meals on wheels

See DOMICILIARY CARE

Means testing

In SOCIAL SECURITY provision this describes the process of assessing a CLAIMANT's means in order to determine ENTITLEMENT TO BENEFITS. Means-tested BENEFITS (also called INCOME-RELATED or TARGETED) are those paid only to CITIZENS who have resources of income and/or capital falling below a fixed level. Such BENEFITS are usually part of SOCIAL ASSISTANCE protection and aim to focus support upon those in proven NEED. Because of this, means-tested BENEFITS can lead to STIGMA (only paid to the poor) and to low TAKE-UP (many not realizing their ENTI-

TLEMENT). The term is often used pejoratively. Means testing can also cause POVERTY and SAVINGS TRAPS. (PA)

Medicalization

The process whereby certain conditions, forms of behaviour or SOCIAL PROBLEMS are viewed as pathological rather than structural in origin and hence as medical problems controllable or treatable on an individualized basis by medical practitioners or similar therapeutic expertise. In some cases it can be seen as the consequence of deliberate efforts by doctors to take responsibility for certain issues; in others it is a consequence of the public expectations placed on them. It has been heavily criticized by those who argue that practitioners have made claims or been asked to give attention to conditions for which their intervention may not be appropriate. These critiques draw attention both to the neglect of broader structural factors and the extent to which definitions of illness by medical practitioners are often no more valid than people's subjective judgements. They are subject to variation over time and between experts, and conditional upon the dominant paradigms in medical knowledge. There have been many criticisms of the use of medical rather than social models in policy making. These are controversial and raise major definitional and boundary issues. The underlying issue, however, is about the recognition of the limits to medical expertise. See also DISABILITY. (MJH)

Mental handicap

An outdated term used in social legislation and policy documents up to the late twentieth century to refer to the experience of people with cognitive IMPAIRMENTS. It has been largely superseded by the preferred term LEARNING DIFFICULTIES. (MP)

Mental health

Has largely replaced the term 'mental illness', although both are still used. Thus provision may be described as 'mental health services', while service USERS have 'mental health problems', or experience 'mental/emotional distress'. Traditionally, segregation and coercion characterized official responses to those believed to have mental health problems, with large numbers incarcerated in asylums. However, since the 1960s there has been a move to more COMMUNITY-based provision, influenced by the escalating costs of maintaining large-scale institutions, and a shift in beliefs about mental health. The developing service USER or 'survivor' movement challenges an emphasis on the danger posed by a minority who commit acts of violence, and resultant policies of control and surveillance. Instead, mental health provision is promoted as INDEPENDENT LIVING for those experiencing mental distress, seeking to address the STIGMA, DISCRIMINATION and SOCIAL EXCLUSION experienced by those labelled as mentally ill. (HM)

Mental illness

See MENTAL HEALTH

Merit goods

Goods or services where governments may have better information about the benefits of the provision than an individual consumer, such as an immunization programme or basic education. There may be a case for government raising taxes to pay for these and requiring CITIZENS to use them. (HG)

Meritocracy

A society where social position is achieved through the personal qualities of individuals, such as their skills, abilities and work, rather than based upon their social background or their wealth. (AE)

Middle way

MACMILLAN, in his 1938 book *The Middle Way*, argued that there was a need to move towards a managed form of capitalism and increased state welfare provision if the adverse social and economic effects of LAISSEZ-FAIRE were to be countered. This Middle Way perspective, which has also been characterized as reluctant collectivism, can be observed in the ideas of Liberals such as BEVERIDGE and KEYNES as well as a number of ONE-NATION CONSERVATIVES such as Gilmour and Heseltine. Welfare reform is seen as necessary not only to bolster capitalism but also to ensure minimum standards and the eradication of SOCIAL PROBLEMS such as POVERTY. Pragmatism rather than rigid dogma guide the Middle Way in SOCIAL POLICY, with a stress on pluralism and PARTNERSHIP. In the 1960s the term was also used to refer to those nations such as Sweden which appeared to be adopting a WELFARE CAPITALIST approach. This could be distinguished from lightly regulated capitalist societies such as the USA, as well as the state SOCIALIST regimes in the Soviet Union and Eastern Europe. See also BUTSKELLISM and KEYNESIAN WELFARE STATE. (RMP)

Migration

The physical movement of people within and between social systems, which may be short- or long-distance, voluntary or involuntary, permanent or temporary. The factors influencing such movements and their effects are subject to considerable debate, as are the policy responses to them. In terms of possible influences, both 'push' and 'pull' factors have attracted attention. Some studies emphasize short-term, localized influences, others the effects of DEMOGRAPHIC, economic and political changes, warfare, environmental degradation and larger, international processes and shifts in the demand for labour. They also diverge in their assessment of the impact of migration within and between countries, particularly its overall economic benefits and disbenefits and its effects on social and ethnic relations. Further controversy centres on the varying role of IMMIGRATION POLICIES and the treatment of different types of migrants such as ASYLUM SEEKERS, REFUGEES or economic migrants.

The UK population has resulted from both internal and in- and out-migrations and has long since been ethnically diverse. The nineteenth and early twentieth centuries saw large-scale sub-national and regional movements, shifts from rural to urban areas, large-scale emigration, especially to the United States and the then colonies, and substantial inward migration, particularly from Ireland and Eastern Europe. More recently, the largest inward migrations to the UK have been from the Asian subcontinent and the Caribbean, coinciding with labour shortages in particular areas. Historically, however, the UK has been a net exporter of people and the majority of migrants to the UK have been white (from Eire, the Old Commonwealth and Europe). (SP)

Mill, John Stuart (1806–1873)

Regarded as the leading philosopher of his age, John Stuart Mill turned away from the 'philosophic' radical tradition of his father James Mill and

JEREMY BENTHAM because of the absence of a spiritual dimension in UTILITARIANISM. Mill wrote on a wide range of subjects, including a defence of the inductive method of investigation in *The System of Logic* (1843) and *The Subjection of Women* (1869). In his most influential work, *On Liberty* (1859), he outlined his belief that the state should only intervene in cases where the actions of an individual cause harm to others. The importance that Mill attached to FREEDOM sprang from his belief that this would enhance creativity and lead to social progress. Although Mill acknowledged that representative democracy could be a progressive force in society by creating a more responsible CITIZENRY, he was concerned that uneducated majorities might oppress minorities. He advocated that educated people should have additional voting RIGHTS and that legislation should be drawn up by experts rather than elected representatives. In later life Mill modified his support for INDIVIDUALISM and the free market, arguing that state intervention was justified to combat SOCIAL PROBLEMS such as POVERTY and ignorance. (RMP)

Minimum Income Guarantee (MIG)

The term used to refer to the 'guarantee' to pensioners in the UK that their income from state PENSIONS will not be below the INCOME SUPPORT level to which they might be entitled. Like INCOME SUPPORT itself, however, the MIG must be claimed by pensioners and some in receipt of contributory pensions may not in practice TAKE-UP this entitlement. (PA)

Minimum wage

A statutory minimum below which wages are illegal. Rather than hourly wages, minima may be linked to weekly or monthly levels. Minimum wages may be restricted to certain industries or applied to workers above a particular age. In order to maintain its real value, the level of minimum wage needs to be upgraded periodically in line with average wages or inflation. It is common in many countries and was introduced in the UK in 1998. (JC)

Mixed economy of welfare

A shorthand descriptor of the combinations of ways in which BENEFITS and services can be provided and funded. These include the PUBLIC

SECTOR, the PRIVATE and VOLUNTARY SECTORS and INFORMAL CARE. The term has come to have a prescriptive as well as descriptive meaning. The 1990 National Health Service and Community Care reforms required LOCAL AUTHORITIES to commission and contract services from commercial and voluntary agencies rather than directly providing them themselves and most care is now provided by outside agencies and individuals not directly employed by the authority. The term includes the notion that USERS should become CONSUMERS who, faced with a range of providers and charges, can make choices about the types of services they receive and their sources, according to their value for money and affordability. Though with a greater emphasis on PART-NERSHIP, New Labour also emphasizes a mixed approach to social provision. (CU)

Mobility

This may refer to social or geographical movement within the population. A socially mobile society is characterized by upward and downward movement of individuals within the social hierarchy. (AE)

Monetarism

Holds that economic EFFICIENCY depends on sound public finance and, in particular, that aggregate demand in the economy and inflation should be controlled by the manipulation of the money supply. It is premised on an explicit critique of KEYNESIAN economics and KEYNES's belief that incurring budget deficits in order to stimulate aggregate demand through public spending can serve to stimulate economic growth and sustain FULL EMPLOYMENT. Monetarism provided the basis for the economic policy of the NEW RIGHT, its desire to constrain public spending and its willingness to tolerate UNEMPLOYMENT as a 'price worth paying' for economic competitiveness. In practice the govern-ments of Mrs Thatcher were obliged to modify the application of such principles, since the pursuit of targets for government borrowing and money supply did not succeed in securing macro-economic stability. The policies subsequently pursued – which entailed a combination of fiscal prudence and ad hoc interest rate manipulation – have in one sense become the new economic orthodoxy, but do not necessarily conform to the strict principles of monetarism. (HD)

Moral hazard

An economic term used to describe features of insurance markets but which can be extended to other areas too. It is a class of MARKET FAILURE, but also applies to SOCIAL INSURANCE. Car insurance that covers any damage to a car may tempt drivers to drive carelessly, creating a moral hazard. This increases insurance claims costs and causes more deaths, although insurance firms may counter by requiring drivers to meet some of the cost of repairs or medical costs. Similarly, guarantees to meet the costs of LONG-TERM CARE may be a DISINCENTIVE to families to provide care. (HG)

Morbidity

The technical term for illness, used particularly to chart morbidity rates when data are provided on the incidence of illness in general, or of specific illnesses, among various groups in the population. (MJH)

Mortality rate

The technical term for death rates, used in relation to data that highlight differences between nations, regions, classes, genders and other groups. Typically these are standardized to take into account age distributions. Infant mortality rates (deaths in the first year of life) provide particularly striking evidence on health inequalities. (MJH)

Mortgage

A loan provided on the security of land or property, paid off over a period of time under an agreed arrangement with the lender. It is the normal basis for lending for house purchase in Britain, where the lender will advance a loan on the security of the property and this is registered as a charge on the property. If the borrower defaults on repaying the loan, the lender has entitlements to recover the loan through sale of the property. The variety of mortgage products available has increased in recent years and different borrowers have very different agreements with lenders. (AM)

Multiculturalism

A concept developed in the 1980s as a way of making sense of the increasing ethnic diversity of British society. It was informed by two key assumptions. First, differences in language, religion, cultural norms and expectations created misunderstandings between different ethnic groups and particularly between the majority and minority populations. Second, promoting an understanding of different cultures could allay these.

For many, however, such attempts led instead to a preoccupation with differences and the 'problematization' of minority ethnic cultures. Anti-racist critiques in particular emphasized the importance of structural disadvantage in explaining the experience of ethnic minorities and dismissed culturalist approaches as a surrogate form of RACISM. More recently there has been a renewed interest in issues of culture and identity as analysts have begun to highlight the complexity of people's affiliations and the extent to which their sense of identity is more than a product of the RACISMS they experience. The conceptualization of culture within multicultural approaches, particularly the neglect of its social and economic context, was perhaps the problem rather than the concept *per se* and cultural diversity is now presented in more dynamic terms as a creative resource, combining both spatial and temporal elements. (KA)

Multiplier effects

The second-round effects of an investment or the consequences of public spending financed by borrowing. For example, investment for a new school will involve builders and architects, who will then spend all or part of that income and thus generate jobs for workers making the products they buy. This assumes an under-employed economy. If there is no spare capacity in the economy the extra demand will generate inflation. (HG)

Municipal government

The LOCAL GOVERNMENT system within the major cities and urban areas of Britain. (AM)

Mutual aid

Formal and informal material help provided between different disadvantaged populations. For instance, among the working class in

Victorian

Victorian Britain neighbourly help, educational development in the Sunday schools of Christian churches and economic collaboration led to FRIENDLY SOCIETIES and Mutual Societies, which were the forerunners of contemporary BUILDING SOCIETIES and pensions organizations. Twenty-first century examples include CREDIT UNIONS, the development of childminding circles and LOCAL EXCHANGE TRADING SCHEMES (LETS). (DWS)

Myrdal, Karl Gunnar (1898–1987)

After graduating from the law school at Stockholm University in 1923 Myrdal turned his attention to economics, receiving a juris doctor degree in 1927. His early publications were on economic theory. He published an influential text on *The Crisis in Population Question* with his wife Alva in 1934. Myrdal was active in Swedish politics and was elected as a Social Democratic member of the senate in 1934. After a period abroad, he was re-elected to the senate in 1942 and chaired the postwar planning commission. From 1945 to 1947 he was Minister of Commerce.

Myrdal was at home on the international stage and was commissioned by the Carnegie Corporation to study the status of the black population in the USA. This led to his best-known book, *An American Dilemma: The Negro Problem in Modern Democracy* (1944). Later he was head of the United Nations Economic Commission for Europe (1947–57) and subsequently he undertook a study of economic developments in South Asia that led to the publication of *Asian Drama* in 1968. He was awarded the Nobel Prize for economics (jointly with HAYEK) in 1974. (RMP)

N

NAIRU

See NON-ACCELERATING INFLATION RATE OF UNEMPLOYMENT

National Assistance

Term given to the MEANS-TESTED BENEFITS paid to unemployed CLAIMANTS after the BEVERIDGE reforms of 1948. These were SOCIAL ASSISTANCE BENEFITS paid to those who were not adequately covered by the NATIONAL INSURANCE scheme. They were largely discretionary in form and were administered by the National Assistance Board. They replaced previous support under the POOR LAW and were themselves replaced by SUPPLEMENTARY BENEFITS in 1966. (PA)

National Child Development Study

Information for this birth cohort study has been gathered at intervals on all those born between 3–9 March 1958. They were followed up at ages 7, 11, 16, 23 and 33, in order to assess their progress and experiences. (MH)

National curriculum

A prescribed set of subjects, first introduced in 1988 and since modified, which all pupils of compulsory school age (i.e. 5–16) in state schools must study, with their performance assessed against set criteria (STANDARDIZED ATTAINMENT TESTS) at various ages. (DEG)

National efficiency

A term summarizing the concerns of many Edwardian commentators of different political persuasions about the condition of the British population, symbolized by the quality of recruits to and Britain's defeats in the Boer War campaign (1899–1902). In order to create a more efficient nation-state they advocated social reform, the restructuring of government, universal military training and the extension of state education. See also SOCIAL IMPERIALISM; EUGENICS. (DEG)

National Health Service (NHS)

A publicly funded and managed system established in the UK in 1948 with the aim of providing comprehensive, universal health care free at the point of ACCESS to all who needed it on the basis of clinical NEED. It is funded primarily by general taxation (with a small NATIONAL INSURANCE input), and though originally an entirely free service, soon after its inception a system of CHARGES for prescriptions and dental and optical treatment was developed.

The NHS consists of hospital services, family or PRIMARY CARE practitioners (GPs, dentists, opticians and pharmacists) operating outside the hospitals, and other COMMUNITY-based services (community nursing, health visiting and preventative medicine). The Secretary of State for Health is responsible for the health service in England. In Wales, Scotland and Northern Ireland it is the responsibility of the devolved governments. In Britain local health authorities are responsible for the planning of services in their areas; in Northern Ireland four health and social services boards are vested with 'area' responsibilities. Responsibility for COMMISSIONING health services is devolved to self-managing PRIMARY CARE Trusts. Hospitals and COMMUNITY services are run by National Health Service Trusts, wholly public bodies but with some managerial AUTONOMY. Patients ACCESS the service, except in emergencies, through the PRIMARY CARE practitioners. Direct self-referral is accepted in the event of accidents and emergencies. Once under hospital care, individuals may be treated as in-patients or out-patients.

The NHS was originally organized on a centralized, unified basis, but reorganized by the Conservative government in the 1990s on a PURCHASER-PROVIDER or QUASI-MARKET basis with health authorities and FUNDHOLDING GPs procuring services from hospitals (organized in

NHS trusts). More recently this INTERNAL MARKET system has been restructured with the formation of PRIMARY CARE Trusts.

Compared with CITIZENS of most other European Union countries people in the UK get their health services for a remarkably low overall cost per head. While this may be partly because a tax-funded service is cheaper to run than an insurance-based or private one, it is often suggested that what is on offer is relatively inferior in quality. While the service's record in dealing with emergency health problems has been good, it has attracted widespread concern about its overall funding and staffing levels and the length of time people have to wait for services. Recent policy has focused both on increasing expenditure on the service and raising standards. The extent to which this will lead to improvements, however, is contested and partly depends upon the rates at which salaries, wages, medicine and equipment costs increase. On past experience these are likely to rise at well above the ordinary inflation rate.

There is also controversy about the extent of unmet NEED. Some argue that a great deal more should be spent, particularly on HEALTH SCREENING and prevention. An opposite view is that people should be encouraged to become more self-reliant and make greater use of self-medication, so that practitioners can concentrate on the more serious cases.

The UK model of health service organization is criticized by politicians on the right as a 'producer' monopoly, in which the activities of doctors and their costs are very hard to control. More consumer control might be achieved through the use of an INSURANCE model, in which individuals belong to insurance organizations (such as HEALTH MAINTENANCE ORGANIZATIONS) that commission care. However, this could make the service more costly and insurance systems do not necessarily enhance PATIENT CHOICE; some people may find it hard to find insurance cover if they are considered a high risk.

Alongside the NHS there is a PRIVATE SECTOR of health care providers. Defenders of private medicine argue that the resources involved are extra ones, enhancing health care. But there is controversy about the support the PRIVATE SECTOR receives from a variety of links, including recent contract or PARTNERSHIP arrangements, with the NHS. NHS doctors can take on private patients, and NHS trusts may offer private PAY BEDS. There is a substantial hidden SUBSIDY to private medicine because doctors are trained in the NHS, and much medical research is publicly funded. Furthermore, private hospitals are able to turn to the PUBLIC SECTOR in emergencies. All this facilitates the use of public resources for private patients and 'queue-jumping' when public beds are scarce and has led to recent attempts to reform consultants' contracts.

The NHS has been criticized for being in reality a 'national illness service', ignoring the need for more preventative medicine and HEALTH PROMOTION. The health progress of the nation has depended perhaps more upon changes in the environment and in behaviour than upon medical advances. Governments have important regulatory responsibilities to help protect our health.

The evidence on health inequalities highlights these issues. Epidemiological studies of the differential impact of MORTALITY and MORBIDITY show considerable differences in the experience of ill-health between different regions of the country, social classes, women and men, and ethnic groups. As MORTALITY RATES have declined overall these differences have not decreased; in many cases they have increased. These differentials are attributable to differences in the availability of health services, but also to other factors such as low income and poor housing. They nevertheless present a continuing challenge to the principles of the NHS. (MJH)

National Insurance (NI)

The SOCIAL INSURANCE scheme introduced in the UK in 1948 following the recommendations of the BEVERIDGE Report. The main CLAIMANT groups were the short-term unemployed, workers off sick, widows, women during maternity and pensioners. Unlike continental SOCIAL INSURANCE schemes, which were EARNINGS-RELATED, NI initially paid FLAT-RATE BENEFITS to CLAIMANTS in return for flat-rate contributions from workers and their employers. In order to pay BENEFITS to CLAIMANTS immediately the NI scheme was introduced on a PAY AS YOU GO basis, although in order to receive BENEFITS CLAIMANTS were required to have made a specified number of contributions into the NI scheme. Initially these were paid as a weekly stamp. Later reforms replaced the stamp with an earnings-related contribution base; and EARNINGS-RELATED BENEFITS were paid to unemployed CLAIMANTS between 1966 and 1982 and to pensioners after 1978. The Inland Revenue now administers the NI contribution scheme. (PA)

National Lottery

The National Lottery was established in November 1994 to provide a national weekly prize draw for CITIZENS. It is managed by a private company, but regulated by legislation via a department of the Home Office, and with reference to OFLOT that deals with consumer COM-PLAINTS. The distribution of income from the lottery is broadly: prizes (50 per cent), taxes (12 per cent), retailers (5 per cent) and organizers (5 per cent). The remaining resources are distributed to public causes through six boards: Arts, Charities, Heritage, Millennium, New Opportunities Fund and Sport. The National Lottery Charities Board (NLCB), now the Community Fund, distributed over £1.3 billion through twelve regional offices in the first five years of operation, while many CHAR-ITIES also received grant aid via the other boards. In particular, the New Opportunities Fund (NOF) funded initiatives in education, health and the environment, often drawing in VOLUNTARY SECTOR organizations, such as healthy living centres and after-school clubs. (DWS)

National minimum standards

Though seldom explicitly defined, a concept of the basic level of human welfare, which a nation should guarantee to its CITIZENS, and which underpinned the classic WELFARE STATE. This was to ensure that everyone was provided with the minimum necessary upon which to flourish and build. (HD)

National Vocational Qualifications (NVQs)

A work-based assessment system introduced in 1986 in an attempt to standardize a plethora of vocational qualifications and accrediting bodies through a five-level framework specifying competence in the performance of occupationally-specific work skills and tasks. 'Lead bodies' representing the main sectors of employment were empowered to specify the required standards for each level. (DEG)

Natural rate of unemployment

See NON-ACCELERATING INFLATION RATE OF UNEMPLOYMENT

Need

Need is a concept which is central to social policy making. While markets are intended to allocate resources according to demand, SOCIAL

POLICIES are concerned with allocating resources according to need. However, there are two particular difficulties with the concept of need. First, what are the distinctions between need and other related concepts such as demand, want or desire? Second, on what basis can needs be ASSESSED?

The term 'need' is usually used to refer to either biological or social needs which some would argue are absolute – the need for shelter, food, human contact, etc. On the other hand, some argue that needs are socially and historically determined and needs differ at different times, in different societies and in different cultures. A distinction can be drawn between what it is we wish to have – a desire, preference or a want – and what we need to make us a human being. While the two are connected, in that our needs may be expressed as wants, they are not the same. However, to decide what are universal human needs is more difficult.

For SOCIAL POLICY the discussion of needs is not entirely abstract because if welfare provision is to address need, it is important to have some way of ASSESSING the needs that do exist in the population. However, given that need is such a contested concept it becomes difficult to do this in anything but a pragmatic way. In so doing state welfare provision becomes open to attack by those who argue that because needs cannot be defined, what are spoken of as needs are merely demands and wants and as such would be better rationed by the market rather than through democratic state structures. (AE)

Negative equity

The condition associated with a significant decline in property values so that a house purchaser who borrowed money to buy a property finds that the property they own has declined in price to a level that means that they could not recover the loan by selling the property. The equity remaining in the property is less than the amount that they had borrowed in order to purchase the property. Hence they have 'negative' equity. See HOME OWNERSHIP. (AM)

Negative income tax

An alternative to the current mixture of SOCIAL INSURANCE and SOCIAL ASSISTANCE BENEFITS provided in the UK that would replace these with a MEANS-TESTED BENEFIT paid to all individuals or families whose income fell below a fixed level. For those in employment this payment would be paid as a credit against INCOME TAX due. Such payments would replace existing means-tested BENEFITS and means-tested TAX CREDITS, such as the Working Families Tax Credit, with one single scheme administered by the Inland Revenue. (PA)

Neighbourhood renewal

The physical, social and economic refurbishment of local urban areas usually inhabited by no more than a few thousand people. Typical activities include attention to housing stock, gardens, play areas and small-scale economic development. The organization of such initiatives frequently attempts to embody the concepts of PARTNERSHIP between the state and local groups and SOCIAL CAPITAL – the development of local leaders and networks. See COMMUNITY DEVELOPMENT. (DWS)

Neo-liberalism

An intellectual tradition premised on a critique of centralized social and economic state planning, which holds that a truly free and prosperous social order can only be achieved within a competitive market economy. Neo-liberal ideas have played an important part in NEW RIGHT thinking. (HD)

Neo-Marxism

See MARXISM

New Deal (UK)

The popular term for WELFARE TO WORK policies implemented by the Labour government in the UK after 1997. It emphasizes paid work as the central element in the attempt to reduce POVERTY and represents a more conditional approach to CITIZENSHIP RIGHTS to SOCIAL SECURITY, stressing obligations individuals owe in claiming their RIGHTS to welfare. Different New Deal programmes are directed at different groups of unemployed people, such as younger people, LONG-TERM UNEMPLOYED, disabled people or LONE PARENTS out of work. In general, all New Deal policies involve assistance with job search activities, options for training or education, wage SUBSIDIES for employers, intensive counselling, advice and guidance. Some schemes, especially for younger unemployed people, involve compulsory participation in a programme. (JC)

New Deal (USA)

Introduced by President F. D. ROOSEVELT between 1933 and 1939, in the aftermath of the Great Depression, it was aimed at providing economic relief as well as reforms in industry, agriculture, finance and SOCIAL POLICY. The New Deal generally embraced the concept of a government-regulated economy. Much of the legislation was enacted within the first three months of Roosevelt's presidency. With the aim of alleviating the suffering of the huge number of unemployed workers, agencies such as the Works Progress Administration (WPA) and the Civilian Conservation Corps (CCC), dispensing emergency and short-term governmental aid and providing temporary jobs, were established. The National Recovery Administration (NRA) was granted authority to help shape industrial codes governing trade practices, wages, hours, child labour and collective bargaining. After 1935 the New Deal greatly increased the authority of the federal government in industrial relations and strengthened the organizing power of labour unions. The most far-reaching programmes were the SOCIAL SECURITY measures of 1935 and 1939, providing old-age and WIDOWS' BENEFITS, UNEMPLOYMENT compensation and DISABILITY insurance. (JC)

New Deal for Communities

The term NEW DEAL has also been used to refer to other Labour government programmes in the UK in the early twenty-first century, in particular the New Deal for Communities, a programme of NEIGH-BOURHOOD RENEWAL funded by central government and operating in a small number of deprived local areas to support COMMUNITY-based projects promoting SOCIAL INCLUSION and COMMUNITY DEVEL-OPMENT. (PA)

New Earnings Survey

National annual survey utilizing PAY AS YOU EARN data conducted by the Office for National Statistics. It measures the gross earnings (including overtime but excluding back pay, tips, gratuities, etc.) of a 1 per cent sample of the full-time (over 30 hours a week) workforce on adult rates whose pay has not been affected by absence. (TM)

New public management

A shorthand term for the remodelling of state services according to the presumed structures and processes of private enterprises. It encompasses a range of measures introduced during the 1980s and 1990s to redress the deficiencies of BUREAU-PROFESSIONALISM identified by NEO-LIBERAL and PUBLIC CHOICE theorists and make provision more resource-EFFECTIVE and consumer-centred. These included organizational restructuring and the importation of commercial financial and human resource practices. Previously large-scale unitary organizations were split into semi-autonomous units. PURCHASER-PROVIDER and strategic-operational roles were separated. Competition within state services and with external bodies was introduced. Organizational hierarchies were de-layered and day-to-day responsibilities were devolved to redesignated budget-holding and line-management posts. These developments were complemented by an emphasis on market mechanisms, strategic plan-ning, cost-effective performance management and staffing policies designed to foster a flexible, customer-driven culture, dilute traditional collectivism and facilitate managerial control.

The extent to which these measures were implemented across welfare services in the UK and elsewhere has been questioned, as have the under-lying premises – notably the implicit MANAGERIALIST ideology and devaluation of public service. Some argue that change in public services has been more complex than the term suggests. But it is still widely used and has been reapplied in analyses of more recent attempts to revalue and modernize state services on more publicly accountable but still entrepreneurial and change-oriented lines. (MM)

New Right

A term applied to a broad group of political thinkers that came to prominence in the latter part of the twentieth century and/or to the ideology that they espoused. The ideology, while clearly drawing on established right-wing ideas, was 'new' in that it distinctively combined NEO-LIBERAL and 'neo-CONSERVATIVE' intellectual traditions with a radical challenge to the post-Second World War political consensus with regard to the WELFARE STATE. At the heart of the New Right project lay the classical eighteenth-century liberal doctrines associated with ADAM SMITH, subject however to an element of nineteenth-century SOCIAL DARWINISM and the interpretation of twentieth-century writers like HAYEK. The central premise of the New Right is that a competitive free market represents the essential and the only institution by which a spontaneous social order may be achieved. The idea that social order may be contrived by human design – or that human WELFARE may be assured by collective state intervention – is rejected as a fallacy. The New Right argue that it is neither possible nor desirable for a truly free society to reach agreement upon a common purpose; rather it should agree the means by which to permit its members to achieve their individual purposes. The New Right critique of the WELFARE STATE was on economic, political and social grounds, although the elements of the argument are interwoven.

At the economic level the New Right not only regards the market as a superior mechanism to that of state planning, but also considers KEYNESIAN economics, upon which the WELFARE STATE was founded, as fundamentally flawed. KEYNESIANISM undermines productive investment and the profit motive in the market sector, while legitimizing deficit budgeting by governments. Economic growth is argued to be the best guarantee of human WELFARE, since the wealth created will TRICKLE DOWN and benefit even the poorest members of society. In turn, the best guarantee of economic growth is seen as an unfettered market in which free choice and the price mechanism function together to ensure that the myriad individual decisions taken by producers and consumers are self-orchestrated to achieve optimum EFFICIENCY. The imperative for government is to adopt strict MONETARIST controls to keep inflation in check and restrict public spending.

At the political level the New Right draws on PUBLIC CHOICE THEORY and its critique of the dangers that arise when choices are exercised not 'privately' in the market-place, but 'publicly' through the democratic process by voters, politicians and bureaucrats. Those dangers are essentially twofold. First, competition by politicians for votes results in escalating promises of public spending that eventually undermine the sustainability of the economy. Second, state bureaucrats and welfare professionals establish a powerful coalition whose interests are served by promoting an increasingly monopolistic and inefficient PUBLIC SECTOR.

At the social level the New Right critique departs from a strictly NEO-LIBERAL perspective which holds that individual self-interest may be productively harnessed by market forces. It holds a more authoritarian or neo-CONSERVATIVE view of human nature: the idea that people are not just self-interested, but self-centred, and that they need the discipline of INCENTIVES and punishment. According to the New Right, the social effects of the WELFARE STATE are principally threefold. First, it is argued that the WELFARE STATE fosters DEPENDENCY, perpetuates cycles of DEPRIVATION and/or creates an UNDERCLASS. Second, the WELFARE STATE undermines such essential 'traditional' institutions as the family by taking over a variety of functions and responsibilities. Third, by promoting social RIGHTS, the WELFARE STATE undermines our sense of individual responsibility to work and to provide for ourselves.

There is a wide spectrum of opinion within the New Right school of thought. Some New Right thinkers emphasize the need to minimize government intervention and to dispense with REGULATION. Others acknowledge a clear role for the state in order to guarantee the necessary conditions for markets to operate freely. Some argue for the wholesale abolition of state welfare. Others accept the need for a minimal welfare SAFETY NET. Although elements of the New Right critique remain highly controversial and several aspects of it have been challenged empirically, its impact upon the policy agenda has been considerable. The legacy of the New Right may arguably be found in several current policy trends, even when these are being advocated or developed by commentators or policy makers who claim to be acting purely pragmatically or even to be opposed to New Right thinking. Many Western governments could be argued to be influenced by New Right thinking and the emphasis it places on the efficacy of market forces, FREEDOM of CHOICE and personal responsibility. (HD)

New social movements

From the 1960s onwards Western Europe was swept by collective social protests against many aspects of the economic and social structures dominating advanced capitalist society in the postwar era. Such protests crystallized around, for example, the anti-nuclear, peace, environmental and women's movements, and the term 'new social movements' was used to distinguish these from older movements such as trades unionism. New social movements are distinctive in terms of their location in relation to the existing polity, their aims, their organizational structure and their modes of action.

Traditional movements have tended to work within existing political institutions, adopting the prevailing bureaucratic and hierarchical forms of social organization and seeking to influence existing political parties. In contrast, new social movements by-pass the state and operate outside of established parties. They question assumptions about the role of economic growth that underpin the ideology of older movements representing capital or labour.

While the aims of older movements tend to focus on gaining political integration through legislative political reform, new social movements seek cultural changes in values and lifestyles, achieved through the mobilization of CIVIL SOCIETY and public opinion. They seek to defend CIVIL SOCIETY against excessive power of the state. Their mode of operation depends on participatory democracy and is usually informal and decentralized with repertoires often including confrontation and direct action, not always within the law. Participants in new social movements tend to fall outside the two traditional classes of labour and capital. Instead they are predominantly drawn from what has been termed the 'new middle class'. The contraction of manufacturing industry and an accompanying growth in the service sector in the latter half of the twentieth century produced a major shift in occupational structures, with a decline in the blue-collar working class mirrored by an expansion of the white-collar sector. Together with improving living standards, the massive expansion in HIGHER EDUCATION and the information revolution, this shift led to a blurring of traditional class divisions and loyalties in the 'post-industrial society'. It has been suggested that a new class has emerged which includes people who are highly educated and economically secure, with jobs which are professional or located in the welfare sector. It is argued that this new middle class is in some respects more alienated from the political system than the traditional working class and, crucially, is more able and willing to criticize established parties, the BUREAUCRACY and the dominant materialist agenda.

Other groups active in new social movements are either peripheral to the labour market, such as students, housewives and pensioners, or are independent and self-employed members of the 'old' middle class, such as farmers, shop-owners and artisans. Nevertheless, the predominance of the new middle class is such that new social movements, like ENVIRONMENTALISM, have been dismissed by some as an expression of middle-class elitism.

The characterization of new social movements as democratic, participatory and geared to informed public opinions applies only to an 'ideal form' of a movement in its most radical initial stages. Once established, compromises are usually made and conventional organizational structures and strategies are gradually adopted. The radical potential of new social movements tends to dissolve as they become transformed into pragmatic reformist movements closely connected to established politics. (MEH)

New towns

New communities built in the period after 1946 under legislation which provided powers to establish New Town Development Corporations to build new planned COMMUNITIES. Initially these new towns were designed to relieve congestion and rehouse people from urban areas; but in the 1960s a new generation of new towns was designed to create new centres for economic growth. The largest group of new towns in Britain is associated with the Greater London area, but other major cities also have new towns associated with them. (AM)

New vocationalism

A concept encapsulating the increasing emphasis within both SEC-ONDARY EDUCATION and post-compulsory education on employability training and the acquisition of work-related skills, emanating from concerns over the need to provide for increasingly flexible, technologically based labour markets and sustain Britain's international competitive edge. (DEG)

Next Steps agencies

Semi-autonomous executive bodies to which, following the 1988 Ibbs Report (Improving Management in Government), most UK central government departmental services have been devolved – sometimes referred to as QUANGOS. Varying in size and function, they range from the BENEFITS and CHILD SUPPORT to the Food Standards and Environmental Agencies and were central to NEW RIGHT-inspired attempts to recast the civil service on consumer-oriented, businesslike lines. Headed by chief executives, they are responsible for operational as distinct from strategic matters and subject to framework documents set by the Treasury and parent department, specifying their responsibilities, resources and performance targets. To meet these they have considerable

FREEDOM, particularly to develop distinct corporate identities, NEW PUBLIC MANAGEMENT processes and personnel policies, including recruitment, pay and grading (previously determined commonly across the civil service), as well as the use of performance-related pay and personalized contracts for senior staff. Some commentators suggest that the aim was to curtail public provision, and during the early 1990s a number of agencies were contracted out or privatized. Opinion on the extent to which they offer more responsive, efficient provision remains divided, as do views on their impact on the traditional public service ethos and the separation of policy making from administration. More recently policy has focused on enhancing the entrepreneurial role of agencies while tightening REGULATION and securing greater co-ordination. (MM)

Non-accelerating inflation rate of unemployment (NAIRU)

In economic theory the level of UNEMPLOYMENT is not clearly determined, but there is a 'natural rate of unemployment', or NAIRU, which is a level of unemployment that is consistent with a constant rate of inflation. In other words, reducing the level of unemployment below this level would result in accelerating inflation. (JC)

Non-contributory benefits

Financed from the general revenue of the government, rather than from INSURANCE contributions. ELIGIBILITY may depend upon membership of a category and/or on proof of NEED and lack of means (see MEANS TESTING). (DM)

Non-governmental organizations (NGOs)

Traditionally associated with economic and social developmental action in the Majority (or Third) World. Three overlapping shifts of meaning have conceptualized NGOs as international agencies linked to the United Nations; non-state, non-profit agencies from developed societies; or non-government agencies indigenous to developing societies. (DWS)

Non-profit sector

See COMMUNITY SECTOR; THIRD SECTOR; VOLUNTARY SECTOR

Non-statutory sector

See COMMUNITY SECTOR; INFORMAL CARE; OCCUPATIONAL WELFARE; PRIVATE SECTOR; THIRD SECTOR; VOLUNTARY SECTOR

Normalization

Originally a Scandinavian principle, opposing the institutionalization of people with LEARNING DIFFICULTIES and supporting their inclusion in normal, everyday living. Their NEEDS are seen as similar to those of others, although it is acknowledged that they will need extra support to live independently. It was originally taken to mean that people with LEARNING DIFFICULTIES should be ENABLED to reproduce the lifestyles of other ordinary CITIZENS: having a normal rhythm to the day, being able to develop sexual relationships, progress through the LIFE COURSE and achieve a good standard of living.

More recently there has been a rejection of LABELLING people according to their DISABILITIES and an increasing emphasis on USERS' RIGHTS. Mencap, a major national voluntary organization for people with LEARNING DISABILITIES, has introduced a new general assembly, one third of whose members have learning disabilities but have real power in all aspects of Mencap's decision making. The national picture is still patchy, however. Transition of young people with LEARNING DISABILITIES from full-time education to COMMUNITY services is often problematic where the latter resources are lacking. There is also evidence of exclusion of adults from normal health and dental services and very limited opportunities for paid employment. (SB)

Normative theory

The purpose of theory is to help explain the nature of the world. As such a theory helps to organize observation, speculation or analytical thought. Normative theory, however, goes beyond merely acting to assist in describing, analysing or explaining the world, by seeking to establish how it should be. In this sense SOCIAL POLICY as a subject is intimately connected to norms: it seeks both to prescribe how things should be and describe how things are. (AE)

Nurseries

A generic term for educational and care provisions for children below the starting school age, including playgroups (usually run by parents and VOLUNTARY organizations), day nurseries, classes and schools provided by public and private bodies, and workplace nurseries provided by employers. (DEG)

Nursing homes

Establishments which provide RESIDENTIAL and nursing care for sick, disabled or elderly infirm people and those with MENTAL HEALTH problems. They may be run (rarely) by the NATIONAL HEALTH SERVICE or (usually) by commercial or VOLUNTARY agencies. They have to be registered with the Care Standards Authority in England and Wales. (CU)

O

Occupational welfare

Usually refers to BENEFITS and services provided for employees by employers in addition to their basic remuneration, but also sometimes used more broadly to refer to other forms of work-related BENEFITS provided by trades unions and professional associations. Employer-sponsored welfare includes financial assistance (encompassing BENEFITS for those unable to work, such as PENSIONS and SICK PAY, and income supplements such as health INSURANCE or help with MORTGAGES and education fees); personal care services (including counselling and FAMILY-FRIENDLY schemes); health care; education and training; and leisure services. Such provision, often termed 'fringe benefits', forms part of many employers' overall recruitment and retention strategies. It has also been fostered by legislation and FISCAL POLICIES.

Traditionally ENTITLEMENT, particularly financial BENEFITS, was restricted to full-time employees, with those in the upper tiers of organizational hierarchies accessing the most generous and the widest range of support. European Union pressures combined with broader labour-market changes have forced pro-rata provision for part-time and other 'non-standard' workers. But employer-sponsored WELFARE remains unevenly distributed between different groups of employees and differentiated on gender and ethnic lines. It also varies between product areas and organizations, the most extensive provision being in large, corporate enterprises in financial services, retailing or capital-intensive manufacturing and some public services, the lowest among small businesses and VOLUNTARY organizations.

The resultant inequities and the ways they have been reinforced by state interventions have attracted considerable criticism. Expanding employer-sponsored WELFARE was, however, central to attempts to cut public spending and restructure WELFARE in the 1980s and 1990s and remains a key element of more recent policy. Initiatives such as STAKE-HOLDER PENSIONS and work-based training are enlarging employers' WELFARE responsibilities, while subjecting them to greater REGULATION and pressure to increase a related form of company WELFARE, supporting COMMUNITY-related services, often in PARTNERSHIP with VOLUNTARY and statutory agencies. (MM)

Official statistics

Data, usually in numerical form, produced by governments. The Office of National Statistics (ONS), formerly the Central Statistical Office (CSO), is responsible for the UK Government Statistical Service and provides parliament and the public with a range of demographic, social and economic data. The government also conducts a number of regular surveys, including the decennial census of population, the annual BRITISH HOUSEHOLD PANEL SURVEY and the regular FAMILY RESOURCES SURVEY, GENERAL HOUSEHOLD SURVEY, LABOUR FORCE SURVEY and Survey of English Housing. Various government departments also publish their own statistics; for example, the Health and Personal Social Services Statistics for England, published annually by the Department of Health, and the annual Social Security Statistics. Key national statistics are published by the Office of National Statistics in the annual publication, *Social Trends*.

Many other countries have comparable government statistical services, and the European Commission has a statistical service known as EUROSTAT, which publishes regular comparative data. Organizations engaged in the collection of international comparative statistics include the United Nations, the International Labour Office, the Organization for Economic Co-operation and Development (OECD) and the World Bank. (MJH)

Ombudsman/ombudsperson

Statutorily appointed non-judicial investigators of maladministration, such as the Parliamentary Commissioner, the Commissioner for Local Administration and the Health Service Commissioner, and also including specially appointed arbitrators, such as the Housing Ombudsman. The concept originated in Scandinavia, where these 'people's champions' had far-reaching powers. (HD)

One Nation

A Conservative Political Centre pamphlet entitled *One Nation: A Tory Approach to Social Problems* was published in 1950 with contributions from, among others, Robert Carr, Edward Heath, Iain Macleod, Angus Maude and ENOCH POWELL. Although this document confirmed the party's broad acceptance of the post-1945 WELFARE STATE, it also attempted to forge a distinctive Conservative approach to SOCIAL POLICY. Rejecting the egalitarian objectives of the Labour Party, One Nation advocates argued that the goal of the WELFARE STATE should be a basic minimum for all. SELECTIVITY rather than UNIVERSALISM was the best way of realizing this aim. Although the term 'One Nation' has come to be associated primarily with those on the left of the Conservative party (particularly during the Thatcher era when it was equated with being 'wet' rather than 'dry'), the pamphlet was sufficiently broad for some of those on the right to claim it as 'part of their inheritance'. (RMP)

Opportunity costs

Economists suggest that everything has a price, which must be borne directly or indirectly by someone. For example, time or other resources used in one activity cannot then be used in another. One way or another someone pays for everything. (HG)

Opportunity state

The opposite of a WELFARE STATE, which in the language of the political sound bite would offer 'a hand up, not a hand out'. It would provide opportunities for education, training and jobs in preference to welfare BENEFITS. The notion is consistent with elements of NEW RIGHT thinking, but has been championed, for example, through WELFARE TO WORK policies both in the USA under the New Democrats and in the UK under New Labour. (HD)

Opted-out schools

Schools which, under the Conservative government's 1988 Education Reform Act after a decision by the governors and a ballot of parents, have voted to opt out of LOCAL AUTHORITY control and assumed self-governing status with funding directly provided by central government. The policy was designed to weaken LOCAL EDUCATION AUTHORITY control and extend PARENTAL CHOICE. See GRANT MAINTAINED SCHOOLS. (DEG)

Owner-occupation

See HOME OWNERSHIP

P

Parental choice

A central theme in recent education policy, particularly under Conservative administrations, designed to extend the CHOICE which parents could exercise on behalf of their children. In practice it involves open enrolment, increasing the range and diversity of schools, especially at SECONDARY level, the publication of school-based information and national LEAGUE TABLES. (DEG)

Parental leave

Leave from employment for parents to ENABLE them to care for children, usually for babies and infants and/or during periods of childhood illness or DISABILITY. European Union countries are required to make provisions, but there is significant variation across countries in the terms and conditions. Parental leave is more often taken by mothers than fathers. (JM)

Pareto principle

Whether a policy is an improvement on the present situation depends upon whether at least someone is better off and no one worse off. If someone is worse off we cannot know whether the change is for the better. (HG)

Parole

Convicted prisoners may be released on parole upon their promise of good behaviour following a partial remission of their sentence. Its routine use is criticized for undermining the EFFECTIVENESS of prison, but defended for its role in controlling prisoners and the prison population. (HD)

Participation

The involvement and incorporation of USERS and CITIZENS more generally in service planning and delivery, providing an opportunity to voice their concerns and contribute to policy formation. In terms of welfare services, it is part of a broader shift in the processes of PUBLIC POLICY making towards EMPOWERMENT and inclusive CITIZENSHIP, intended to increase ACCOUNTABILITY and secure more responsive, sensitive provision. The concept itself, however, remains both elusive and contested. At a practical level many commentators argue it reflects consumer models of involvement rather than user-EMPOWERMENT models based on clearly defined RIGHTS and starting with the experiences of service USERS themselves, rather than from the interests and concerns of providers. This points to the need for more radical approaches, based not only on understanding how CITIZENS might be able to play a more active part in policy-making processes, but the issues on which they might want to have a say and what these imply for the practice of service professionals. (TM)

Partnership

An increasingly popular form of organization for the delivery of services, the development and planning of activities or the implementation of a programme or project based upon a formal agreement among a number of agencies to achieve a common purpose. (AE)

Paternalism

Personal or governmental regulations, policies or practices that curtail the FREEDOMS and responsibilities of individuals or groups in their supposed best interests. (TM)

Paternity leave

Leave from employment for fathers at the time of the birth of a child. Some countries (e.g. Norway) reserve part of PARENTAL LEAVE to men, thus giving a form of paternity leave. (JM)

Path dependency

A term used to explain why systems of social welfare that begin in different ways tend to stay different despite common economic and demographic pressures. Systems tend to keep the characteristics with which they began. The UK pattern of SOCIAL SECURITY began as a FLAT-RATE system and has retained that feature. Australia began with a MEANS-TESTED PENSION scheme and retains it. Once in place a service or activity develops its own expertise and creates its own set of institutional assumptions about how things are 'naturally' done. The NATIONAL HEALTH SERVICE is an example of this. (HG)

Patient choice

The ability of health service USERS to select between different primary and secondary care providers. State health services are often criticized for not giving patients choices. Markets may offer more CHOICE, for those with the cash to pay. The NATIONAL HEALTH SERVICE traditionally limited choices by requiring registration with a particular GENERAL PRACTITIONER and by structuring ACCESS to secondary care. Other European Union state systems leave more scope for choice. (MJH)

Patriarchy

Used by FEMINISTS to describe a social, economic and political system based on male domination and oppression of women, most closely associated with radical feminists. The concept is contested within feminism, particularly in its radical feminist form, which tends to emphasize essential biological differences between women and men. It has, nevertheless, also been used within other strands of feminism and in SOCIAL POLICY to underline the pervasiveness and holistic nature of women's subordination. But here the emphasis is on structures and systemic practices, which are historically and culturally specific, rather than on the unchanging oppression of individual women by individual men. A number of interlocking patriarchal structures have been identified, each of which has implications for SOCIAL POLICY: the state, the economic system and labour market, the family, sexuality and reproduction, male violence, and cultural institutions. Broadly, these can be divided into public and private forms of patriarchy. It has been argued that, as women have moved increasingly into the public sphere, there has been a shift from private to public forms of patriarchy. (RL)

Pauperism

A nineteenth-century term denoting both those dependent on the state-provided POOR LAW and their condition. It was argued, especially by those who favoured the abolition of the Old POOR LAW, that a legal ENTITLEMENT to relief merely created the paupers it set out to relieve. This conclusion was based on several interrelated arguments. First, the existence of the POOR LAW undermined people's willingness to work and therefore responsibility both for personal well-being and national wealth. Second, since it was believed that only a certain proportion of the national wealth was available in the form of wages, poor relief could only be increased at the expense of independent workmen, thereby worsening their condition and forcing them to become paupers also. Third, the provisions of allowances under the SPEENHAMLAND system both fostered improvidence and discouraged hard work. Such thinking underlay the introduction of LESS ELIGIBILITY and the stigmatization of those claiming relief under the New POOR LAW as paupers. (DEG)

Pay as you earn (PAYE)

The practice whereby employers collect INCOME TAX on behalf of the Inland Revenue from wage and salary payments. Participation in PAYE ensures that most employees in the UK pay income tax in a steady flow throughout the year, and also means that most do not have to submit an annual tax return. (DM)

Pay as you go (PAYG or PAYGO)

CONTRIBUTORY BENEFITS, particularly old-age PENSIONS, may be paid for either by building up a PENSION FUND or by a PAYG arrangement. Under PAYG, the contributions of current workers are used to pay current pensions. When the workers retire, their pensions are paid by the next generation of contributing workers. (DM)

Pay beds

May refer to the use of public hospital beds by private patients, in return for payment for their care costs. But it may also refer to beds occupied for a supplementary payment by NHS patients, which gives them extra amenities, in particular privacy. (MJH)

Pension fund

Where pension contributions are invested in financial assets in a pension fund, and when the contributor retires, these assets are used to purchase an ANNUITY. Pension funds may be managed by the state or by private fund managers. (DM)

Pensions

Several different types of regular payments by the government, employers or other providers. Occupational pensions are payments made by employers to employees who have retired (see RETIREMENT) or have ceased to be able to work due to DISABILITY. ELIGIBILITY for such payments may be a BENEFIT due under the contract of employment (OCCUPATIONAL WELFARE). Another type is the ANNUITY payable by a PERSONAL PENSION provider. However, the most common usage refers to different types of state pension. For example, the NATIONAL INSURANCE system provides pensions for contingencies such as old age, DISABILITY and widowhood. The use of the term 'pension' carries connotations of ENTITLEMENT that the more general term BENEFIT does not. Historically, the payment of pensions by governments before the advent of the WELFARE STATE was a mark of honour or distinction conferred upon the recipient. In Britain, the use of the term 'pensions' to describe INSURANCE BENEFITS draws attention to the element of contractual ENTITLEMENT that derives from the CONTRIBUTORY PRINCIPLE. However, receipt of a pension does not have to be supported by payment of contributions. For example, War Pensions are paid to injured ex-servicemen by virtue of their service, while the earliest general old-age pension scheme introduced in Britain in 1908 was NON-CONTRIBUTORY. See MINIMUM INCOME GUARANTEE. (DM)

Performance indicators

Measures for assessing performance within and between organizations, set and collected for LOCAL AUTHORITIES by the Audit Commission and for other services by central departments, often in conjunction with the Commission. Under BEST VALUE general health indicators provide evidence of a LOCAL AUTHORITY's overall performance and service-specific indicators that of individual departments. (SB)

Performance reviews

Performance (or BEST VALUE) reviews require the review of all of a LOCAL AUTHORITY's services every five years, prioritizing poor performance, and one cross-cutting theme review each year. Reviews apply the four Cs (challenge, consult, compare, compete) and the five Es (economy, EFFICIENCY, EFFECTIVENESS, EQUITY and environment). (SB)

Personal pensions

PENSIONS that are arranged by an individual with an insurance company or other pension provider, in contrast with occupational pensions which are arranged via the beneficiary's employer. (DM)

Personal social services

A term which some argue was invented for the Seebohm Committee (1965–8), which reviewed the organization of LOCAL AUTHORITY health, welfare and children's services in England and Wales to secure an effective family service. Others point to the closeness of the term to the much older concept of personal SOCIAL WORK or personal social service supported in the nineteenth century by the CHARITY ORGANIZATION SOCIETY in opposition to what it saw as impersonal state welfare. Today it is used to encompass a changing mix of VOLUNTARY, statutory and private social care provision.

While provision of welfare in Britain has always been mixed, it was dominated in the nineteenth and early twentieth century by the VOLUNTARY SECTOR. As late as 1911 gross annual receipts of CHARITIES exceeded PUBLIC EXPENDITURE on the POOR LAW. Even in the postwar period BEVERIDGE argued that the community should accept responsibility for supplying the basic NEEDS of its CITIZENS for both income and social services. With social services therefore omitted from postwar reconstruction, demands on the VOLUNTARY SECTOR grew substantially in the 1950s and 1960s as the POVERTY of families and older people on low incomes intensified along with inflation.

The 1959 Younghusband Report on LOCAL AUTHORITY social workers recommended a large increase in their numbers, following which the Seebohm Report recommended unifying LOCAL AUTHORITY services for children, older people and PUBLIC HEALTH in England and Wales into one large SOCIAL SERVICES DEPARTMENT (SSD). Set up under the 1970 Local Authority Social Services Act, SSDs were intended to be based on universal and generic principles, with social workers able to work with the whole range of individual and family problems and with an individual or family served by a single service. In practice, social workers continued to specialize in work with particular client groups – children and families, older people, people with physical and sensory DISABILITIES, MENTAL HEALTH problems and LEARNING DIFFICULTIES – while families still had to cope with the interventions in their lives of unrelated health, social care, housing and other agencies. The new SSDs, however, confirmed the reversal of the importance of voluntary and statutory services, with the VOLUNTARY SECTOR becoming the less than equal partner.

The contraction of PUBLIC EXPENDITURE in the late 1970s restricted resources for SSDs and encouraged those on both the left and right of the political spectrum to support an enlarged role for the VOLUNTARY SECTOR. Conservatives supporting greater economy and EFFICIENCY argued for a reduction of public provision, while welfare pluralists supported more participative and DECENTRALIZED services. PARTNERSHIP between the sectors was briefly stimulated through COMMUNITY WORK and the 'patch-based' approach which encouraged SOCIAL WORK to become more integrated with neighbourhoods and informal caring networks in liaison with local VOLUNTARY agencies. In the 1983 Barclay Report on social workers' roles and tasks, a minority report dissented against this development, seeing it as undermining specific SOCIAL WORK skills. Support for this view has been provided by horrific child-abuse cases, of which subsequent reports have blamed both social workers and departmental management.

While commercial provision was minimal at this time, it received an unexpected boost through the 1984 Residential Homes Act, which allowed those in receipt of SUPPLEMENTARY BENEFIT (now INCOME

SUPPORT) and assessed in need of RESIDENTIAL or NURSING HOME CARE to receive this with funding from the Department of Social Security. The resulting growth in private RESIDENTIAL CARE cost government £2.57 billion by 1993 in comparison with £39 million in 1982 and flew in the face of developing COMMUNITY CARE policy which was requiring the closure of institutions and the support of people in the COMMUNITY. By the 1990s the PRIVATE SECTOR had become established as the main provider of nursing and RESIDENTIAL home care for the growing numbers of frail older people, but as LOCAL AUTHORITIES purchased most of these services they held considerable power in the market.

The 1988 Griffiths Report, 'Agenda for Action', provided the basis for the 1989 White Paper 'Caring for People' and the 1990 National Health Service and Community Care Act, implemented in 1993. This ended for the time being a debate about placing COMMUNITY CARE services under health service jurisdiction and reaffirmed both the MIXED ECONOMY of care and the shift away from institutional provision. SSDS were required to become purchasers of care from VOLUNTARY and commercial suppliers and develop care packages for people assessed as eligible with the aim of maintaining them in their own homes. LOCAL AUTHORITY RESIDENTIAL and DOMICILIARY services were increasingly privatized or replaced by contracts with independent providers. This process, along with the switch to DOMICILIARY CARE, is continuing, with RESIDENTIAL provision peaking at the end of the 1990s and over half of home care services provided by non-statutory agencies.

Several other significant developments have also affected social services delivery. EMPOWERMENT of service USERS has become an acknowledged goal, in theory if not always in practice, and legislation has ENABLED USERS to purchase their own services. The role of INFORMAL CARE has been further recognized, with the 1995 Carers (Recognition and Services) Act and the Carers and Disabled Children Act 2000 providing some support for the estimated 6 million people who care for family and friends. A Commission for Long Term Care has called for all personal care to be provided free rather than incur MEANS-TESTED LOCAL AUTHORITY CHARGES. Concerns over the quality of provision have also led to new initiatives to improve standards. These include the establishment of a Care Standards Commission to regulate quality in RESIDENTIAL and home-care services, the Quality Protects programme for children's services, a performance assessment framework, joint reviews by the Social Services Inspectorate and the Audit Commission and the BEST VALUE scheme. Finally, the importance of supporting the million-strong social care workforce has been brought home by severe recruitment shortages and the knowledge that 80 per cent of this work-force is made up of unqualified female staff.

The future direction of the personal social services, however, remains uncertain. Difficulties around working in PARTNERSHIP with health authorities, particularly with hospital discharge, have revived the call for COMMUNITY CARE to be integrated into PRIMARY CARE. In the long run this may spell the demise of large SSDs and may once again affect the balance of service provision between PUBLIC, VOLUNTARY and PRIVATE SECTORS. (SB)

Perverse incentives

Rewards for actions that run in the opposite to the desired direction of policies. For instance, MEANS TESTING may aim to restrict government spending on BENEFITS by TARGETING these on poor CLAIMANTS, but if CLAIMANTS manage to increase their income they lose some BENEFIT, thus discouraging attempts to raise individual income and reduce BENEFIT costs. (HG)

Philanthropy

The philosophies and related practices allegedly reflecting individual and institutional 'love of humanity', although sometimes more narrowly taken to mean the pledging or donation of money to particular activi-ties or organizations. Debate frequently polarizes between the ALTRUIS-TIC (rewards are marginal or absent) and instrumental (rewards are satisfaction, status, influence) bases of philanthropy, although empirical studies reveal more mixed motivational influences in practice, both at individual and institutional levels. Philanthropic activities vary across social classes and ethnic groups, between societies and over time, and there are no simple correlations between economic health and levels of philanthropy. (DWS)

Policy networks

Denote the relationships and the degrees of communication that exist between groups and government. They exist at different levels of gov-ernment, in different policy areas and around particular issues, and can be ranked on a continuum from issue networks that lack coherence and consensus to closed policy communities. (SB)

Poll tax

A flat-rate tax levied on each person in the population. See COMMUNITY CHARGE. (PA)

Polytechnics

Usually refers to those thirty leading technical institutions designated polytechnics as part of the binary system of HIGHER EDUCATION introduced in the late 1960s. Their distinctive vocational orientation gradually gave way to more comprehensive and broad-based arts and social science provision; and, with the abolition of the binary system in 1992, they were redesignated as UNIVERSITIES. (DEG)

Poor Law

A residual system of financial and SOCIAL ASSISTANCE for those unable to support themselves which is conventionally divided in England and Wales into the Old Poor Law (codified in 1598 and 1601) and the New Poor Law of 1834. In theory, the former provided different types of provision (poorhouses, WORKHOUSES and houses of correction) for different CLAIMANT categories (the aged, disabled, able-bodied and persistent idler). Locally, it was administered by parish overseers appointed by magistrates and financed by local rates on property. A concern with the rising cost of relief was one factor that led to the 1834 Poor Law Amendment Act. This was fashioned according to the tenets of LIBERAL INDIVIDUALISM and the developing market economy and assumed that POVERTY was a personal rather than a structural problem. Hence provision was governed by the deterrent principle of LESS ELIGIBILITY and the WORKHOUSE test. Despite the administrative CENTRALIZATION introduced by the Act, localism remained a feature of the New Poor Law just as it had been of its predecessor, and policy and practice were often at variance. The Poor Law came to an effective end in 1929 and was finally abolished in 1948. By that time a new infrastructure of statutory social welfare had been created which went beyond the 'reserved for the poor' principles of the Poor Law. (DEG)

Poplarism

A term applied to the attempts by Labour councillors in the East End London borough of Poplar in the late 1910s and 1920s to safeguard working-class conditions, including those of POOR LAW CLAIMANTS. Led by George Lansbury, the Council Leader, they achieved notoriety on two accounts. First, he and thirty others were imprisoned for six weeks for refusing to levy a rate that included a substantial contribution to general London County Council expenditure. They sought instead a greater rate equalization across London in which poorer boroughs like Poplar would be subsidized by richer districts. Second, many Poplar councillors also served as POOR LAW Guardians, in which capacity they attempted to pay more generous poor relief allowances than those authorized by central government. Other Labour-controlled Boards of Guardians during the 1926 General Strike replicated their action. It led to stronger central controls over the Boards and the creation of larger units of LOCAL GOVERNMENT in 1929, which took over POOR LAW administration and in which PAUPER votes counted for little compared to those of the ratepayers. (DEG)

Positional good

According to economists, when a product is in short supply its price will rise and then firms will produce much more and the product may become a mass-consumption good. However, positional goods are things that are valued because they are rare and distinctive or not accessible to the mass market, such as an original painting. Education is also a positional good, in part. High qualifications may be of value in improving individual HUMAN CAPITAL, but they also distinguish holders from other CITIZENS. If everyone had the same qualifications, that advantage would go away. (HG)

Positive discrimination

The explicit shaping or TARGETING of practices to ensure that disadvantaged or under-represented groups have fair ACCESS to services and past imbalances are redressed. See also AFFIRMATIVE ACTION. (GC)

Post-Fordism

See FORDISM

Postmodernism

It is argued that the 'modern' era, once characterized as the 'Age of Enlightenment' and dominated by Western culture and the rise of capitalism, has been superseded or is in the process of fragmentation. Post-modernism may denote a variety of disparate strands of thinking. On the one hand, it is a profoundly sceptical critique of modernity arguing that modernity's claims for the beneficence of scientific reason and the pursuit of human progress and emancipation have been proved at best hollow or at worst fraudulent. The grand ideological narratives of both LIBERALISM and even its challenger, SOCIALISM, are now discredited. On the other hand, it is a call to new forms of analysis of the global economy and the scope within it for locally DECENTRALIZED post-FORDIST economic and welfare systems. It focuses upon the emergence of new forms of political expression based on social difference and social movements in place of the politics of class. It points to emergent forms of popular cultural expression; the significance of social and cultural identity and the processes by which identities are socially constructed; the constitutive nature of discourse and the analytical possibilities of deconstruction. (HD)

Poverty

Among both academics and policy makers there is disagreement about both the definition of poverty and the extent of the problem. However, there is some agreement that the existence of poverty is a problem: poverty is perceived to be a bad thing, and most people expect SOCIAL POLICY planners to seek to remove or ameliorate it.

Disagreement about the definition of poverty has been character-ized as a dispute over whether poverty is an absolute or a relative phenomenon. Absolute poverty exists where people do not have suffi-cient resources to provide for their basic NEEDS of food and shelter. This is also referred to as being below the level of subsistence. Some argue that absolute poverty no longer exists in affluent industrial soci-eties, but others argue that HOMELESSNESS is an example of absolute poverty amid affluence. Relative poverty exists where people may have some resources but do not have enough to take part in the kind of activ-ities accepted as normal by the conventions of the society in which they live. They are poor relative to the standards of their society. This concept has been popularized by research carried out in the UK by Peter Townsend. It is also sometimes referred to as deprivation or SOCIAL EXCLUSION.

Both absolute and relative definitions of poverty have been subject to criticism. It is difficult to conceive of absolute NEEDS independent of the social context in which people are placed, and subsistence is therefore often defined relatively – what do people need to subsist on in Britain in the twenty-first century? Relative poverty can be confused with inequality – are people who are relatively poor simply those who are at the bottom of an unequal distribution of resources within society?

Researchers have attempted to produce measures of poverty, which combine both absolute and relative approaches. These include Budget Standards measures, which seek to fix the minimum cost of the weekly budget for individuals or families living in Britain today; or DEPRIVATION Indicator measures, which ask representative samples of the population what they regard as the essential material requirements for a basic standard of living. These definitions can then be operationalized to measure the extent of poverty in society by counting the numbers of people with incomes below the budget standard or those lacking the agreed basic requirements.

One of the earliest poverty researchers in the UK was B. S. ROWNTREE, who pioneered the budget standards approach. He also made a distinction between primary and secondary poverty:

- Primary poverty was experienced by those who did not have a sufficient income to meet their subsistence NEEDS.
- Secondary poverty was experienced by those who had an income above subsistence level but still went without essential items because of poor budgetary planning.

This distinction has not been widely adopted, but it has influenced debates about the behaviour of poor people. For instance, some critics have argued that poor people who spend some of their minimum income on tobacco or alcohol are contributing to their own deprivation, and should not therefore be provided with additional resources. However, qualitative research on the experience of poverty casts doubts on such a simplistic view. Such research reveals the very real difficulties that individuals and families experience in surviving on very low incomes, in particular, for instance, when exceptional NEEDS must be met (such as a broken cooker) or when indebtedness reduces even further weekly spending power.

In practice most measures of poverty used in affluent countries are based upon a proxy measure taken from statistical evidence about the distribution of income or wealth within the society. The most common measure here is to count as poor those families or households with an annual income below 50 per cent of the average income within that society. This is clearly a relative measure. It has been adopted by the UK government in its annual publication of the numbers of HOUSE-HOLDS BELOW AVERAGE INCOME; and it is also used by the EU and the OECD to make comparisons of poverty levels in different countries.

However, such measures cannot reveal the extent of the 'poverty gap'. This is the distance between the incomes of the poor and the fixed average level. For those with very low incomes this gap is much greater. This may be of concern to policy makers, for large numbers of people facing a large poverty gap are evidence of a much more serious poverty problem. It may also influence the outcome of anti-poverty measures, as raising incomes that are far below the fixed level will require much more extensive REDISTRIBUTION.

Another aspect of poverty not measured by simple counting is the problem of 'poverty dynamics'. This is the length of time that people experience problems of poverty and deprivation. Research has revealed that those who spend long periods of time living on low incomes experience much more hardship than those who are poor only for short periods. Although most periods of poverty are relatively short, there are a significant number of people experiencing extended spells of deprivation. For these people both surviving within poverty and escaping from it are much more serious problems.

Although most research on poverty is concerned primarily to identify the numbers of individuals or families who are poor or the extent of their poverty, there is also evidence that both the risk of poverty and the experience of it vary across different social groups. Thus women are more likely to be poor than men and to experience higher levels of deprivation. The same is true of members of some ethnic minority COMMU-NITIES. Experience of poverty is also closely linked to age, with children (and their parents) and pensioners experiencing much higher levels of poverty than the rest of the population. (PA)

Poverty trap

Because MEANS-TESTED supplements to people receiving low wages are withdrawn when wages rise, the value to recipients of any such wage increases is reduced and people are thus trapped in poverty. In the 1970s some recipients could lose more in BENEFITS than they gained in a wage increase. Now the average rate of loss is around 70 per cent of increased wages, but large numbers of low-wage earners are affected. (PA)

Powell, John Enoch (1912–1998)

Conservative MP for Wolverhampton from 1950 until his resignation from the party in 1974 and then an Official Unionist member for South Down, Northern Ireland, Enoch Powell presided over an ambitious hospital-building programme while serving as Minister of Health (1960–3). His economic LIBERALISM led him to oppose higher forms of state welfare expenditure that he believed would have inflationary consequences. He resigned from the MACMILLAN government along with the Chancellor Peter Thorneycroft and Nigel Birch in 1958 after Treasury plans for a £50 million cut in PUBLIC EXPENDITURE were rejected. A fierce opponent of Britain's entry into the EEC, Powell is best remembered for his controversial views on IMMIGRATION and repatriation in the late 1960s. His infamous 'rivers of blood' speech in 1968 led to his dismissal from Heath's shadow cabinet. His publications include *The Social Services: Needs and Means* (with Iain Macleod, 1954) and *The Welfare State* (1961). (RMP)

Power-resources model

See SOCIAL DEMOCRACY

Pre-school education

Takes a variety of forms and is provided by public, VOLUNTARY and commercial organizations. Within the PUBLIC SECTOR, LOCAL EDUCATION AUTHORITIES may provide NURSERY schools or nursery classes in PRIMARY SCHOOLS, both of which are free of charge and which children usually attend for five half-day sessions in term time. In addition they provide reception classes in primary schools for the 'rising fives', i.e. those just below compulsory school age, attendance at which may be part-time or full-time. Though there is no legal requirement for them to provide pre-school education, they are required to make provision for children over two who have SPECIAL EDUCATIONAL NEEDS. Pre-school children may also attend day NURSERIES provided by LOCAL AUTHORITY SOCIAL SERVICES DEPARTMENTS for which a charge may be payable. In the independent sector provision ranges from COMMUNITY-based playgroups (run primarily by parents and VOLUNTARY groups) to day NURSERIES and INDEPENDENT SCHOOLS provided by commercial companies and VOLUNTARY organizations on a fee-paying basis. It is generally acknowledged that children who have had some form of pre-school education perform better when compulsory schooling begins and recent policy has aimed to increase provision and its TAKE-UP, especially among those from disadvantaged backgrounds. It has also been subject to increasing REGULATION and INSPECTION. In England this is undertaken by the education inspectorate, and in Wales by the social service inspectorate, reflecting a wider debate about the balance between 'play' and 'education' in provisions for young children. (DEG)

Prescription charges

Payments determined by the Department of Health for each item of medicine prescribed by UK NATIONAL HEALTH SERVICE practitioners. Hospital in-patients, children, the elderly, people with low incomes and sufferers from certain chronic conditions are exempted from these. (MJH)

Pressure groups

Formal organizations based around the promotion or protection of particular interests, which members share, such as the alleviation of child POVERTY and HOMELESSNESS, or the protection of animals and the countryside. Unlike the more loosely formed NEW SOCIAL MOVEMENTS, they seek to influence policy through links with administrative and political institutions such as LOCAL AUTHORITIES, central government departments and financial institutions. (DWS)

Preventative medicine

Interventions designed to pre-empt the onset of disease, including not only HEALTH PROMOTION, HEALTH SCREENING and GENETIC SCREENING, but also other efforts to influence people's incomes, work lives, lifestyles, environments and consumption. (MJH)

Primary care

First-line care for people with medical NEEDS. For those who are ill, it has a particular significance in the UK because patients cannot, except in emergencies, refer themselves directly to specialist practitioners or hospitals. They have to go first to the GENERAL PRACTICE with which they are registered. GENERAL PRACTITIONERS (GPs) are therefore the 'GATE KEEPERS', making judgements about when referral to more specialized secondary services is appropriate. GP services are free (though patients may have to pay PRESCRIPTION CHARGES) and they are paid on a capitation basis, with allowances for administrative expenses and special payments for particular procedures such as HEALTH SCREENING or immunization.

Traditionally GPs were organized on a single or group-practice basis and focused on diagnostic and treatment services, with patients being referred directly for in- or out-patient hospital care. Recent governments, however, have emphasized the GPs' role in HEALTH PROMOTION, PREVENTATIVE MEDICINE and minor surgery, as well as general medical care, and various health and care professionals are increasingly based in their practices. Their role in the overall management of local provision has also been expanded through the introduction of Primary Care Trusts, responsible for primary and COMMUNITY health services and COMMISSIONING secondary services in their area, and managed by a governing board including GP, community nursing and SOCIAL SERVICES representatives.

Other primary care provision includes NHS Direct (which offers a state-run, free telephone advisory service from nurses) and dentists, opticians and pharmacists who offer both state and privately funded services and are paid on a fee-for-service basis for the latter. In addition there are a few commercial general practices, some operating on a 'walk-in' basis. (MJH)

Primary education

Defined in the 1944 Education Act as schooling for children aged between 5 and 11, though in practice a distinction was made between infant schools for those aged 5 and 7, and junior schools for 8–11-year-olds. An alternative mode emerged from the 1960s when some LOCAL AUTHORITIES introduced first and middle schools (for 5–8s and 8–12s respectively). The 1988 Education Reform Act reinforced the infant–junior divide with the introduction of key stage, standard assessment tests at the ages of 7 and 11. At the end of key stage 1 pupils undertake practical classroom-based tasks and written tests in English and maths. At the end of key stage 2 at age 11 there are written tests in English, maths and science. Primary schools in the state sector are non-selective.

In urban areas, they are often neighbourhood schools. Village primary schools, especially in isolated rural areas, however, have often faced the threat of closure because of insufficient pupil numbers. (DEG)

Private finance initiative

Introduced by the UK government in the 1990s as a means by which private funds can be used to supplement public investment in capital projects such as hospitals, schools or housing. This saves the government having to borrow money and hence add to PUBLIC SECTOR borrowing, while the private developer carries the risk that the facility may not be needed after the contract has ended. (HG)

Private health insurance

Protection against the expenses associated with illness provided by financial service organizations or employers enabling individuals to claim the cost of treatment. INSURANCE can take a number of forms. Medical, dental and ophthalmic insurance provides for treatment for specified conditions. Critical illness insurance offers a lump sum in the event of a serious condition. LONG-TERM CARE insurance covers the costs of continuing care. Permanent health insurance provides an income replacement in the event of loss of employment due to illness or DISABILITY. (MM)

Private rented sector

This sector of housing comprises properties that are privately owned but are let for rent. It was the major source of housing at the beginning of the twentieth century, but has declined dramatically since then, though it still retains a significant role. It is a diverse sector including expensive housing directed at mobile professionals, a niche market for students, and a low-quality market that is the source of some significant housing problems. (AM)

Private schooling

Fee-charging INDEPENDENT SCHOOLS. There is considerable diversity in the sector, with provision ranging from ancient foundations, usually with a high proportion of residential pupils, to smaller less well-known day and boarding schools and former DIRECT GRANT GRAMMAR SCHOOLS. They are exempt from the NATIONAL CURRICULUM and tend to have more favourable teacher–pupil ratios than state schools. This, it has been argued, produces better results in competitive examinations and hence entry into HIGHER EDUCATION and into certain types of professional career. For those on the political left their existence has been seen as a barrier to EQUALITY of educational opportunity. In practice, however, there have been few attempts to alter their position, while recent Labour policies have emphasized collaboration between the private and state sectors. (DEG)

Private sector

This refers to those industries and services financed for profit by shareholding individuals or organizations and is generally contrasted with the PUBLIC SECTOR of organizations owned and managed by the state. It comprises corporate and non-incorporated enterprises and the self-funded purchasing activities of individuals and households. In SOCIAL POLICY it is generally used to refer to one part of the MIXED ECONOMY OF WELFARE, the others being the state, VOLUNTARY and INFORMAL sectors). Unlike these, private-sector providers sell welfare BENEFITS and services on a for-profit or commercial basis to those prepared to buy such provision.

Statutory and voluntary organizations may charge for their services, and INFORMAL CARE may also involve some financial exchange, but these CHARGES are not designed to generate an operational profit and in practice are driven by very different sets of values to those governing PRIVATE WELFARE. In recent times, private-sector welfare providers have been subject to tighter state REGULATION. However, it continues to attract criticism from those who question the role of markets in welfare and the applicability of business models to state provision. (MM)

Private welfare

Sometimes loosely used to denote all forms of non-statutory welfare, but primarily refers to the production and consumption of welfare BENEFITS and services on a profit-making or commercial basis. In this usage it comprises diverse product markets varying in size and competitiveness, with differing mixes of suppliers and purchasers trading under different institutional and regulatory conditions. Some trade in services such as health and social care, housing or education; others in financial benefits such as MORTGAGES, PENSIONS, long-term savings and INSURANCE.

Production is preponderantly in the hands of profit-making, proprietary enterprises, though mutual and not-for-profit companies are significant in some markets. In financial services markets provision is dominated by large multinational and corporate businesses, although purchasing may involve smaller intermediaries or individual advisers as well as direct funding. In other markets the range of providers is more diverse, extending from self-employed single traders to large conglomerates.

Purchasing also varies. Some markets primarily serve individuals buying or investing on their own behalf or their dependants' behalf, but many are geared to volume purchasing by employers procuring various forms of OCCUPATIONAL WELFARE and, increasingly, other 'proxy purchasers'. These include VOLUNTARY and, particularly, public agencies contracting administrative services or provision for state-aided end-USERS, sometimes through QUASI-MARKETS.

The use of such QUASI-MARKETS has expanded in recent times, as has the use of FISCAL and other INCENTIVES to encourage self-provision and commercial production. Both have also been boosted by PRIVATIZATION. This has resulted in increased REGULATION and an enhanced role for the state as a market player, which means that private welfare is more complex and dependent on non-market processes than its representation in traditional SOCIAL POLICY literature might suggest. Nevertheless fundamental questions remain about its distributional consequences and the place of MARKETS IN WELFARE more generally. (MM)

Privatization

In its narrowest sense this refers to the transfer of the ownership of public assets and services to individuals or NON-STATUTORY agencies. More broadly it is a shorthand term for the many government initiatives in the 1980s and 1990s designed to reduce state involvement in the production, funding or control of services and increase market-based provision. In the case of welfare BENEFITS and services it involved not only transfers to commercial organizations but also to VOLUNTARY agencies and INFORMAL CARERS and increased self-provision. This process varied from service to service and took a number of forms:

- The sale of land, property and other assets to individuals or non-statutory providers.
- Replacing or partially replacing tax finance by new or increased CHARGES.
- Transferring administrative responsibilities to employing organizations.
- Promoting self-funding and alternative suppliers (commercial, VOLUNTARY and INFORMAL) through cuts in public provision and SUBSIDIES.
- Facilitating self-provisioning through fiscal and other concessions.
- CONTRACTING OUT the management and delivery of state-funded services.
- Employing private capital in public-service projects under the PUBLIC FINANCE INITIATIVE.
- DEREGULATING the controls exercised over welfare providers.

Implemented in tandem with the restructuring of public services on PURCHASER-PROVIDER market-oriented lines, these measures were intended to increase the EFFICIENCY, cost-EFFECTIVENESS and responsiveness of welfare agencies, although their success in achieving these has been questioned. What is clear, however, is that they contributed to a blurring of the traditional boundaries between statutory and non-statutory provision and an expansion of the MIXED ECONOMY OF WELFARE. (MM)

Professionalism

The knowledge, expertise and integrity of highly trained and qualified staff are among the main characteristics associated with professionalism. The competence and ACCOUNTABILITY of welfare professionals have been questioned following scandals in health, education and social services, while USER groups and managers have challenged their traditional independence and self-REGULATION. (SB)

Progressive taxation

Takes a higher share of income the more that one earns and can be contrasted to a REGRESSIVE TAX which takes a smaller share the richer one becomes. INCOME TAX is a progressive tax in most countries, including the UK. SOCIAL SECURITY taxes are mildly regressive; people stop paying more when their incomes rise above a given point. The FLAT-RATE contributions BEVERIDGE recommended were very regressive. (HG)

Provident associations

Ethical banking organizations that make loans to projects considered to be of social or environmental value; for example, to a MULTICULTURAL COMMUNITY, a company importing only sustainably produced timber or an organic farming group. Depositors become part of the association by choosing projects for investment. (DWS)

Public assistance

In the UK prior to the BEVERIDGE reforms of 1948, those not covered by SOCIAL INSURANCE BENEFITS could claim MEANS-TESTED DISCRETIONARY assistance from local Public Assistance Committees. This was in effect a continuation of the nineteenth-century POOR LAW, and was therefore much STIGMATIZED. However, some CLAIMANTS were also able to seek support from the National Unemployment Assistance Board, although this too employed a MEANS TEST and was regarded as a stigmatized form of support. (PA)

Public choice theory

A body of thinking based on the application of classical economic theorizing to political processes. It is premised on the twin assumptions that all social entities comprise sets of egoistic individuals operating rationally to maximize their own self-interests, and that economic and political behaviour are analogous. In WELFARE STATES ALLOCATIVE decisions are thus construed as taking place in a political market in which parties compete for power by offering different welfare packages and voters shop around for the best personal deal rather than considering the wider collective interest.

Unlike the economic market, however, there is no visible price mechanism connecting the costs of welfare production to consumption. Hence the political market is held to induce fiscal irresponsibility, a process reinforced by the activities of welfare professionals and bureaucrats. Rather than operating with a sense of public duty, they are similarly seen as self-interested, and therefore motivated only to expand their agency's remit and their own status within it, irrespective of USER NEEDS. Thus, while each set of political actors is operating rationally (i.e. self-interestedly), the combined effect is held to generate an unsustainable expansionism that threatens to destabilize both the economy and democratic GOVERNANCE. The solution is seen to be the dampening down of demand by returning welfare to the costed realism of the economic market where individuals can directly meet their own needs. Such approaches contributed to the late-twentieth-century restructuring of state welfare, although both their premises and empirical base have been widely criticized. (MM)

Public expenditure

All expenditure by all levels of government – central and local – within which the 'control total' denotes the totals set for each government department for three years ahead. The annually managed total is set a year at a time for those services affected by events beyond their control, such as SOCIAL SECURITY. The COMPREHENSIVE SPENDING REVIEW sets spending targets for three years ahead. (HG)

Public goods

An economic term for those goods or services that cannot be sold on the market and are 'non-excludable'. Everyone benefits from such things as clean air, the police force or the defence of the nation. They may also be 'non-rival', which means they can be provided without denying someone else access – like an extra car driving on an open road. It costs nothing to do so, and it is not economic to charge for the space. Crowded roads are another matter. (HG)

Public health

The maintenance of the health of the public at large. While it embraces the concerns of a wide range of agencies, including health services, it tends to be particularly applied to immunization and related programmes, environmental protection, food safety and the REGULATION of consumer services. (MJH)

Public policy

SOCIAL POLICY is concerned with one aspect of public policy – a wider term used to encompass foreign policy, defence policy, energy policy, environmental policy, etc. Most elements of public policy have some relevance for SOCIAL POLICY, but traditionally SOCIAL POLICY has been more concerned with a narrower focus on policies explicitly concerned with well-being and welfare. (AE)

Public schools

In the UK, schools that provide private education to children whose parents pay fees are sometimes, perhaps misleadingly, called public schools. See INDEPENDENT SCHOOLS; PRIVATE SCHOOLING. (PA)

Public sector

The public sector consists of central government, LOCAL AUTHORITIES and public corporations. It is contrasted with the PRIVATE and VOLUNTARY (or THIRD) sectors. (AE)

Public sector borrowing requirement (PSBR)

The total amount that local and national government and the nationalized industries borrow to finance their activities. This includes borrowing to cover both capital expenditure and the budget deficit (the cost of government services not covered by tax receipts that year) and has been replaced by the term 'the public sector net cash requirement'. More emphasis is now given to three measures that correspond to the Exchequer's rules of budget management:

- The surplus or deficit on the current account – whether spending on everything but buildings is covered by tax receipts that year.
- Public sector net borrowing – to fund capital spending on buildings.
- The public sector net debt ratio – the balance between the total debt of government built up over many years and the value of government assets (schools, hospitals, houses, parks and amenities). (HG)

Purchaser/provider split

The division of public welfare services into distinct units responsible on the one hand for supplying provision (perhaps in competition with other statutory and often NON-STATUTORY agencies) or, on the other, for COMMISSIONING and contracting services from potential deliverers. It was central to the restructuring of welfare on business lines in the late twentieth century and the creation of QUASI- or INTERNAL MARKETS and remains a key principle of much current welfare management. The aim was to generate more EFFICIENT, cost-effective services and enhance consumer CHOICE, but achievement of these has been questioned. (MM)

Q

Quality adjusted life years (QUALYs)

A technique for assessing the benefit of a medical intervention through quantifying improved LIFE EXPECTANCY. It is a rationalistic device offering a possible solution to some of the ethical dilemmas about the rationing of expensive resources. (MJH)

Quality assurance

A planned scheme of procedures and techniques designed to ensure that services or products meet national or local standards within agreed resources and time scales. The interactive nature of welfare provision and the range of potential STAKEHOLDERS mean that developing and implementing such schemes is a highly complex and contestable process. (MM)

Quality control

MANAGERIALIST rather than USER-derived measures for assessing whether specified input, process and output service standards have been met and maintained. (MM)

Quangos (quasi-autonomous non-governmental organizations)

Quangos have become a significant element within the institutional structure of government in Britain, in particular in taking over aspects of public administration previously run directly by government as part of the NEXT STEPS initiative, such as the Benefits Agency and health service trusts. They are organizations that are not directly accountable to parliament or to LOCAL GOVERNMENT. Boards appointed by government manage many Quangos, and questions about the extent of their democratic ACCOUNTABILITY are common. (AM)

Quasi-market

Simulations of market conditions in public services through the separation of the purchasing from the provision of services and the introduction of competition, businesslike processes and consumer CHOICE. Unlike conventional markets purchasing is undertaken on behalf of consumers by care practitioners working to earmarked budgets, while provision is publicly funded and accountable and may be confined to statutory agencies or include not-for-profit as well as commercial organizations. (MM)

R

Racism

Can be understood both as an ideology and a source of ('racial') identity, demarcating boundaries between 'self' and the 'other' at the individual and collective levels. As an ideology, it structures power, privilege and socio-economic opportunities in favour of a particular group deemed to be superior, while attributing negative qualities to those held to be inferior. It thus legitimizes the former and the prejudicial, discriminatory and oppressive practices stemming from the construction of the term 'race' to denote innate biological–physiological or intellectual and cultural differences between people.

The notion of biologically distinct 'races' was first deployed in the nineteenth century when depictions of the conquest of the 'savage', non-European, pagan 'other' by 'civilized' Europeans served to legitimize colonial expansion, the expropriation of the land and RIGHTS of indigenous communities and their incarceration and extermination. It was furthered in the first part of the twentieth century by the development of EUGENICS as a theory and movement. In a major historical and ideological shift, EUGENICISTS also addressed the 'other' closer to home. Drawing on Darwin and MALTHUS, they reconstructed the notion of certain groups being racially, intellectually and politically inferior, as well as socially contaminating, legitimizing the segregation and incarceration of those defined as physically, socially or psychologically abnormal or pathological. In the UK EUGENICISTS' views on 'race' became intertwined with crosscutting discourses on class, gender and DISABILITY and wider concerns about those perceived as a threat to the moral and physical well-being of English society. These encompassed Irish as well as other immigrants and groups held to be 'unfit', such as single mothers, the unskilled, DISABLED people or those with MENTAL HEALTH problems or LEARNING DIFFICULTIES.

It was partly in reaction to this, as well as earlier theories of biologically based 'races', that the term 'racism' appears to have entered the British lexicon during the 1930s. It gained currency as the pseudo-scientific claims used by the Hitler regime to justify the genocide of Jewish and other people came under increasing scrutiny. In the wake of these, racism thus came to be defined along the lines developed by UNESCO as falsely claiming that there is a scientific basis for placing people in hierarchical groups according to presumed immutable cultural and psychological differences.

However, in the face of the experiences of those who migrated to the UK and Europe in the immediate postwar years this equation of racism with belief in a presumed scientific theory of 'race' was increasingly challenged. Instead, analysts during the 1960s began to highlight the extent to which prejudice or DISCRIMINATION against 'other' groups involves deterministic belief systems about differences between people grounded in perceptions of their culture, history or descent. Hence the term came to be seen as relational rather than fixed, and as encompassing the ways in which the notion of 'race' as a basis of prejudice and/or DISCRIMINATION is deployed as a metaphor for the social, political, cultural and moral fabric of the group construed as the 'other'. This process, sometimes referred to as racialization, involves the use of language not merely as a descriptor, but as a symbol that conjures up certain images and myths involved in the moral or NORMATIVE judgements made about the people it refers to.

More recent analysts have emphasized the emergence of a new form of racism in the UK that draws on presumed cultural differences between ethnic groups rather than notions of racial superiority or inferiority. This new form of cultural racism invokes traditional ideas about 'British nationalism' and the 'British way of life', and deploys a notion of fixed, homogeneous and static cultures that denies a right to a 'British identity' for 'immigrants' and their descendants. It can be argued that even though the term 'ethnicity' has replaced 'race' as an ostensibly neutral concept it only veils underlying cultural racism and serves the same function of constructing cultural difference as pathological.

It has, therefore, been suggested that racism cannot be conceptualized as a coherent discourse with neatly drawn boundaries. Rather, the contradictions and discontinuities inherent to this, as to any social discourse, persuade us to think of 'racisms' as well as forms of resistance operating within a discontinuous history of ideas and practices legitimized through particular loci of power and knowledge. (SC)

Rates

One of the oldest forms of tax used since the sixteenth century to fund the activities of LOCAL GOVERNMENT, including the poor rate – the tax once used to fund relief of the poor in local parishes. Rates were a tax on the value of property. They lasted until the end of the 1980s, when the COMMUNITY CHARGE (or POLL TAX) replaced them. Rates were paid by householders and the owners of offices and factories, based on a valuation of the worth of their property. They could thus be somewhat regressive. After the introduction of the COMMUNITY CHARGE (now COUNCIL TAX), rates remained as a tax on offices and firms, collected nationally and redistributed to LOCAL AUTHORITIES on a per capita basis. This is now called the national non-domestic (or business) rate. (HG)

Rathbone, Eleanor Florence (1872–1946)

After studying at Somerville College, Oxford, Eleanor Rathbone examined various social conditions in her home town, Liverpool, becoming convinced, like other reformers of the period, of the need for increased state action if such problems were to be addressed. She was an independent member on Liverpool City Council from 1909 to 1934 and was elected as an independent MP for the combined universities from 1929 to 1945. She was a vociferous campaigner for equal CITIZENSHIP for women and succeeded Millicent Fawcett as President of the National Union of Societies for Equal Citizenship in 1919.

Her name is most closely associated with the introduction of FAMILY ALLOWANCES. Through the Family Endowment Society, which she established in 1917, Rathbone attempted to persuade policy makers and opinion formers of the need for reform of this kind. When Family Allowances were finally introduced in 1945 it was not the arguments of Rathbone and the Family Endowment Society that carried the day, but rather the part such payments could play in controlling wage demands. Her publications include *The Disinherited Family* (1924) and *The Case for Family Allowances* (1940). (RMP)

Rational choice

A body of thinking closely associated with PUBLIC CHOICE THEORY. It maintains that individuals are essentially egoistic, self-interested, calculative beings, making decisions solely according to the relative costs and benefits of available options in meeting their welfare NEEDS or other goals. (MM)

Reciprocity

A mutual transaction rests upon reciprocal relations based upon a shared understanding of the norms governing the transaction. Reciprocity implies the mutual, internalized, sharing of the conditions of exchange rather than these conditions being imposed by an external order. An exchange based upon reciprocity gives rise to obligations. For example, we may give blood freely and we expect others will also do so, thus ensuring that if we need blood it will be given to us. (AE)

Redistribution

The distribution of income, wealth, consumption or other indicators of welfare across households can be analysed to measure POVERTY and inequality. Redistribution refers to the way an initial distribution (usually taken to be that generated by the market) is modified by taxes, TRANSFERS and/or the provision of free goods and services by the WELFARE STATE. Welfare provision can be said to have a high redistributive impact if the level of POVERTY and inequality generated by the market is substantially lowered after these transactions are taken into account. (DM)

Redress

The procedures by which grievances may be resolved or expressed, which may entail litigation before the courts; administrative procedures such as APPEALS, reviews, COMPLAINTS or references to an OMBUDSPERSON; or resort to less formal consultative mechanisms involving elected representatives or local groups or fora. (HD)

Redundancy

Denotes the loss of a job due to reduction in the demand for workers in a particular industry. In 1965 a statutory system of redundancy, or severance, pay was introduced in the UK, including lump-sum payments, the costs of which are met in part from a general levy on employers. (JC)

Refugees

Under the 1951 UN Geneva Convention, a refugee is an individual who, 'owing to a well-founded fear of being persecuted for reasons of race, religion, nationality, membership of a particular social group or political opinion, is outside the country of his/her nationality or habitual residence and unable or unwilling to return to it' on grounds of personal safety. Governments may challenge whether refugees have 'well-founded' fears, conflate 'inability' with 'unwillingness', or assert that 'political' refugees are 'economic migrants' to refuse refugee status. (GC)

Regeneration

Embraces a wide variety of different interventions to improve the opportunities for (particularly urban) local COMMUNITIES adopted since the 1990s. Regeneration policies are often AREA BASED. In the past they have had a major focus on property development, but more recently have been aimed at improving economic opportunities through training and employment opportunities for local residents. In Scotland PARTNERSHIPS were established to develop policy in deprived urban areas. In England the major funding regime is the Single Regeneration Budget (SRB), now run by the Regional Development Agencies (RDAs). (AM)

Regionalization

A range of different organizations in the SOCIAL POLICY field have regional bodies which seek to co-ordinate activities at a regional level. DEVOLUTION and separate legislative and administrative arrangements established for Scotland, Wales and Northern Ireland can be seen as part of this regionalization. Within England, Government Offices for the Regions (GOR) co-ordinate central government's programmes within each of the regions and a variety of planning and policy developments have a strong regional component. Regional Development Agencies (RDAs) and Regional Chambers were set up in 1998 to further strengthen regional GOVERNANCE in England. (AM)

Registered Social Landlords

See HOUSING ASSOCIATIONS; SOCIAL HOUSING

Regressive taxation

A tax where those on lower incomes pay a higher percentage of their income in tax, the lower the income the higher the share paid in tax. This is true of a POLL TAX or flat-rate SOCIAL SECURITY contribution. (HG)

Regulation

The maintenance, monitoring and enforcement of standards or codes of practice regarding the provision of goods and services and professional conduct required by legislation or voluntarily agreed by trades associations, professional organizations and other bodies. It encompasses measures to ensure the financial probity of providers, protect consumers or vulnerable groups and secure quality. These may include specifying who is permitted to provide BENEFITS and services, how they should be delivered or ensuring PERFORMANCE INDICATORS or other targets are met, and involve a variety of procedures at different points in welfare production and consumption:

- Input regulation requires potential providers to meet key minimum criteria regarding, for instance, their financial stability, facilities, staffing levels and qualifications, and management structures.
- Process regulation covers operational matters and modes of delivery, including the conditions attached to provision, such as USER consultation, COMPLAINTS procedures and EQUAL OPPORTUNITIES POLICIES.
- Output regulation involves evaluating the quality, efficacy and cost-effectiveness of provision in terms of national or local BENCHMARKS or other impact indicators.

Where these requirements are stipulated by legislation, compliance is secured through registration, licensing or other approval procedures backed by systems of AUDITING, INSPECTION, monitoring and EVALUATION overseen by the relevant central or LOCAL GOVERNMENT departments or specially constituted independent regulatory agencies which report to the government. Compliance may also be secured through the structuring and monitoring of contracts with external suppliers or SERVICE AGREEMENTS with in-house statutory providers.

Similar measures may also be implemented on a voluntary basis through the establishment of codes of practice and other forms of self-regulation by associations of suppliers. These too are designed to control entry and provide a form of consumer protection by limiting association membership to those who maintain industry-wide standards. Traditionally a parallel system of self-regulation applies to some PROFESSIONS, particularly medical practitioners, whose associations control entry through various registration processes based on specialized training and ensure only approved practitioners are employed. They also guarantee standards and protect USERS through establishing codes of conduct and practice and are empowered to discipline or debar those breaching these standards. In the case of other welfare professions, such as teaching and SOCIAL WORK, although associations uphold their own codes of conduct and standards of professional ACCOUNTABILITY, disciplinary powers remain with their employers.

Recent decades have seen considerable policy shifts in the use and form of regulatory mechanisms which have increasingly come to be seen as an alternative to the more visible forms of public welfare, direct provision and FISCAL POLICY. From the 1970s state regulation was subject to extensive criticism, especially from NEO-LIBERAL analysts who held that it distorted both the supply and demand for services and the in-built regulatory disciplines of the free market. Their influence led to attempts to deregulate the economy, liberalize the financial and other markets and reduce what were perceived as unnecessary and burdensome restrictions on providers.

At the same time, however, PRIVATIZATION and the associated introduction of QUASI- and INTERNAL MARKETS in publicly funded welfare services led to the establishment of a new range of regulatory agencies and systems which affected VOLUNTARY and commercial as well as state providers. The government's bid to control PUBLIC EXPENDITURE and reduce variations between local services also necessitated increased monitoring and EVALUATION. In the process traditional methods of AUDITING and checking their use of public funds were given an enhanced regulatory role. This was most manifest in the creation of a new 'watchdog' agency, the Audit Commission, set up in 1982 to ensure that LOCAL AUTHORITIES made economic, EFFICIENT and EFFECTIVE use of resources. It was also marked by the increasing use of PERFORMANCE INDICATORS as an indirect means of regulating public service providers and the deployment of more directive forms of INSPECTION, symbolized by the establishment of OFSTED to conduct inspections of state-funded education providers.

There has also been the development of new regulatory regimes for PRIVATE WELFARE, as governments came under increasing pressure to re-regulate or tighten protection for those purchasing their own services or BENEFITS, for instance private PENSIONS. Requirements imposed on the UK government as a result of EU membership have added further to these developments.

Some have suggested that recent restructuring of UK welfare involved a shift from a public provider state to an evaluative or regulatory state. Current policy points in the same direction. Public services are increasingly expected to meet explicit performance agreements and are subject to a wide range of input, process and output regulatory mechanisms. Commercial providers of some services such as STAKEHOLDER PENSIONS are obliged to adhere to government standards or 'kite marks' and others are encouraged to adopt them. Consumer protection legislation has been strengthened and welfare professionals subject to closer regulation through, for instance, the implementation of CLINICAL GOVER-NANCE, related reforms to medical self-regulation, and the development of new regulatory agencies to oversee care standards and the training of care practitioners. (MM)

Regulations

Legally enforceable rules usually contained in delegated legislation approved by parliament, specifying the terms and conditions governing ELIGIBILITY for BENEFITS and services, the administration of these, and standards of provision. (MM)

Reproduction policies

Reproduction of the next generation is one of the key functions of families. It encompasses both the bearing of children and their upbringing and care. Reproduction policies are focused in particular on issues related to the bearing of children, while issues of upbringing and care would usually come under the heading of FAMILY POLICY. There are two main areas of reproduction policy.

First, governments may wish to intervene to influence the level of reproduction; that is, the number of babies being born. France is the best-known example of a country that has sought to follow a pro-natalist policy, encouraging a high birth rate for political and economic reasons. China is the best-known example of the other extreme, seeking to control the birth rate through the 'one child' policy in order to reduce population size. Many countries will, at some time or another, have pursued policies intended to influence levels of reproduction, sometimes in a highly coercive manner.

Second, governments may be keen to influence, not just the overall level, but also the type of individuals or groups who are able to reproduce. The EUGENICS movement, which was strong at the end of the nineteenth and early twentieth centuries, aimed at policies to prevent people with mental or physical defects from reproducing. This justified the use of ABORTION and enforced sterilization of those considered unsuitable for bearing children. For example, Nazi Germany followed a population policy which excluded certain families from state support and imposed sterilization on 'hereditary inferior' individuals. Much less extreme, but also concerned with control of reproduction, are measures intended to encourage or discourage certain sectors or groups from parenthood. Until fairly recently, reproduction was closely linked to marriage and this provided one mechanism of control – only those who married were expected to reproduce – and so control over marriage included a degree of control over fertility. However, this is no longer the case. Current policies therefore seek to influence fertility decisions in other ways. For example, the British government has recently adopted a target to reduce by half the rate of conceptions among under-18-year-olds in England by 2010. This will be pursued by a mixture of information and advice, and by promoting ACCESS to relevant health care services.

There is a wide range of possible measures that can be adopted to encourage or discourage child bearing. These include financial INCENTIVES and penalties, services to support parents, EMPLOYMENT POLICIES, housing policies and so on. But the most direct measures are those that prevent conceptions and those that terminate pregnancies – contraception and ABORTION. These are the key areas affecting reproductive behaviour, and governments can both determine the legality of these and influence their availability and cost. The UK, in common with other Western countries, has generally adopted a more liberal approach to these policies over time. In the early years of the century campaigners such as Marie Stopes sought to make information about contraceptive techniques known and acceptable both to women and men and to the medical profession. The introduction of the contraceptive pill in Britain in 1964 made contraception much easier to use and much more reliable. The National Health Service (Family Planning) Act of 1967 permitted FAMILY PLANNING advice to be given on the NATIONAL HEALTH SERVICE and allowed the free prescription of contraceptives, initially to married women only. The Abortion Act of the same year legalized ABORTION under certain conditions.

The advent of new reproductive technologies in recent years has raised many complex issues about the use and REGULATION of these. The Warnock Report of 1984 (the report of the Committee of Inquiry into Human Fertilization and Embryology) led to the 1985 Surrogacy Arrangements Act and the 1990 Human Fertilization and Embryology Act. The former banned commercial surrogacy agencies, making surrogacy a private arrangement between individuals. The latter set out the regulatory framework for the use of techniques such as in-vitro fertilization (IVF). Clinics that offer fertility treatment must be licensed and ACCESS to assisted parenthood must take account of the needs of any children subsequently born and have regard to any risk to the child, parental motivations, health and age. Treatment may therefore be denied on social, as well as medical, grounds. There are regular media stories highlighting concerns about the social consequences of the use of such techniques. Recent examples include the issue of the 'elderly' mothers (aged 50-plus) receiving fertility treatment, the dangers and problems of multiple births following assisted conception, and the rights to insemination following the death of the sperm donor. IVF treatment remains expensive and there is a high failure rate, but the development of assisted conception techniques challenges many of our ideas about the 'natural' relationship between parents and children. (JM)

Reserve army of labour

According to MARX capitalism inevitably goes through cycles of economic expansion and contraction. In periods of expansion the demand for labour increases and employment levels will grow, reducing the size of the reserve army of labour – the number of those who are unemployed. Increased demand for labour will push up its price, thereby reducing profit rates, which will lead to reduced aggregate demand and a slowing down of economic activity. As a consequence, UNEMPLOYMENT will rise, or the size of the 'reserve army of labour' will grow. MARX therefore regarded the 'reserve army of labour' as an inevitable product of capitalism, and as a product that had a useful function for employers by putting pressure on the wages of those who are in employment. (JC)

Residential care

Services provided for those who require LONG-TERM CARE on a live-in basis. They include residential care homes, NURSING HOMES and CHILDREN'S HOMES. Many are now run by commercial or, to a lesser extent apart from CHILDREN'S HOMES, by VOLUNTARY organizations. LOCAL AUTHORITIES meet fees for CHILDREN'S HOMES. Adults, especially elderly people, are expected to contribute all or part of the cost of their care on a MEANS-TESTED basis. In practice only a minority are totally self-funding. Under COMMUNITY CARE policies DOMICILIARY CARE has been promoted in preference to residential provision for adults, partly because it avoids the problems associated with institutionalization, but also because it is thought to be more cost-effective. However, residential services are now increasingly seen as one component of a continuum of care. Concerns remain though over the qualifications, training and pay of staff, most of whom are women. See INSTITUTIONAL CARE. (CU)

Residential child care

Those arrangements whereby children in public care are LOOKED AFTER in group establishments on a 24-hours-a-day basis by paid staff. Homes take two main forms: residential units (commonly known as CHILDREN'S HOMES) and residential schools, where formal education is provided on the premises. Small numbers of young people with severe difficulties are placed in secure accommodation. Although large establishments caring for 50 or more children remain common in many parts of the world, the majority of residential units in Western Europe cater for 5–20 children. In the UK it is rare for young children to be placed in residential care, which is seen to lack the personalized, continuous care required for the long-term upbringing of children. However, many young people in their teens who are estranged from their birth families prefer residential care to an alternative family. Living in residential care tends to be a stigmatized status and there is often a high turnover of residents and staff. Key policy issues concern the need for vigilance against staff who might abuse children, how best to achieve a better-trained and more professional workforce, and the provision of support to young people once they leave. (MH)

Residential schools

See RESIDENTIAL CHILD CARE

Residual welfare

Refers to a selective provision of public welfare services and BENEFITS, providing modest levels of support and TARGETED at the poor and others without alternative resources. TITMUSS distinguished between a residual and INSTITUTIONAL (or UNIVERSAL) WELFARE. Residual welfare prioritizes and actively encourages individual provision, PRIVATE WELFARE, family SELF-HELP and support provided by VOLUNTARY organizations. Statutory forms of support are provided as a safety-net only, largely reserved for marginal and DESERVING groups and taking responsibility only when families and market fail. (JC)

Resource Allocation Working Party (RAWP)

Set up in 1974 to develop a formula for allocating resources to health authorities in England, weighted according to varying health NEEDS. It was abolished in 1994, but similar principles are still used. (MJH)

Respite care

Services for people with chronic special NEEDS living in the COMMUNITY, which are primarily designed to give their INFORMAL CARERS a rest. There are many different types of respite care. For example, some VOLUNTARY organizations arrange for VOLUNTEERS to look after the person in need of care in their own homes while the INFORMAL CARER goes away. This can be for as little as an afternoon or as much as a fortnight. Other forms of respite care include DAY CENTRES and short-term RESIDENTIAL CARE whereby the USER leaves their home for a day or a week at a time and thus allows their CARER a chance to stay at home without having the responsibility to care. Respite care is widely regarded as the way in which INFORMAL CARERS can best be supported, although there is evidence, particularly in the case of USERS with senile dementia, that respite care can deepen confusion and upset on the part of the USER. Some argue that respite care denigrates USERS by construing them as a burden and is not necessarily appropriate to their

NEEDS, while others argue that access to respite care should be a RIGHT of all CARERS. (CU)

Retirement

A product of the provision of state, occupational and private PENSIONS during the twentieth century that enabled individuals to withdraw from paid employment when they reached a certain age. It is thus a socially constructed concept, and the main mechanism by which capital could remove what LLOYD-GEORGE called 'worn-out workers' from the labour force. Payment of the state PENSION initially set at age 70 and subsequently 65, was lowered to 65 for men and 60 for women in the 1940s, a pattern followed by occupational PENSION providers. The growing availability of retirement PENSIONS led to marked withdrawal of men over 65 from the labour market. In the late nineteenth century nearly 75 per cent were in paid employment; in the 1950s it was one-third, falling to 10 per cent in 1980 and 3 per cent at the beginning of the twenty-first century. The numbers of retirees increased further during the last decades of the twentieth century when economic restructuring led many employers to launch early retirement schemes and their staff to find other routes out of the labour market. In consequence retirement (associated with receipt of a pension) is no longer the recognized entry point to old age and is becoming obsolete as a way of distinguishing older people. Increasing numbers of individuals, particularly men, are leaving the labour force in their fifties rather than later and in different ways, through early or partial retirement, REDUNDANCY, UNEMPLOY-MENT, on the grounds of DISABILITY or ill-health or, in some cases, through ACCESS to secure occupational or PERSONAL PENSIONS and private savings. Recent government policy, however, emphasizes continued labour-force participation by those in their fifties and early sixties and a more flexible approach to the process of retirement, ENABLING individuals to continue working into their seventies on a full-time, part-time or gradual 'withdrawal' basis. EQUAL OPPORTUNITIES concerns have also led to the phasing in of a similar retirement age for women and men. (TM)

Right to buy

Introduced under the Housing Acts of 1980, this provided a right for secure tenants (principally COUNCIL TENANTS) with a minimum period of tenancy (initially 3 years and subsequently 2 years) to buy the property in which they live. It gave them RIGHTS in relation to the process of purchase and the price at which they bought, including very generous discounts. Between 1980 and 2000 some 2 million of the 6.5 million COUNCIL TENANTS in the UK bought their properties in this way. (AM)

Rights

These relate to the substantive ENTITLEMENTS to which the policy-making process gives rise and they provide the basis of the rhetorical claims which drive debates and struggles over welfare. Lawyers define the first kind of rights as 'positive' or 'black-letter' rights, and the latter as 'moral' rights. In common with other social sciences, however, SOCIAL POLICY recognizes that all rights are in fact socially or ideologically constituted. A distinction can be made between doctrinal rights (rights based on principles prescribed 'from above') and claims-based rights (rights based on demands voiced 'from below'). To understand where rights come from, we must recognize that what once may have been asserted as claims-based rights, may now have the character of doctrinal rights that appear or are presented as being inherent to the human condition.

In premodern times the arbitrary power of the sovereign to govern was regarded as a divine right and was reflected in the people's 'natural' right to be governed. As the commercial and industrial middle classes began to wrest power from the crown and the aristocracy, this characteristically CONSERVATIVE view of rights was displaced from the seventeenth century onwards by LIBERAL conceptions of rights. T. H. MARSHALL famously characterized the process that followed in terms of the emergence first of CIVIL RIGHTS (to FREEDOM and security under the law) and later to political rights (to democratic PARTICIPATION). The development of modern CITIZENSHIP was completed, according to MARSHALL, with the emergence of social rights – the rights enjoyed within a SOCIAL DEMOCRATIC WELFARE STATE to SOCIAL SECURITY, health and social care, and education. The modern conception of rights became enshrined in the doctrine of universal human rights encapsulated in the 1948 United Nations Declaration of Human Rights, which encompasses not only civil and political rights, but social, economic and cultural rights.

There is another distinction between negative rights and positive rights. 'Negative' rights relate to the liberties and immunities by which we may demand the forbearance of others. 'Positive' rights (here the term is being used differently than in the legal sense mentioned above) relate to the claims and powers by which we may demand some substantive performance or provision by others. Characteristically, many of our civil and political rights are negative, in the sense that they involve FREEDOMS from interference, whereas social rights are positive in the sense that they involve an ENTITLEMENT to some service or BENEFIT. NEO-LIBERAL critics argue that while certain kinds of negative rights are or should be universal, positive rights demand resources that not every society can afford and which governments cannot extract without offending the more fundamental rights of the individual. MARXIST or neo-MARXIST critics argue that under capitalist relations of production negative rights provide only illusory protection, whereas positive rights are always conditional in nature and serve not to emancipate, but to regulate their beneficiaries. FEMINIST critics argue that rights, though they may purport to be 'gender blind', are 'man made' and tend to reflect patriarchal assumptions that systematically disadvantage women.

Defenders of positive rights to welfare usually point out that, although WELFARE RIGHTS are costly, civil and political rights are not cost-free, since they too require extensive administrative machinery. And in any event, if people do not have a right to have their basic NEEDS met, they will not be able to take advantage of the FREEDOMS that civil and political rights bestow. Even if we reject the doctrinal basis of our rights and the idea that rights are vested in the human individual by virtue of eternal moral verities, then the rights we define through SOCIAL POLICIES represent the codified objectives by which a society may properly regulate itself. Rights, in other words, are creatures of policy. They define – among other things – our claims on the WELFARE STATE and they specify the conduct of the administrators and professionals who provide welfare BENEFITS and services. However, if our rights are the sum of the obligations we can enforce against others, what of the obligations that others can enforce against us? An enduring controversy concerning rights relates to the way in which they may correlate with the fulfilment of obligations. For example, the British Labour Party, both in an amendment to its constitution in 1995 and in the policies it pursued in government since 1997, sought explicitly to promote a society in which 'the rights we enjoy reflect the duties we owe'. This implies, controversially for some, that none of our rights can be unconditional, but depend upon our fulfilment of social obligations to work and, so far as possible, to provide for ourselves and our families.

Another controversy relates to the manner in which rights may be enforceable. In liberal democracies it is the judiciary or the courts which provide REDRESS when the rights of an individual are breached. In the British context, however, the judiciary has been inclined to observe a legal tradition in which CIVIL RIGHTS take precedence over other kinds of rights. The consequences of this have been, first, that the enforcement of social rights has tended to remain the preserve of various kinds of administrative forum, such as TRIBUNALS, OMBUDSPERSONS and COMPLAINTS procedures. Second, broader concepts of human rights have tended to remain the preserve of international law and until recently have not been directly enforceable in British courts. This has changed with the enactment of the Human Rights Act 1998 which has incorporated into British law the provisions of the European Convention on Human Rights (itself modelled on the UN Convention referred to above). Significantly for SOCIAL POLICY, however, the European Convention relates primarily to civil and political rights; its sister document, the Council of Europe's SOCIAL CHARTER (first promulgated in 1961 and which expressly encompasses social, economic and cultural rights), has not been incorporated. (HD)

Risk assessment

Risk can be defined as the chance of suffering loss, injury or damage. Professionals and CARERS are continuously involved in assessing the risk individuals pose to themselves and others – particularly people with LEARNING DIFFICULTIES or older people with dementia. Concern for public safety is also at the forefront of MENTAL HEALTH policy. Attitudes to risk range from the negative, seeing risk as a need for protection and security in which the views and RIGHTS of the individual concerned are not significant, to a positive stance in which taking a gamble and acknowledging the RIGHTS of the person to do so are more central. At either end of the spectrum the need for accurate assessment procedures is crucial, but these are more likely to be comprehensive if the individual's views are also included.

Though it is agreed that early intervention and preventative services can minimize risk, most responses are to crises where risks have escalated and are less easy to manage. Older people with dementia, for example, may only receive risk assessments once their condition has deteriorated from mild to severe dementia, when CARERS can no longer cope, and it can be difficult to decide who is most at risk of harm. See also ASSESSMENT. (SB)

Risks

These fall into three overlapping categories in SOCIAL POLICY. First, there are the individual risks associated with the ordinary human life-course – childhood, ill-health and DISABILITY, UNEMPLOYMENT, old age – to which the classic WELFARE STATE was directed. Second, there are social risks and the DISWELFARE that is associated with a market economy and capitalist social relations, including the risk of POVERTY, exploitation and various kinds of disruption which welfare provision is calculated to ameliorate. Third, there are environmental risks, including not only the hazards posed by nature itself, but those that have been manufactured by human intervention. The WELFARE STATE was once regarded as a bulwark against a variety of risks. Some now argue that the nature of risk is changing. This is a result of processes of GLOBAL-IZATION and the less manageable forms of economic insecurity it creates; because of POSTMODERNITY and the associated crisis of trust in science, technology, professional expertise, economic planning and political processes; and because people's awareness and perception of risk are therefore being transformed. In such circumstances the role of the state and its capacity for enabling individuals to manage risks has lately been brought more sharply into focus. (HD)

Roosevelt, Franklin Delano (1882–1945)

Born into a prosperous family, Roosevelt entered politics in 1910 as candidate for the New York Senate and became Assistant Secretary of the US Navy from 1913 to 1920 during the presidency of Woodrow Wilson. He was the running mate for James Cox in the Democratic Party's unsuccessful presidential campaign in 1920. Roosevelt became Governor of New York State in 1929. He became the 32nd President of the United States during the Great Depression, which had been triggered by the stock market crash of 1929, serving a record four terms in office (1933–45). Following a special session of Congress held shortly after he first came to office, Roosevelt introduced wide-ranging legislation intended to restore credibility to the banking system and put the economy on an even footing. He introduced a raft of interventionist measures under his NEW DEAL programme (1933–8). This included the Federal Emergency Relief Administration, the Civilian Conservation Corps and the National Recovery Administration. Undoubtedly, the most far-reaching reform enacted by Roosevelt was the Social Security

Act of 1935. This Act saw the introduction of UNEMPLOYMENT INSUR-ANCE, old-age PENSIONS and aid for dependent children. (RMP)

Rough sleeping

HOMELESS persons sleeping outdoors on a permanent or temporary basis. Some rough sleepers will spend shorter or longer periods in hostels or other accommodation. Consequently the numbers of rough sleepers identified at any one time is lower than the population which is, at some stage, involved in rough sleeping. A rough-sleepers initiative established by government provides funding for projects TARGETED on rough sleep-ers and increased provision of hostels and other services has been made. See HOMELESSNESS. (AM)

Rowntree, Benjamin Seebohm (1871–1954)

JOSEPH ROWNTREE's son Seebohm joined the family cocoa business in York in 1889 after studying at the Quaker school in York and Owens College in Manchester. He helped in the development of the firm's enlightened employment practices, including the introduction of an 8-hour day (1896), PENSION scheme (1906) and works council (1919). His deep interest in social issues led him to conduct a survey in 1899 that investigated the social conditions of the working class in York. He also explored the incidence of POVERTY, introducing the concepts of primary and secondary poverty. This study was highly influential in shifting debate away from behavioural explanations of poverty towards structural factors such as UNEMPLOYMENT, low income and old age. Rowntree conducted two further studies in 1936 and 1950. The find-ings of the 1936 survey were taken into account, but not followed, by BEVERIDGE in his deliberations over BENEFIT levels for his *Report on Social Insurance* in 1942. The study of 1950 with G. R. Lavers gave rise to the suggestion, subsequently questioned, that the problem of POVERTY had virtually been resolved as a result of FULL EMPLOYMENT and the introduction of the WELFARE STATE.

Rowntree was also involved more directly in PUBLIC POLICY. During the First World War he was responsible for overseeing the welfare of munitions workers and for devising the postwar housing programme. During this period he also developed his interest in the notion of a MINIMUM WAGE, publishing *The Human Needs of Labour* (1918). (RMP)

Rowntree, Joseph (1836–1925)

The son of a grocer, Joseph Rowntree joined his brother Henry's cocoa works in York in 1869 and helped oversee a major expansion in the firm's activities. He became the owner of the firm on the death of his brother in 1883. The firm was renowned for its farsighted EMPLOYMENT POLICIES and excellent working conditions. Workers were provided with educational opportunities as well as free medical and dental services. He built a model village for low-income workers at New Earswick in 1901, which was designed by the influential architect Raymond Unwin. Rowntree took a keen interest in the problem of POVERTY, publishing *Pauperism in England and Wales* in 1865. He was also an active member of the temperance movement and published widely on the subject, including *The Temperance Problem and Social Reform* (1900). He was a supporter of the Liberal Party and the sponsor of a number of 'cocoa press' publications, including *The Nation*. Today, the Joseph Rowntree Foundation is a major sponsor of research in areas such as housing and social care. (RMP)

Royal Commission

A UK government committee charged with investigating and making recommendations on major policy issues. Its members are typically a mixture of experts and interest-group representatives, with a prominent public figure as chair. (MJH)

S

Safety net

Like the net provided for a trapeze artist at a circus, the WELFARE STATE may provide a safety net to ensure the survival of its CITIZENS if they experience an economic or social fall. Its key characteristics are that it is there for everyone and operates regardless of the cause of the fall, and that it provides only the minimum necessary for survival. (DM)

Sample of Anonymized Records (SARs)

Two sets of data extracted from the CENSUS and anonymized so that it is impossible to identify anyone from the information. One set comprises a 1 per cent sample of individuals and the other a 2 per cent sample of households. (HJ)

Savings trap

Because MEANS-TESTED BENEFITS are reduced or removed where CLAIMANTS have capital holdings, then those who have saved money over time may be penalized by loss of MEANS-TESTED support to which they might otherwise have been entitled. (PA)

Schumpeterian workfare state

After the Second World War WELFARE STATE arrangements were based on the ideas of KEYNES and BEVERIDGE, geared towards securing FULL EMPLOYMENT and reliant on policies of demand management with the aim of securing better living standards for the working class. Drawing on the ideas of Schumpeter, since the economic crisis in the mid 1970s many policy analysts have viewed WELFARE STATES as being in the process of transformation towards Schumpeterian workfare states, in which SOCIAL PROTECTION is subordinated to the needs of flexible labour markets and international economic competition. Increased economic internationalization and a shift from FORDISM to post-FORDISM require a restructuring of traditional welfare programmes. The aim is to reduce the scope of public involvement in SOCIAL PROTECTION, to increase individual responsibility and private provision in order to make SOCIAL POLICY more compatible with attempts to strengthen the structural competitiveness of national economies – rendering SOCIAL POLICY secondary to economic growth. (JC)

Scottish Resource Allocation Working Party (SCRAW)

The Scottish version of the RESOURCE ALLOCATION WORKING PARTY (RAWP). (HJ)

Scrounger

A popular term generally used to describe (derogatively) those who cheat the SOCIAL SECURITY system. Those who cheat the tax authorities are not usually described in this way. The most usual forms of cheating are claiming BENEFIT when working on the side, not declaring income or savings or not declaring help from a living-in partner. MEANS-TESTED BENEFIT systems are more prone to this kind of abuse. (HG)

Secondary education

Compulsory schooling for children and young people usually between 11 and 16, though pupils may remain up to the age of 19. The post-1944 TRIPARTITE SYSTEM of secondary education was largely replaced from the 1960s by COMPREHENSIVE schools. The past twenty years has seen a growing variety of provisions within the state system and increasing emphasis on specialist secondary schools. (DEG)

Secondary modern schools

Part of the TRIPARTITE SYSTEM of SECONDARY EDUCATION introduced under the 1944 Education Act. Pupils were selected according to ability by the ELEVEN PLUS examination, and those with 'practical' skills, in practice the majority, went to secondary modern schools. They were incorporated into COMPREHENSIVE schools in the 1960s. (PA)

Secure accommodation for children

A form of RESIDENTIAL CARE in which children's liberty is restricted in a closed unit. The main grounds for admission are that the child is likely to harm themselves or others, or is at risk as a result of absconding from previous placements. (MH)

Select Committee

Committees of either the House of Commons or House of Lords in the UK parliament set up to conduct enquiries on topical issues. These must be distinguished from the Standing Committees that consider legislation. There are select committees to consider public accounts and to deal with the work of each of the main government departments. (MJH)

Selectivity

TARGETING services or BENEFITS on a MEANS-TESTED basis selectively benefits those in most NEED. However, selectivity may be used to mean focusing support on particular individuals or groups by the use of other means of selection, such as family status (LONE PARENTS) or age (pensioners). More generally, therefore, selectivity in SOCIAL POLICY is contrasted with UNIVERSALISM, which provides the same level of support or service to all, irrespective of means or circumstances. (PA)

Self-advocacy

Self-advocacy, with training and support provided to service USERS and CARERS to represent themselves effectively, is central to user EMPOWERMENT. It goes beyond normal advocacy in which a representative speaks on behalf of an individual and ENABLES service USERS to express their views on the services and outcomes they want. (SB)

Self-help

The efforts of small groups of people experiencing similar economic, health or social conditions to resolve or ameliorate their situation. Some agencies have grown to international proportions (e.g. Alcoholics Anonymous) and are no longer purely self-help. There are individual-istic traditions of self-improvement, in contrast to more collective emphases. See MUTUAL AID. (DWS)

Service agreements

Arrangements governing the delivery and standard of provision con-cluded between agencies involved in purchasing and supplying welfare. The latter may be an independent sector provider or an in-house sup-plier. SOCIAL SERVICE DEPARTMENTS may also make an agreement with a USER to provide services following a needs ASSESSMENT. (SB)

Settlement laws

Specified the criteria under which an individual could claim poor relief from a particular parish in terms of birth, marriage or apprenticeship. Those who did not fulfil these criteria could, in theory, be returned to their place of settlement if it was thought they might become a charge on the poor rate. (DEG)

Settlements

First established in the 1880s as centres for educational and welfare activ-ity by university students and academics, for the benefit of low-income groups in urban areas. Toynbee Hall in the East End of London was the first (see S. A. BARNETT). Over time they have become more formalized and developed different portfolios of work, often involving COMMUNITY DEVELOPMENT strategies. Since 1974 there has been a British Association of Settlements and Social Action Centres (BASSAC). (DWS)

Sexism

Attitudes, policies or practices based upon stereotyped assumptions about women and men, usually to the disadvantage of the former. An example is the initial exclusion of married women from ENTITLEMENT to the invalid care allowance, paid to CARERS, on the grounds that they would normally be at home anyway. (RL)

Sheltered employment

The provision of paid work in specialist centres outside the mainstream labour market for certain groups of people, predominantly those with DISABILITIES. Such work was traditionally segregated, low paid, low skilled and stigmatized, and has been largely replaced by supported employment initiatives in mainstream settings. (MP)

Sheltered housing

Individual OWNER-OCCUPIED or rented accommodation, which is usually purpose-built within a setting or grouped on a single site, offering different degrees of support and protection for those unable to live completely independently. (TM)

Sick pay

An income for a person who is normally employed but is unable to work because of illness or injury. The minimum RIGHTS to sick pay laid down by the government in law are referred to as statutory sick pay (SSP). Provisions contained in the worker's contract of employment (OCCUPA-TIONAL WELFARE) may supplement SSP. (DM)

Sickness benefit

SOCIAL INSURANCE BENEFITS paid to those unable to work due to illness. In the UK they have now largely been replaced by SICK PAY for illness up to 26 weeks. (PA)

Sink estate

Housing estates that have very low reputations and are associated with a variety of SOCIAL PROBLEMS. The term has generally been associated with specific areas of COUNCIL HOUSING with concentrations of problems. The reasons for the development and continuation of problems in these estates have often been associated with the operation of housing ALLOCATION policies and the CHOICES made by tenants and potential tenants. These processes result in a concentration of certain types of households in particular areas. As areas become regarded as less desirable, households who are able to obtain accommodation elsewhere do so, and the households that are housed in these estates are those with the least choice. It is argued that the quality of a variety of services on these estates is likely to be affected by the concentration of problems and the reputation of the estate actively makes the problems faced by individual households worse. (AM)

Smiles, Samuel (1812–1905)

The importance attached to self-reliance in mid-nineteenth-century Britain can be traced in part to the works of Samuel Smiles. Having practised as a doctor in Haddington, Smiles moved to Leeds in 1834, where he became editor of the *Leeds Times* for four years. Smiles came to public attention in 1859 when the earlier lectures he had given to a group of young men at an evening class on mutual improvement were published under the title *Self Help*. The book was translated into a number of languages and sold over 250,000 copies by the time of his death in 1905. Although Smiles was sympathetic to MUTUAL AID, it was his stress on the importance of individual effort, perseverance, sobriety and self-improvement that captured the public imagination both at home and abroad. Having bettered himself through hard work and abstinence, Smiles saw no reason why others should not do likewise rather than rely on 'character-sapping' forms of external help. The popularity of *Self Help* and Smiles's other publications on *Character* (1871), *Thrift* (1875) and *Duty* (1880) can be explained in part by the fact that they provided the growing middle classes with reassurance concerning the intrinsic fairness of prevailing economic and social arrangements. (RMP)

Smith, Adam (1723–1790)

A political economist and philosopher, born in Kirkcaldy, Scotland. Smith was educated at the University of Glasgow and Balliol College, Oxford. He was appointed to the Chair of Logic (1751) and subsequently the Chair of Moral Philosophy at Glasgow (1752). In his most influential work, *The Wealth of Nations* (1776), Smith explored how economic wealth was generated and distributed. He rejected the need for the tight economic REGULATION associated with mercantilism. Smith used the term 'invisible hand' to describe the intangible process whereby the self-interested actions of individuals in a competitive society inevitably lead to a situation in which the economic well-being of society would be enhanced. His ideas concerning free trade and non-interventionism proved highly influential and by the mid-nineteenth century economic LIBERALISM was embraced across the political spectrum. Although Smith has been regarded as the pre-eminent representative of LAISSEZ-FAIRE, he did believe that government had a role to play, albeit a limited one, in the provision of PUBLIC GOODS such as education. (RMP)

Social Administration

An alternative term for SOCIAL POLICY in academic circles. Many current SOCIAL POLICY courses were previously called Social Administration. More specifically, however, the term focuses attention on the processes of policy development and delivery, rather than the wider social and theoretical context within which these are situated. (PA)

Social assistance

Generally refers to those aspects of SOCIAL SECURITY provision where ENTITLEMENT to BENEFIT is based upon MEANS TESTING, and may be contrasted with SOCIAL INSURANCE (NATIONAL INSURANCE in the UK) where BENEFITS are paid in return for contributions. However, the term 'social assistance' also has a wider meaning, especially within a broader European and EU context. Here social assistance refers to those SOCIAL POLICY measures that aim to relieve POVERTY through the provision of a minimum income (or equivalent) to people who are poor or deprived. Such assistance is contrasted with INSURANCE or universal provision, which aim to provide INCOME PROTECTION or guaranteed services to a wider range of the population. (PA)

Social capital

Social networks are connections between individuals based upon RECIPROCITY and trust. Social capital theorists argue that these social networks have value and that strengthening relationships of trust and reciprocity improves societal well-being. (AE)

Social Chapter

The Agreement on Social Policy (Social Chapter) is part of the Treaty on European Union which was signed in Maastricht in 1992. Because of a British veto it appeared as an annex, but provided the legal basis for the (then eleven) other member states to adopt qualified majority voting in areas such as HEALTH AND SAFETY at work, working conditions, EQUALITY between men and women and other issues. (JC)

Social Charter

A set of social RIGHTS adopted by the Council of Europe, a pan-European body. The countries which have committed themselves to the revised version of the Social Charter have also signed up to a monitoring system that allows independent experts to measure national laws against the Social Charter's standards. (JC)

Social control

Social structures and social systems act as mechanisms by means of which individuals are controlled in the way that they think, act and behave. Social control can be understood in both a positive and negative sense. On the one hand, social control ensures that individuals in society can co-operate, communicate and coexist. On the other hand, social control restricts FREEDOM and action. In this sense, WELFARE STATE policies can be understood as a means by which social control is exercised by forcing people to take paid work, through imposing a particular family form on households or in controlling the behaviour of particular groups. One view of state welfare, influenced by MARXISM, would see it as a way in which an unequal society is made to seem fair and legitimate, thus exercising social control over the population by ensuring that the social order is not questioned. (AE)

Social Darwinism

In the latter part of the nineteenth century various social and political thinkers such as HERBERT SPENCER, William Sumner and Benjamin Kidd attempted to demonstrate how Darwinian theories of evolution could be applied to human society. See also HERBERT SPENCER. (RMP)

Social democracy

Over the last century European social democracy has undergone a process of increasing revisionism and deradicalization. Initially close to MARXIST and SOCIALIST positions by rejecting capitalism and aiming to abolish private ownership of the means of production, a process of revisionism has led to the acceptance of capitalism subject to democratic control and curbed by welfare statism and KEYNESIAN macroeconomics. Social democrats share the view that class divisions between workers and capitalists are the fundamental axis of power and of political struggles in industrialized capitalist democracies. However, unlike MARXISTS they do not accept that capitalism would inevitably lead to a worsening of the position of the working class, nor that capitalist markets are necessarily prone to crisis. Instead, social democrats have always regarded capitalism as capable of reform via democratic means. Indeed, with the help of political REGULATION and planning, the market logic could be used to promote both economic growth and social EQUALITY. State power, rather than control of the means of production, would therefore be the aim for the labour movement, since it would mean gaining political control over economic power and thus gradually transforming capitalist societies into SOCIALIST societies.

Democracy matters, therefore, because electoral processes make it possible for the labour movement to become organized and to displace class struggle from the industrial to the political arena. Winning parliamentary majorities is the key for acquiring the authority to enable social and economic transformation. Political control also allows the use of the (welfare) state as an instrument for redistributing income and ACCESS to resources in favour of the working class. Consequently, for social democrats, WELFARE STATE instruments have become a crucial vehicle for achieving their aspirations of creating a more socially just and solidaristic society within a capitalist market economy.

Social democracy, as a political movement and ideology, has often been regarded as the historically strongest political force for WELFARE STATE expansion. This is the premise for a school of thought that was dominant in cross-national WELFARE STATE research for most of the 1980s. According to the 'social-democratic' model of WELFARE STATE development, the strength of national labour movements (in terms of parliamentary power of leftist parties, degree of unionization, etc) is the most important single factor that determines the scope and degree of national WELFARE STATE programmes. Invariably, Sweden figured as the social democratic prototype, where, until the 1980s, the 'power resources' of the capitalist class (control over capital assets) were incapable of preventing the labour movement from making effective use of its 'power resources' (high degree of labour-force organization, centralized union system, virtually continuous rule of the social democratic party since the 1930s). As a consequence, working-class strength led to an expansion of social RIGHTS and the creation of an increasingly universal, REDISTRIBUTIVE and comprehensive WELFARE STATE. This includes not only universal BENEFITS and services financed by PROGRESSIVE TAXATION, but extends to wages policy, active labour-market programmes and industrial-relation policy.

Historically, social democrats did not differ from SOCIALISTS as far as their aims were concerned (creating a SOCIALIST society) but by the methods applied in order to achieve those aims (LIBERAL parliamentary democracy and universal WELFARE STATES). However, while a commitment to the use of interventionist power is still distinguishable, since the mid-1990s modern social democratic parties in several European countries have introduced policies which include retrenchment in welfare spending and making social RIGHTS more conditional. Critics have argued that this indicates the increasing irrelevance of traditional social democratic aspirations such as EQUALITY, SOCIAL JUSTICE and REDISTRIBUTION. By contrast some social democrats have argued that the political centre-left has always been concerned with an employment-based social policy as an attempt to enhance skills and adaptability in the interests of the employability of wage earners and maximizing the opportunities for individuals. Others have pointed to the need to adapt to changed socio-economic contexts and the imperatives of international competitiveness. At least implicitly, this indicates a continuation of the revisionist and reformist path that has been a characteristic trait of social democracy since the beginning of the movement. (JC)

Social Dialogue

After the Social Agreement of the MAASTRICHT TREATY in 1992, the Social Dialogue became a central institution in European Union social policy making. It seeks to involve the social partners (employer organizations and trades unions) in matters of EU SOCIAL POLICY and requires the Commission to consult social partners before initiating policy in the area related to employment. Within the remit of the Social Dialogue, the Commission's role is to provide relevant information for policy making and to facilitate negotiations between the social partners. As the key actors in the area, social partners can initiate and formulate policy and determine which form of legislative instrument should be chosen for policy implementation, including collective agreements rather than formal adoption by the European Council. (JC)

Social dimension

As one aspect of integration among member states of the European Union, the social dimension refers to areas of SOCIAL POLICY competence where minimal standards are set at the EU rather than national level. The process of European integration has largely been a process of economic rather than SOCIAL INTEGRATION. Yet the so-called 'social dimension' has gained prominence since the 1970s in two respects. First, legislative progress has been made in matters concerning workers residing in a member state other than their own, or moving between member states. Second, the EU has also increased its competencies in labour-market related areas such as equal treatment, HEALTH AND SAFETY measures and working conditions. See also SOCIAL DIALOGUE. (JC)

Social dividend

See BASIC INCOME

Social division of welfare

A concept devised by TITMUSS to signify the various ways in which welfare BENEFITS and services could be delivered and their differing distributional consequences. He distinguished three such modes: direct provision by the state, and (less visible) FISCAL and OCCUPATIONAL WELFARE systems. Though functionally equivalent they operated on different bases, with the UNIVERSALIST, REDISTRIBUTIVE potential of publicly funded and delivered welfare being contrasted with the selective nature of the OCCUPATIONAL WELFARE and tax systems. In practice these benefit the already privileged, the mainly white male holders of secure, well-paid professional and managerial posts.

This conception has been criticized for omitting other channels of both non-statutory and state provision, particularly REGULATION, and eliding OCCUPATIONAL with other forms of PRIVATE WELFARE. It has increasingly given way to a broader term, the MIXED ECONOMY OF WELFARE. TITMUSS's underlying concerns, however, remain central to SOCIAL POLICY analysis. Subsequent writers have continued to highlight the inherent tensions between a CITIZENSHIP- or RIGHTS-based approach to welfare guaranteed by the state, and the use of provision based on other, more discretionary allocative processes. They have also re-emphasized the social differentiations arising from variations in provision, with FEMINISTS in particular pointing not only to those stemming from market and OCCUPATIONAL WELFARE, but also to the ways in which VOLUNTARY and informal welfare may often entrench rather than reduce social inequalities. (MM)

Social dumping

Used to denote one possible outcome of economic and political integration between the member states of the European Union. It refers to companies which might decide to move to countries where wages and wage-related social contributions are low, in order to reduce the costs of labour. (JC)

Social economy

Those organizations, such as COMMUNITY-owned businesses, CO-OPERATIVES and development trusts, which trade for social or ethical purposes rather than in order to generate a profit for shareholders. Such organizations try to reconcile the discipline of the market with a primary commitment to their USERS or members. Most individual organizations in the social economy are small in terms of turnover and paid staff and operate only within a small local area, and they frequently rely upon VOLUNTEERS and local networks. It is argued that organizations operating within the social economy can help to improve local employment levels, COMMUNITY CAPACITY BUILDING, and the supply of goods and services to local COMMUNITIES. (DWS)

Social engineering

A term used to describe attempts at creating a particular (desired) social outcome through intervention in social relations by state REGULATION or public action. (AE)

Social exclusion

Widely used in the UK and Europe in the early twenty-first century to describe a SOCIAL PROBLEM that is linked to, but different from, POVERTY. Whereas poverty is generally taken to refer to the problem of inadequate resources, specifically low income, social exclusion is taken to refer to the wider aspects of DEPRIVATION, which prevent people from participating in social activities or using public and private services. Social exclusion is also often thought of as affecting particular social groups or local neighbourhoods. Social exclusion also draws attention to the processes by which people are excluded, thus underlining the role played in perpetuating the problem by those who exclude others. (PA)

Social expenditure

Often used interchangeably with PUBLIC EXPENDITURE in the UK, where much social-service activity is financed out of taxation. In other European countries much social welfare, health and housing expenditure is funded out of SOCIAL INSURANCE contributions and spent by VOLUNTARY or religious bodies who may add their own forms of revenue. Social expenditure is thus a broader term than simply tax-funded expenditure by the state. It includes spending by all kinds of collective agency – HOUSING ASSOCIATIONS, CHARITIES, social service agencies, local and central government – on SOCIAL POLICY functions in some way regulated by social legislation. (HG)

Social Fund

Part of the UK SOCIAL SECURITY system designed to meet exceptional NEEDS over and above the weekly allowance payable under INCOME SUPPORT, through the provision of grants and loans. The Social Fund is a cash-limited fund and is distributed to BENEFITS Agency offices for disbursement under national guidelines.

The term is also used to refer to the European Social Fund, a measure implemented by the European Commission as part of the European Structural Funds. It provides resources for programmes of social REGENERATION in regions experiencing industrial restructuring and underdevelopment. (AE)

Social housing

Housing provided by organizations whose objectives are to meet social NEED and where policies relating to ACCESS, allocation, management and charging reflect social objectives. In the British context this embraces both COUNCIL HOUSING (PUBLIC SECTOR housing) and housing provided by REGISTERED SOCIAL LANDLORDS (or HOUSING ASSOCIATIONS). The term 'social housing' has not always been used in Britain and is not always favoured in other countries. It has implications associated with welfare housing. These imply that the sector caters purely for households in need, whereas the tradition of public housing in Britain and elsewhere has been to give priority not to people with social need, but to provide high quality housing suitable for people to continue to live in as their circumstances change. Consequently the tradition of public housing was associated with a greater degree of social mix than could be implied by the term 'social housing'.

Use of terminology in this field remains equivocal. Social housing can be used to embrace a range of very different types of housing catering for very different groups. In this sense it is a 'catch-all' to include a diverse set of housing provision, housing a diverse population. It generally refers to housing where rents are below the levels that would apply in the market and to types of landlord (LOCAL AUTHORITIES and REGISTERED SOCIAL LANDLORDS) as distinct from private landlords or HOME OWNERSHIP. It is important to recognize a considerable shift in terminology in this area. Most of the literature prior to the 1990s refers to COUNCIL HOUSING and to HOUSING ASSOCIATIONS. After 1996 HOUSING ASSOCIATIONS were relabelled as REGISTERED SOCIAL LANDLORDS and the term 'social housing' is much more widely used. The term 'social rented housing' or SOCIAL RENTED SECTOR is a common alternative.

Because of a significant programme of transfers of ownership from LOCAL AUTHORITIES to REGISTERED SOCIAL LANDLORDS there has been some blurring of the distinctions within the social housing sector. The balance within the sector is shifting from COUNCIL HOUSING to REGISTERED SOCIAL LANDLORDS because the latter have the bulk of new building in the sector and are the recipients of stock transfers. The relative shares of different types of landlord within the sector have consequently shifted in recent years and are expected to further shift in the future as government embarks upon a major programme of stock transfer. (AM)

Social imperialism

Has been used to highlight the way in which social reforms in the late nineteenth and early twentieth century were constructed and promoted in order to bolster Britain's imperial interests and create a sense of SOL-IDARITY based on nation rather than class. From this perspective, Britain's imperial strength, both economic and military, would be undermined if the 'fitness' of the population were neglected. Both New Liberal and FABIAN thinkers argued that greater degrees of state intervention were necessary if Britain was to maintain its supremacy in the world. A number of the Liberal reforms between 1906 and 1914 in areas such as health and education were underpinned by the need to improve the 'fitness' of the population. See FABIANISM; HERBERT SPENCER; SOCIAL DARWINISM. (RMP)

Social inclusion

The goal of measures taken to combat the problem of SOCIAL EXCLU-SION extends beyond the provision of material resources to poor people. They include measures to improve service delivery and service ACCESS in deprived areas across both public and private services, measures to build up the capacity of local people to become more active CITIZENS, and measures to promote local economic REGENERATION. Social inclusion is assumed to benefit all CITIZENS by promoting a more cohesive and harmonious social structure for all. (PA)

Social indicators

Statistics that provide help with the analysis of the outputs or outcomes of SOCIAL POLICIES. They are usually produced by government and appear in collections of OFFICIAL STATISTICS. Crucial issues on which social indicators are available are POVERTY, UNEMPLOYMENT, inequalities in health, and illiteracy. There has been considerable interest in cross-national data, enabling the efforts of different countries to be compared. International organizations, in particular the Organization for Economic Co-operation and Development (OECD), the United Nations, the World Bank and the International Labour Office (ILO), produce compilations of social indicators from various countries. There are academic ventures that have contributed to this activity, notably the LUXEMBOURG INCOME STUDY, which assembles data which can be used to assess SOCIAL SECURITY policies in a cross-section of countries. (MJH)

Social insurance

Developed by many advanced industrial countries in the twentieth century, social insurance operated alongside other forms of SOCIAL SECURITY protection. However, it became the dominant form of provision in most of the countries of the European Union throughout most of the twentieth century, although in Britain social insurance protection took on a particular form and in the latter quarter of the century declined in importance relative to SOCIAL ASSISTANCE protection.

Use of the term 'insurance' suggests that protection under such schemes is based upon the principles of INSURANCE now widely used to protect people and property in the PRIVATE SECTOR. In fact social insurance does not operate strictly under such principles.

Private insurance is largely voluntary, it covers specific and limited contingencies, premiums are related to the extent of coverage and the estimate of RISK, and the contributions collected are invested to provide a fund to meet demands from insured parties. Social insurance is compulsory (for those included within it), it covers a wide range of social needs, premiums are FLAT-RATE or EARNINGS-RELATED, and the contributions collected are not invested but rather are used each year to meet the needs of existing beneficiaries – a system known as PAY AS YOU GO. In general, therefore, social insurance is a form of public welfare provision rather than private insurance protection.

The social insurance model was first developed in Germany in the late nineteenth century under the then Chancellor, BISMARCK. This model of provision is still widely followed in continental Europe. BISMARCK's aim was to provide some protection for workers in times of labour MARKET FAILURE, by utilizing the contributions made by them when in employment. The basis of provision was self-protection rather than REDISTRIBUTION of resources, and the focus of protection was on the more secure members of the working class (those in employment) in order to diffuse the political conflict which UNEMPLOYMENT and other forms of labour MARKET FAILURE might otherwise fuel.

The model was therefore one of work-based protection, and it was extended in a number of countries to provide not just INCOME SUPPORT but also funding for, and ACCESS to, other welfare services such as PUBLIC HEALTH. The basis of protection within social insurance is, however, SOCIAL SECURITY BENEFITS to replace lost income; and most social insurance schemes pay such BENEFITS only to those falling within defined contingencies outside the labour market, usually:

- UNEMPLOYMENT;
- RETIREMENT;
- SICKNESS;
- WIDOWHOOD;
- MATERNITY.

Because the focus of protection is on existing workers many social schemes provide EARNINGS-RELATED payments to those claiming BENEFITS in protected contingencies – emphasizing the focus on self-protection rather than POVERTY relief. There is generally an upper-earnings limit to the amount of money paid, fixed in relation to average wages. Protection is, however, limited to those who have contributed to the scheme, as established by fixed contribution conditions. Thus there may be many unemployed and retired people or people with DISABILITIES who have not made the requisite contributions and are not protected under the scheme.

The great strength of social insurance is the image of self-protection that it projects and the related belief in a right to protection because of membership in a scheme that has been purchased through contribution to it. Conversely its great weakness, especially as a form of SOCIAL SECURITY for all, is the exclusive nature of the contribution 'contract', which results in many needy CITIZENS being excluded from any (or adequate) protection.

The 'BISMARCK' social insurance schemes of continental Europe, paying EARNINGS-RELATED BENEFITS to ex-workers, nevertheless do provide a major aspect of the extensive and generous public SOCIAL SECURITY protection available in those countries. In the UK social insurance has taken on a different and more restrictive role. Here it is called NATIONAL INSURANCE and is largely based on the recommendations of the BEVERIDGE Report of 1942, although BEVERIDGE's proposals drew heavily on the forms of protection developed in the country by the FRIENDLY SOCIETIES in the latter half of the nineteenth century.

FRIENDLY SOCIETIES were mutual protection agencies established by groups of workers, usually covering one or more industries. They offered CONTRIBUTORY protection similar to the public protection provided by the BISMARCK schemes elsewhere. BEVERIDGE's aim was to 'nationalize' these and incorporate them with the limited state insurance protection developed in the country in the 1920s. However, he rejected the EARNINGS-RELATED basis of BISMARCK schemes. His priority was to use public insurance protection to prevent POVERTY, and thus both contributions and BENEFITS were fixed at minimum FLAT-RATE levels.

BEVERIDGE's proposals were largely introduced as NATIONAL INSURANCE (NI) by the postwar Labour government in Britain, providing protection in specified contingencies linked to contributions paid – initially recorded as a weekly insurance stamp. Contributions into the NI fund were also made by the employers of all workers and by the Treasury from general taxation. Since the initial reforms British social insurance has moved onto an earnings-related contribution basis, although the BENEFITS are still paid at a low FLAT RATE (with the exception of the PENSION protection under SERPS, and those with private PENSION cover can opt out of this). The balance of contributions to the scheme has also altered, with the Treasury supplement being reduced in later years. The British NI scheme retains the key features of social insurance, however. In particular, BENEFITS are only paid to those workers who have contributed to the scheme. And in the latter part of the century these contribution conditions were tightened, effectively excluding more and more people, especially women, from protection, and increasing the number forced to rely on SOCIAL ASSISTANCE BENEFITS.

Social insurance in Britain and elsewhere, therefore, remains a restrictive form of public SOCIAL SECURITY protection. For those included within the scheme social insurance protection is secure and (sometimes) generous; for those excluded it is an example of the partial nature of some public welfare provision. (PA)

Social integration

Seen by some as the opposite of SOCIAL EXCLUSION, this term has its roots in continental European countries with their concern for social cohesion and order. As a policy objective, it can be contrasted with an Anglo-Saxon concern with personal liberty and ensuring minimum standards, or a Scandinavian concern with social inequality. (AE)

Social justice

One of the most powerful yet elusive of the terms used in SOCIAL POLICY, which is essentially a NORMATIVE concept or moral ideal. It is concerned with the extent to which social arrangements may be

regarded as 'right' or 'fair'. One's belief in social justice and one's definition of it therefore depend on one's ideological stance. The term
'justice', conventionally, has two distinct meanings: one relating to the
principles of restitution or corrective punishment in the legal context
and the other relating to the distribution of resources and/or opportunities in the social context. Social justice relates to the latter. At the heart
of debates about social justice lies a tension between two political
values, FREEDOM and EQUALITY. Social justice does not necessarily
ensure complete freedom (since it may entail constraints associated with
collective responsibility – such as an obligation to pay taxes) or complete EQUALITY (since some kinds of inequality might be unavoidable or
even legitimate).

Within the spectrum of those who espouse a commitment to social
justice there are, on the one hand, LIBERALS who seek as much FREEDOM
for the individual as is consistent with ensuring that such inequalities
as exist between individuals are fair. On the other, there are SOCIAL
DEMOCRATS or SOCIALISTS who seek as much EQUALITY within society
as is consistent with the FREEDOM of its individual members. Beyond
this spectrum there are, at one extreme, NEO-LIBERAL or NEW RIGHT
thinkers who reject the idea of social justice, since distributive processes
ought, they believe, to be based on the self-equilibrium of a free market
rather than artificially contrived principles of justice. At the other
extreme, there are some MARXISTS or neo-MARXISTS who argue that
notions such as social justice are fundamentally misleading and serve to
distort our understanding of the inherently exploitative nature of capitalist society. FEMINIST and other thinkers have expanded the concept
of social justice to encompass not only distributive justice, but also
issues relating to the recognition of social difference. They argue that
struggles for REDISTRIBUTION should be linked to struggles for parity of
PARTICIPATION for women, gays and lesbians, minority ethnic and religious groups and others who suffer socially constituted injustices.

Social justice is therefore concerned with who ought to get what –
and upon what terms. This implies competing principles of REDISTRIB-
UTION and fairness. Broadly speaking, REDISTRIBUTION – through tax-
financed WELFARE STATE systems – can achieve social justice in either of
two ways. Justice may operate in accordance with formal or proportional principles on the one hand, or with substantive or individualized
principles on the other. The distinction is closely associated with other
distinctions, such as that which is often made between rules-based and
discretionary welfare provision and between 'simple' and 'complex'
EQUALITY. Just treatment requires that the provision of BENEFITS and

services is procedurally consistent and calculable. Just outcomes, however, may require that people should be treated differently according to their actual circumstances. The first concept presents social justice as a technical matter to be determined through the proportionate application of predetermined policies. The second presents it as a matter requiring the creative intervention of beneficent experts or administrators. Proponents of each are inclined to accuse proponents of the other of acting 'unjustly' and neither concept necessarily accords with popular perceptions of what is 'just', especially when they are applied to justify service rationing. In practice, however, the administration and allocation of SOCIAL SECURITY BENEFITS, health and social care, education and housing may entail a combination of principles.

The pursuit of social justice may also call upon one or more of three principles of fairness: RIGHTS, DESERT and NEED. Any particular distribution of resources or opportunities may be defended on the basis of a discourse of RIGHTS, such as the right of ownership, though 'negative', property-based notions of RIGHTS, often associated with NEO-LIBERAL thinking, do not generally support the idea of social justice. However, the concept of RIGHTS has been widened by advocates of social justice to encompass social RIGHTS and the idea that full CITIZENSHIP requires not only the rule of law and political democracy, but guaranteed ENTITLEMENTS to social welfare, health care and education. This classic linkage of social justice to CITIZENSHIP through the concept of social RIGHTS rests on a belief in the equal worth of all CITIZENS. Equal worth, however, may translate into either a universal EQUALITY of resource allocation or a more conditional EQUALITY of opportunity. Increasingly SOCIAL POLICY, even under SOCIAL DEMOCRATIC governments, is moving away from universal RIGHTS and towards conditional RIGHTS designed to promote social justice based more upon the second principle of fairness, DESERT.

As a principle to underpin social justice, DESERT can be interpreted in two quite distinct ways. On the one hand, it may be argued that people should be rewarded on the basis of merit or achievement, for the work they do, the care they provide or for the contribution they make to society. On the other hand, it can also be argued that people who have been in some way disadvantaged deserve to be compensated for the injury or DISWELFARES they have suffered. For example, social justice may require that disabled people should be compensated for the ways in which they are socially excluded or that members of a particular minority ethnic group should be compensated for the way in which they (or their forebears) have been persecuted in the past.

The final principle of fairness on which social justice may depend is that resources should be REDISTRIBUTED in order to meet human NEED. Once again it is a principle with two interpretations: the UNIVERSALIST and the selective. The UNIVERSALIST interpretation is that every person's basic human NEEDS – the things they require to establish health and AUTONOMY – should be unconditionally guaranteed. The selectivist interpretation – currently in the ascendant – is that REDISTRIBUTION should be TARGETED on those in the greatest NEED and that BENEFITS and services should be MEANS TESTED. (HD)

Social market economy

Used mainly in Germany to denote the broad compromise between the major political parties and social partners. This compromise was forged in the late 1950s and 1960s in favour of a market economy embedded within a strong system of SOCIAL SECURITY for workers, which extends to industrial relations, labour law and SOCIAL PROTECTION codified in collective agreements. (JC)

Social polarization

The process of separating society into opposite groups with conflicting interests such as taxpayers and BENEFIT CLAIMANTS. (AE)

Social Policy

Refers both to the process of developing and implementing measures to combat SOCIAL PROBLEMS in society, and to the academic study of these measures and their broader social context. The academic study of social policy is sometimes contrasted with SOCIAL ADMINISTRATION, which pays less attention to broader contextual analysis. (PA)

Social problems

There is no single approach to explaining why or how certain social conditions, behaviour or groups came to be viewed and dealt with as problematic. Analysts differ in how they perceive and account for such phenomena, the type of research they undertake, their evidence-base, and their prescriptions. A number of broad perspectives can, however, be identified, clustering along differing and not necessarily directly overlapping polarities. One fundamental divide hinges on the extent to which social problems are seen as objectively given or socially constructed. This division between 'realists' and 'constructionists' is paralleled by variations between those who view society in primarily consensual terms and those who emphasize its conflictual base and, relatedly, to whether they are held to breach widely shared norms and values or the interests of dominant groups. A further division is that between structural and more individualist explanations.

In addressing these, recent studies have made considerable use of the distinction between private troubles and public issues developed by C. Wright Mills. Whether it be UNEMPLOYMENT, domestic violence or ROUGH SLEEPING, individual difficulties, it is argued, only enter the public realm when they either involve large numbers and/or appear to affect the wider society and, by implication, demand a collective rather than an individual solution. Social problems are thus often defined as conditions that pertain to society as a whole, or large sections of it, which are a collective source of concern, and open to social interventions.

As historical and comparative analyses show, however, the processes whereby individual difficulties are transmuted into sources of public concern are far from straightforward and vary both temporally and spatially. Activities or conditions that in some societies warrant collective counter-action, however extensive, may not be questioned at other points in time or in other societies. Rather, they may be seen as part of the normal ordering of life and a matter of personal misfortune to be dealt with through risk-avoidance or assistance from family, friends and charitable bodies.

One central theme in recent literature therefore revolves around exploring how these differential evaluations develop and their outcomes. Here constructionist writers have highlighted a number of possible processes. Some emphasize the key role played by certain individuals, PRESSURE GROUPS or 'moral entrepreneurs' in identifying and defining particular types of behaviour or social conditions as social problems, conducting research to demonstrate its scale, campaigning for solutions and securing countervailing social legislation. Others have pointed to the ways in which media coverage often not only reinforces these processes but may, through sensationalist reporting, amplify such campaigning, and by exaggerating the size and character of the presumed problem generate a moral panic and precipitate legislation.

Once regulated, it is argued, further processes come into play, serving to reaffirm the existence of a 'problem' and the need for continuing, often more extensive, intervention. Agencies established to deal with it, while claiming to have the necessary skills, contend that the issue is larger and more complex than initially thought and requires further action. Social legislation, moreover, does not imply agreement on the sources of the 'problem', nor its solution. Some of those highlighting it may take an individualist approach; others may emphasize the effects of an individual's upbringing, local environment or broader social and economic changes rather than individual traits or failings, or see it as rooted in deeper structural factors.

The constructionist approach thus points to the highly contestable and unstable nature of social problems. It has been taken further by other writings drawing not only on social interactionist theorizing, but neo-MARXIST and more recent poststructuralist analysis. The first have drawn attention to the impact of various LABELLING processes at both the micro 'street' level and a macro societal level. MARXIST-inspired analysts have focused more on the ways in which the construction of social problems reflects the social and power relations of capitalist society and forms part of a wider legitimating ideology. Dominant groups, it is argued, impose a particular conception of problem issues as stemming from the characteristics of certain groups or areas rather than more fundamental structural inequalities. They differ, however, in their views on the stability of such constructions and the opportunities, given the inherently conflictual nature of capitalism, for alternative characterizations.

Other analysts argue for a more complex approach to how notions of social problems are socially produced and perceptions of them insti-tutionalized, distributed and challenged in ways which reflect a multi-plicity of non-class as well as class-based interests. Discourse studies in particular point to the ways knowledge is constituted along particular lines, particularly the tendency to conceive social problems in medical or loose dichotomous terms that distinguish certain conditions or forms of behaviour as DEVIATIONS from presumed social norms. More broadly, research tends to focus on those construed as 'different', whose views are also often discounted in favour of the findings of designated experts. Such knowledge may become so entrenched that it comes to constitute 'common sense' and, though open to change, is in practice highly resistant to it.

Constructionism and related perspectives have cast new light on divergences in perceptions and explanations of social problems and the definitional issues they raise. But its apolitical, relativist implications have been widely criticized, particularly by those who espouse a more realist approach to social problems. From this standpoint social problems are objectively describable, often pressing, and have real consequences for individuals and the wider society. It is these concerns that provide the basis for the second over-arching perspective within SOCIAL POLICY. As a discipline it is rooted in the attempts of nineteenth- and early twentieth-century reformers to mitigate the social conditions associated with early urban industrialism and the disruptions generated by ongoing economic and social change. These were held to be open to empirical inquiry and many early researchers saw themselves as social explorers, surveying and reporting on the general state of society. Though this imagery has disappeared, the sense of social problems as observable phenomena whose possible causes can be investigated has not; nor has the underlying concern with developing possible countermeasures.

In practice realist and constructionist approaches often merge. Current SOCIAL POLICY analyses increasingly involve questions not only about possible causation, but about what groups are involved in the shifts from personal troubles to public issues, why and with what effects. The role and views of the 'subjects' of these processes are also beginning, albeit unevenly, to be addressed. Equally significantly the focus is moving away from studying social problems, however perceived, as discrete phenomena, but as cross-cutting and often experienced cumulatively. Policy, too, is adapting to this more holistic approach, while revisiting long-standing debates over causation. Social problem analysis thus remains both complex and contested, but pivotal to the study of SOCIAL POLICY. (MM)

Social protection

Collective measures taken by the state to promote the well-being of the population through protection against some of the RISKS associated with the labour market and family life. Different forms of social protection were developed throughout the twentieth century in all advanced industrial economies. (AE)

Social rented sector

See SOCIAL HOUSING

Social security

A term used in two senses. In the first narrow sense it refers to the INCOME MAINTENANCE systems of a country. Social security in this sense is about what is done by the state to provide income for those who have a legitimate claim upon resources from the state. This would include CONTRIBUTORY INSURANCE BENEFITS, NON-CONTRIBUTORY BENEFITS and MEANS-TESTED BENEFITS and take the form of PENSIONS, BENEFITS for children, DISABILITY BENEFITS, BENEFITS for the unemployed, etc. These forms of social security provision became almost universal in advanced capitalist countries during the twentieth century. In some countries, such as the USA, social security has an even narrower sense than this and is used almost exclusively to refer to MEANS-TESTED BEN-EFITS for the poorest.

Social security in the second broader sense refers to the aims of social security rather than the means as discussed above. It may not be through state action that most people and groups achieve social security. Employment, families and wider social networks may be more effective routes to social security than anything done by government. (AE)

Social services

See PERSONAL SOCIAL SERVICES; SOCIAL WORK

Social services departments (SSDs)

The generic departments set up by LOCAL AUTHORITIES following the Local Authority Social Services Act 1970 to administer the full range of generic social services. See PERSONAL SOCIAL SERVICES. (PA)

Social tourism

The notion that individuals might move from one country to another, or from one part of a country to another, solely motivated by the intention of claiming more generous BENEFITS or better welfare services. The potential for social tourism has often been used for main-taining or increasing stricter BENEFIT controls against non-British CITIZENS. (JC)

Social wage

Coined in the 1960s to draw attention to the goods and services received from the state in terms of SOCIAL POLICY protection, e.g. health care, housing, employment BENEFITS etc., all of which add up to make a social wage in addition to wages from paid employment. In some countries the level of the social wage is much higher than others and may be used as part of the arguments in national pay bargaining rounds. (AE)

Social work

Developed in England and Wales from VOLUNTARY 'friendly visiting' services provided for poor, DESERVING families by the CHARITY ORGANIZATION SOCIETY in the nineteenth century and remained primarily a VOLUNTARY SECTOR service until the postwar growth of PERSONAL SOCIAL SERVICES.

Psychodynamic casework and counselling became the preferred methods of social work until the 1968 Seebohm Report and the ensuing LOCAL AUTHORITY SOCIAL SERVICES DEPARTMENTS encouraged generic social work. Professional recognition and qualifications were established through the 1971 Central Council for Education and Training in Social Work (CCETSW). The Barclay Report (1983) suggested social workers should have complementary roles, as counsellors and as social planners arranging networks of support for clients, but following the 1990 National Health Service and Community Care Act, their CARE MANAGEMENT role so intensified that social workers complained about losing their casework skills. Radical social workers also contended that social work had lost sight of its original goal as a means of combating family DEPRIVATION.

As part of the wider attempt to improve training and standards in social care, a General Social Care Council responsible for REGULATING and training social workers and other care staff replaced CCETSW in 2001. The training of social workers has also been revamped. (SB)

Socialism

Over the centuries the term 'socialism' has been equated with the desire to establish a more humane, co-operative and EGALITARIAN society. Over the past two centuries socialism has provided a sustained critique of the exploitative economic and social relations which underpin capitalism. It has a number of different and often competing strands. For example, the idealist utopian ideas of Saint-Simon and Owen were superseded by the scientific socialism of MARXISM, which provided the theoretical underpinning of mainstream SOCIAL DEMOCRACY in Europe up until 1917. Subsequently there was a major division between those who adhered to the revolutionary socialist strategy of communism and those who believed that it was possible to achieve socialism through existing political and social structures. Within this reformist or FABIAN tradition there has been a continuing debate about the overall aim of state action. Fundamentalists wanted to secure a socialist society by transforming capitalism through increased public ownership, while revisionists such as CROSLAND and GAITSKELL believed that a more equal society could be achieved by the appropriate REGULATION of capitalism, high-quality public services and a fairer REDISTRIBUTION of income and wealth. This revisionist strategy has come under severe pressure in recent decades as a result of the FISCAL and LEGITIMATION CRISES of the 1970s and the resurgence of global capitalism in the 1980s and 1990s. While many centre-left governments in Europe have retained their commitment to state interventionism, the accommodation made with capital, including tight controls over public spending and lower tax burdens for high earners, suggest that DEMOCRATIC SOCIALIST strategies are now in the process of being formally abandoned. Moreover, the demise of communist regimes in Central and Eastern Europe in the late 1980s and early 1990s led to renewed doubts over the practical applicability of socialist ideas (RMP).

Solidarity

Unlike in the UK where SOCIAL SECURITY has been developed largely in response to POVERTY, SOCIAL SECURITY programmes in other European countries have a stronger emphasis on notions of mutual support and solidarity. This is particularly the case in countries with developed SOCIAL INSURANCE systems, such as France, Italy or Germany. In German terminology, for example, members of a particular SOCIAL INSURANCE branch are referred to as 'solidaristic community' (*Solidargemeinschaft*). As members and contributors to the system, it links the interests of employers and employees, which are not identical with those of, say, taxpayers or the working class. In other words, members of solidaristic networks have particular responsibilities to each other.

Other solidaristic networks of mutual responsibilities might be family members or local COMMUNITIES. (JC)

Special educational needs

Are defined legally as present when a child has significantly greater difficulty in learning than the majority of children of his or her age or has a DISABILITY which prevents or hinders the use of educational facilities normally provided. Specific duties are laid on LOCAL EDUCATION AUTHORITIES with regard to providing for such needs. Recent policy has favoured integration into mainstream schools. (DEG)

Special schools

Schools designed and operated to provide specialist education for those with SPECIAL EDUCATIONAL NEEDS or other DISABILITIES, including blind or profoundly deaf pupils. (PA)

Speenhamland

A system of supplementary payments to the wages of poor labourers operating under the English POOR LAW in the late eighteenth and early nineteenth centuries, named after the village of Speenhamland where it was reputed to have developed. Such wage SUBSIDIES were intended to disappear after the introduction of the WORKHOUSES in the POOR LAW Amendment Act of 1834, but in practice some local areas continued the practice. The term is now sometimes used pejoratively to refer to indiscriminate welfare support, especially for those in low-paid employment. (PA)

Spencer, Herbert (1820–1903)

After a technical education, Spencer was employed as a railway engineer from 1837 to 1841 before turning his hand to writing, becoming a sub-editor on *The Economist* in 1848. Regarded as one of the first sociologists, Spencer was a prolific writer on a broad range of subjects. In *Social Statics* (1850) he stressed the importance of both individual FREEDOM and the value of scientific enquiry. In 1860 he published a prospectus entitled *A System of Synthetic Philosophy* in which he outlined his plan to establish a unified system of philosophy based on evolutionary precepts which would encompass all existing fields of knowledge. These ideas were developed in *First Principles* (1862), *Principles of Biology* (2 vols, 1864–7), *Principles of Sociology* (3 vols, 1876–96) and *Principles of Ethics* (2 vols, 1892–3). Spencer is best known for his support of SOCIAL DARWINISM. He coined the phrase the 'survival of the fittest' to describe the process whereby the more adaptable individuals and cultures would prosper while the less adaptable would fall by the wayside. Believing that it was inappropriate to intervene in this evolutionary process, Spencer championed the principle of LAISSEZ-FAIRE and opposed collective provision for the 'unfit' poor. See also SOCIAL DARWINISM. (RMP)

Stakeholders

In economic terms stakeholding refers to those people who hold a stake in an economic venture – these may be shareholders and investors or workers and managers. In other words not all the stakes held are equal. In SOCIAL POLICY terms those with an interest in a particular social service or BENEFIT are also referred to as stakeholders. Again not all the stakes are equal; for instance, taxpayers, BENEFIT administrators and CLAIMANTS all hold different stakes in SOCIAL SECURITY provisions. The term aims to capture the idea of investment and commitment which all CITIZENS have in different aspects of SOCIAL POLICY, and also to appeal to the notion that a concern with self-interest can be compatible with support for collective welfare provision. (PA)

Standard spending assessment

The formula which central government uses in assessing the expenditure needs of LOCAL AUTHORITIES in determining the level of grant assistance provided to them. (AM)

Standardized assessment tests

Externally set tests taken by pupils at the end of each key stage in the NATIONAL CURRICULUM at ages 7, 11 and 14, designed to measure their achievement (and that of their schools) in relation to the NATIONAL CURRICULUM attainment targets. (DEG)

State earnings-related pension scheme (SERPS)

Introduced in 1978, having been legislated for in 1975 with cross-party support, the culmination of twenty years of Labour and Conservative effort to improve pension provision for those without an occupational pension. It was a PAY-AS-YOU-GO scheme to provide EARNINGS-RELATED BENEFITS to contributors. In the 1980s successive Conservative governments cut the BENEFITS accruing from contributing to SERPS and increased INCENTIVES to CONTRACT OUT into either occupational or PERSONAL PENSIONS. (DM)

State welfare

See WELFARE STATE

Statutory instrument

A document containing rules and REGULATIONS formulated to amplify or interpret powers given in a UK ACT. These pass through parliament with minimal scrutiny. Many key aspects of SOCIAL POLICY, such as SOCIAL SECURITY BENEFIT rates, are set out in statutory instruments rather than in the original ACT. (MJH)

Stigma

Physical attributes or social positions may become associated with particular characteristics in a way that leads to negative assumptions being made about the person on the basis of these characteristics. For example, a person with a DISABILITY becomes stigmatized as helpless, an unemployed person becomes stigmatized as lazy or an older person may be seen as feeble. Social and institutional processes lead to stigma. MEANS-TESTED BENEFITS in particular have been experienced as stigmatizing recipients as a result of the ways in which they are treated by the state and the historical legacy of the POOR LAW, which was actively designed to stigmatize PAUPERS. Stigmatizing processes may lead to DISCRIMINATION and ideologies that rationalize or explain unequal treatment on the basis that those stigmatized differ from the norm. (AE)

Street-level bureaucrats

A term coined by Lipsky to refer to front-line staff in organizations such as schools, hospitals, police stations and SOCIAL WORK offices who dispense public BENEFITS or have recourse to public sanctions and, in effect, make policy through their own rules and routines. Although their job requires them to work with individuals, in practice they have to develop impersonal procedures for coping with USERS *en masse*. They therefore have to make stressful compromises that can be one cause of their burnout. Only successful rationalization enables them to cope with working in adverse circumstances with a constant lack of resources that negate the ideals with which they probably started work.

Consumers of public services, especially the poor, have to balance their RIGHTS as CITIZENS to object to inferior service with acceptance of the lack of resources and organizational restrictions, knowing that they may be treated less favourably if they complain. The high level of DIS-CRETION allowed to such staff means it is hard to make them accountable for their actions. Though four main types of ACCOUNTABILITY have been identified – to the organization, to consumers, to the law and to professional norms – each is fraught with difficulty. (SB)

Student loans

Introduced in the early 1990s as replacements for MEANS-TESTED maintenance grants. Initially supplements to the grants, since 1998 loans have been the means of support for students' living expenses. They are repayable by graduates when their income reaches a certain level. (DEG)

Subsidiarity

The idea that support should be provided at the most appropriate level, which is the agency closest to the person in need in the first instance. For example, individuals should exhaust their own resources first and, if insufficient (even extended) families should be responsible for providing help. If support is still inadequate, it is LOCAL AUTHORITIES rather than the central state that should step in. Influenced by Catholic social doctrine, the principle is very important in some continental European countries and in certain forms of SOCIAL POLICY in particular. German SOCIAL ASSISTANCE policy, for example, has been strongly influenced by the principle of subsidiarity. Within the European Union subsidiarity has also become an important reference point, underpinning decisions in favour of retaining competencies at national (or sub-national) rather than EU level. (JC)

Subsidy

Generally taken to mean measures to reduce the costs of a good or service through a payment to the supplier from the state. However, subsidies may also be paid to the USERS of services; for instance, subsidies to low wages paid to recipients as TAX CREDITS. (AE)

Subsistence

The basis of sustaining life or the means required to provide for basic survival, often used to refer to the minimum level at which SOCIAL SECURITY BENEFITS should be set. (AE)

Superannuation

Some forms of old age and DISABILITY PENSIONS are referred to as superannuation, particularly in Australia and New Zealand. Superannuation may be payable either by the state or by the employer. The recipient can expect to receive the BENEFIT regularly until death; thus the common root with ANNUITY. (DM)

Supplementary Benefit

This MEANS-TESTED form of SOCIAL SECURITY replaced NATIONAL ASSISTANCE in 1966, and was itself replaced by INCOME SUPPORT in 1988. It was administered by an independent QUANGO, the Supplementary BENEFITS Commission. (PA)

Survivors benefit

Payable to close relatives (spouse and/or children) when a person dies. They are closely connected with other family-based SOCIAL SECURITY provisions, such as the payment of additions for dependants. Survivors' BENEFITS ensure that, if the primary breadwinner dies, his or her insurance contributions and ENTITLEMENTS can be used for the benefit of dependants. WIDOWS'/WIDOWERS' BENEFITS are a type of survivors' BENEFIT. See BEREAVEMENT ALLOWANCES. (DM)

Sustainable development

The idea that social development can only be sustained in the long term if it takes into account the pressures it exerts on the natural environment. The 1987 meeting of the World Commission on Environment and Development defined sustainable development as development that meets the needs of the present without compromising the ability of future generations to meet their own needs. There is a contrast within this definition between environmental protection purely in order to satisfy human requirements (a technocentric approach) and the argument that the natural world has a value in its own right and environmental sustainability can only be achieved through radical social change in patterns of production and consumption (an ecocentric approach). Although there is no consensus about this in practice, there is general agreement about its underlying principles of environmental protection, social EQUITY, COMMUNITY PARTICIPATION, inter-sectoral co-operation and democratic ACCOUNTABILITY. (MEH)

Syndicalism

Syndicalists emphasize the importance of industrial FREEDOM. They reject the idea that change can be achieved through parliamentary means, believing that producer militancy, such as strike action, is the best means of promoting working-class interests. (RMP)

T

Take-up

Means-tested BENEFITS that are not paid automatically but have to be claimed by recipients may have a low take-up because people do not apply for them. This may be due to lack of knowledge, confusion over ENTITLEMENT or fear of STIGMA. Levels of take-up of such BENEFITS are estimated by government in the UK and expressed as a proportion of the eligible population applying for a BENEFIT or the proportion of the total expenditure which would be made if everyone eligible took up their ENTITLEMENT. (AE)

Tapers

Many social BENEFITS are given dependent on the income of the recipient. As income rises so the BENEFIT is reduced. The rate at which this happens is the taper. A 50 per cent taper would mean that BENEFITS would be reduced by a MARGINAL TAX RATE of 50p for each additional pound of income. The impact of tapers can lead to a POVERTY TRAP. (HG)

Targeting

This term has been adopted by recent governments to describe those policies that direct services or BENEFITS exclusively at people in greatest need of them. This was often taken to mean the use of MEANS TESTING in the allocation of provision in order to ensure that only those proven to be poor were targeted and justified as a prudent use of limited public resources. It was contrasted with UNIVERSALISM, under which services and BENEFITS were provided equally to all, irrespective of means or circumstances. In this context targeting is therefore a euphemism for MEANS TESTING.

Targeting is also another term for SELECTIVITY and can include various means for directing services or BENEFITS towards those in need of them. For instance, targeting can apply to the direction of services and BENEFITS to particular social groups (ethnic minorities or LONE PARENTS) or to the ALLOCATION of additional support or new initiatives to specific local neighbourhoods. This form of targeting is also referred to as POSITIVE DISCRIMINATION, and it has been a common feature of many SOCIAL POLICY programmes that have sought to tackle the SOCIAL PROBLEMS experienced by particular sectors of society. (PA)

Tawney, Richard Henry (1880–1962)

An established authority on economic and social history (becoming a professor at the LSE in 1931), he published a number of influential texts in this area, including *The Agrarian Problem in the Sixteenth Century* (1912) and *Religion and the Rise of Capitalism* (1926). He was also an active member of the Workers Educational Association. He served as a member on the consultative committee of the Board of Education from 1912 to 1931 and helped to produce the Hadow Report of 1926. Firmly committed to universal SECONDARY EDUCATION, Tawney was the driving force behind Labour's radical education agenda in the interwar period. Tawney joined the Independent Labour Party in 1909 and stood, unsuccessfully, as a candidate in the general elections of 1918, 1922 and 1924. He drafted the Labour Party manifesto of 1928 entitled *Labour and the Nation*. Tawney is best known for his ethical (Christian) SOCIALIST ideas that are captured in two of his most influential texts: *The Acquisitive Society* (1921) and *Equality* (1931). Tawney castigated capitalism for its unethical lack of social purpose and function. He advocated the REDISTRIBUTION of economic and social power to working people and the creation of remoralized, co-operative, SOLIDARISTIC COMMUNITIES so that the equal worth of all CITIZENS could be upheld. He was a strong supporter of UNIVERSAL welfare services which, he believed, would bond people together. His work has been a source of influence for luminaries such as GAITSKELL, CROSLAND and TITMUSS, as well as for members of the New Labour government. (RMP)

Tax credit

Individuals may be relieved of paying tax on part of their income – a TAX RELIEF (see also FISCAL WELFARE). This has the effect of helping the rich most because they pay more tax on their income than the poor. Tax credits avoid this effect by subtracting a given sum from an individual's tax bill for specific purposes such as care of a child. They can also be made available as cash to families who are not paying tax – rebatable tax credits. The Working Families' Tax Credit is of this kind, and a wider range of such credits to cover child care costs and pensions have recently been developed. It is also possible to TAPER credits so that they lose value as income rises. In the UK tax credits do not appear as PUBLIC EXPEN-DITURE as they are taxes not raised. This has political advantages. (HG)

Tax relief

Taxpayers may be excused the duty to pay tax on part of their income if they spend it on items approved by government, such as buying a house, looking after children or giving to a CHARITY. Such relief helps most those with the highest incomes paying most tax. Relief may be limited to a fixed amount of expenditure or to relief only from the lowest rates of tax. See also FISCAL WELFARE. (HG)

Technical and Vocational Education Initiative (TVEI)

A scheme central to NEW VOCATIONALISM in the mid-1980s by which extra funds were provided for schools and colleges to develop projects in different subject areas that would provide those aged between 14 and 18 with experience of how industry worked and relevant vocational skills. It gave way from the mid-1990s to other work-related training initiatives. (DEG)

Technical schools

SECONDARY technical schools superseded the junior technical schools of the earlier part of the twentieth century in the post-1944 TRIPARTITE SYSTEM. Designed specifically for pupils with 'mechanical' abilities as selected by the ELEVEN PLUS, they remained the smallest sector of SEC-ONDARY SCHOOLING and were incorporated into COMPREHENSIVE schools in the 1960s. (DEG)

Thatcherism

While sometimes used as a synonym for the NEW RIGHT, this is an expression that captures the political style and cultural shifts that were associated with the British Conservative governments led by Prime Min-ister (later Lady) Margaret Thatcher in the period 1979–90. On the one hand, it is associated with a belief in free markets and a desire to 'roll back' the WELFARE STATE, to privatize nationalized industries and to deregulate the economy; on the other hand, with a belief in a strong state and a desire to maintain strict monetary control, to curtail the power of the trades unions, to strengthen the armed services and the police and to centralize governmental and indeed prime ministerial power. The success of the Thatcher governments in fulfilling such specific objectives was in some respects limited, but some would argue that they enjoyed success in promoting popular capitalism and eroding SOCIAL-DEMOCRATIC ideas. Thatcherism is epitomized by Margaret Thatcher's famous aphorism 'There is no such thing as society, only individuals and their families', but also by her nationalism and hostility to the European Union. (HD)

Think tanks

Organizations of academics and politicians aiming to shape the context of policy debate and to influence policy-making processes. They range in size from a handful of staff to hundreds in some US examples. Many are based outside the civil service and government, although there are also examples of 'units' and 'task forces' based within both government and opposition parties. The first significant think tank in UK SOCIAL POLICY was the FABIAN Society, established in 1884 to campaign for gradual change towards SOCIALISM. There has been a steady growth since then, with a dramatic increase in the number of think tanks in the last quarter of the twentieth century. (DWS)

Third sector

A relatively uncontentious way of referring to the VOLUNTARY and COM-MUNITY SECTORS, which avoids definitional debates about the meaning of 'voluntary'. It alludes indirectly to other sectors, not necessarily ranked by their numbering: first PUBLIC, second PRIVATE or for profit, and fourth INFORMAL. (DWS)

Third way

Coined to describe the Blair government's approach to the development of SOCIAL POLICY in the UK. It involves a rejection of previous 'old Labour' approaches based on high taxation and high public spending to deliver state-run services; and a rejection of NEW RIGHT approaches based on automatic preference for private market delivery. The third way is 'between the state and the market'. In practice the third way involves support for WELFARE PLURALISM and a pragmatic assessment that it is a judgement of BEST VALUE that should determine how and where services are provided. (PA)

Titmuss, Richard Morris (1907–1973)

Started out as an office boy before becoming a fire insurance officer at the age of 18. Despite his lack of formal academic qualifications Titmuss applied his command of statistical analysis to social issues, publishing his first book, with his wife Kay, on *Poverty and Population* in 1938. This book established Titmuss's credentials as a social investigator and led to an invitation to write one of the official civilian war histories, *Problems of Social Policy* (1950), which many regard as his finest work. He was subsequently appointed to a chair in SOCIAL ADMINISTRATION at the LSE in 1950. It is a mark of his influence that the subject had taken firm root in HIGHER EDUCATION by the time of his death in 1973. He continually highlighted the negative aspects of market forces, not least in *The Gift Relationship* (1970), where he demonstrated the social and economic advantages of the non-commercial blood-donor system operating in Britain (see ALTRUISM). The essay remained his most favoured means of communication and several of these, including the SOCIAL DIVISION OF WELFARE, have come to be regarded as seminal contributions to the subject. Titmuss was particularly proud of the NATIONAL HEALTH SERVICE because it treated patients by virtue of their medical NEED rather than on the basis of class, status or ethnicity. (RMP)

Total institution

Any establishment where people live on a long-term basis and where all their NEEDS are catered for within that establishment. The regime deliberately, or as a result of procedures, reduces the AUTONOMY of inmates. Such residences can include mental hospitals, prisons, REFUGEE centres and RESIDENTIAL establishments for children. (CU)

Total quality management

A form of service improvement which views it as a continuous organization-wide process involving all staff in the development and maintenance of responsive customer-oriented provision. (MM)

Transaction costs

The costs of making markets or exchanges of any type work, such as information costs, accounting procedures, or legal costs if people do not keep to the contract. QUASI-MARKETS in health and social services have been criticized for the high transaction costs involved in billing for services and setting contracts. However, non-market systems also carry transaction costs, such as the negotiation of annual budgets and the costs of regulating quality. (HG)

Transfers

Economists distinguish between government activities involving the employment of people and the use of buildings and materials (such as the provision of education and health care) and transfers, whereby money is transferred between the government and households but resources are not used or consumed until the transfer is spent by the recipient. Most transfers to households are made through the cash BENEFIT system (in the form of old-age and DISABILITY PENSIONS, MEANS-TESTED BENEFITS, etc.), but they can also take the form of scholarships, student grants and other payments.

It is possible to analyse REDISTRIBUTION by comparing the pre-transfer and post-transfer distribution of income. Transfers can be classified as horizontal or vertical according to their REDISTRIBUTIVE impact. Horizontal transfers take place between households on a similar income level. They arise because the SOCIAL SECURITY system may recognize the NEEDS of one as greater (or more worthy of assistance) than the other. For example, CHILD BENEFIT may lead to horizontal REDISTRIBUTION to families with children from those without. Vertical transfers are those that transfer resources up and down the income scale. For example, to alleviate POVERTY, the WELFARE STATE may transfer resources vertically from rich to poor. PAY AS YOU GO PENSION systems result in INTERGENERATIONAL TRANSFERS from those of working age to the elderly.

In some areas of welfare provision a policy choice may be made about whether to make cash transfers to enable people to purchase the things they need, or whether to provide services directly. For example, a cash payment could be given to a person needing care to enable him or her to purchase care, or, alternatively, PUBLIC SECTOR employees could offer care services. Cash payments allow the operation of competitive markets for provision of services, while direct provision enables the government to exercise more control over what exactly is provided. If the government wants to promote markets but also wants control over how money is spent, it may give VOUCHERS instead of cash.

While the term 'transfer payments' usually refers to payments from the government to households, any payment made unilaterally (i.e. not as part of an exchange) is technically a transfer payment. For example, the payment of maintenance by absent parents is a private transfer from one household to another. (DM)

Transmitted deprivation

See CYCLE OF DEPRIVATION

Tribunals

Independent adjudicative bodies that preside over APPEALS in a wide variety of matters, including several specifically related to social welfare. They are statutorily appointed and though their constitution will depend on their specific terms of reference, tribunals usually consist of up to three persons, of whom one – who must sometimes be a qualified lawyer – acts as Chairperson. A consultative body, the Council on Tribunals, oversees the work of tribunals. Some, such as SOCIAL SECURITY tribunals and immigration APPEAL TRIBUNALS, have been set up to decide appeals against decisions by state administrators. Others, such as employment tribunals, have been created by social legislation to regulate disputes between private parties. The decisions of tribunals can sometimes be reviewed by higher appellate bodies (such as the Social Security Commissioners in the case of SOCIAL SECURITY matters) or by the ordinary courts. However, tribunals have been developed since the beginning of the last century, particularly in the SOCIAL SECURITY field, as a form of administrative REDRESS that is separate from the ordinary courts. Tribunals, though they exercise a 'quasi-judicial' function, are supposed to provide a more informal and accessible forum than the courts. (HD)

Trickle down

Used to describe and justify the effect of NEO-LIBERAL policies, by which the promotion of economic growth creates additional wealth that can 'trickle down' the social order and benefit even the poorest members of society. Such growth, it is argued, is best promoted by increasing the rewards available to potential entrepreneurs and existing business leaders – both directly through market-driven remuneration and indi-rectly through tax cuts. While such an approach is likely to increase the extent of social inequality, this in itself will not matter. As the gap between rich and poor increases, so does the INCENTIVE to succeed, and successful entrepreneurs and the businesses they run or create will provide more jobs and increased living standards for everybody: 'a rising tide lifts all boats'. Empirical evidence for the existence of a trickle down effect is ambiguous. None the less, belief in the trickle down effect con-tinues to inform social development policies in various parts of the world and to be evinced by policy makers in the developed world who hold that economic growth should be sustained at the expense of greater social EQUALITY. (HD)

Tripartite System

The three-fold division in state SECONDARY EDUCATION between GRAMMAR, secondary TECHNICAL and SECONDARY MODERN SCHOOLS established after the 1944 Education Act. It owed much to contempo-rary psychological theories positing three types of mind: the academic, the mechanical and those who deal with 'concrete things rather than ideas'. The ELEVEN PLUS examination was intended to allocate children to the school best suited to their aptitudes and abilities and, in theory, each type of school was to be equal in parity and prestige. Research soon showed otherwise. Children of middle-class parents predominated in the GRAMMAR SCHOOLS, while their working-class contemporaries were disproportionately to be found in the SECONDARY MODERN SCHOOLS. These findings, along with the wide disparity in the distribu-tion of GRAMMAR SCHOOL places, challenged the idea of EQUALITY of educational opportunity as a leitmotif of the 1944 Act. However, eco-nomic considerations about the potential loss of talent represented by the system focused attention on early leavers and 'late developers' and shifted the debate in favour of COMPREHENSIVE schools. Less noticed was the use of quotas so as to ensure similar GRAMMAR SCHOOL entry rates for boys and girls, though more girls tended to 'pass' the ELEVEN PLUS exam than boys. (DEG)

Truancy

Unauthorized absence from school. A legal duty is imposed upon parents to ensure their children of compulsory school age (5–16) attend school regularly. LOCAL EDUCATION AUTHORITIES have a range of powers available to ensure that parents fulfil this responsibility, including legal proceedings, school attendance orders and education supervision orders. The authority's school attendance functions are usually carried out by education welfare officers who base their information on the admission registers which schools are required to keep and the attendance registers on which the presence or absence of pupils is noted at the start of morning and afternoon school. Recently there has been considerable political concern over truancy and its links with juvenile crime, and the police have been empowered to remove truants from public places and return them to school, while schools have been encouraged to develop a range of anti-truancy measures. (DEG)

U

Underclass

The term originated in US policy debates and particularly the work of Charles Murray, who has argued that an underclass developed in the US towards the end of the last century, and that similar trends could be identified in the UK. In this context the term is used to refer to those dependent on welfare, especially where welfare DEPENDENCY is concentrated in particular social groups (e.g. LONE PARENTS) or local neighbourhoods. Here a CULTURE OF POVERTY can develop, and those who share this culture can become socially and ideologically separated from the broader working class to constitute a distinct underclass. Murray's discussion of the underclass has a strongly pathological tone. Others have argued that the creation of such a class is the product of social and economic forces that have isolated some groups from the contracting labour market and created SOCIAL EXCLUSION: it is not due to the failings of those who are so excluded. However, sociological research has found little evidence for the existence of such a separate social class linked to BENEFIT DEPENDENCY and SOCIAL EXCLUSION. (PA)

Undeserving

See DESERVING

Unemployment

Refers to people who are out of work and seeking paid employment. Seemingly a straightforward concept, unemployment can be defined and therefore measured in several ways. National statistics often regard only those people as unemployed who have registered at EMPLOYMENT

OFFICES, can prove that they are looking for a job and are claiming BEN-EFITS or BENEFIT credits. A wider definition might include those who, for whatever reason, do not claim BENEFITS or do not register as unemployed but are nevertheless seeking employment. An even wider concept includes 'discouraged workers', i.e. those who are interested in finding paid employment but are currently not actively looking for a job because of adverse labour-market conditions. Unemployment data can be based on statistics provided by employment offices or derived from labour-force surveys. (JC)

Unemployment trap

A situation where a person out of work is discouraged from taking up employment due to an insufficient increase in income. In other words, a combination of low wages, taxation and BENEFIT withdrawal might lead to a situation in which income from paid work is lower, or only marginally above, the level of income received in BENEFITS when out of work. See also MARGINAL TAX RATE. (JC)

Universalism

The idea of the universal provision of services is often associated with the implementation of the postwar welfare reforms in Britain, sometimes referred to as the creation of the WELFARE STATE. The postwar reformers were keen to avoid some of the unpopular aspects of prewar provision, in particular the PUBLIC ASSISTANCE schemes, which had restricted BENEFIT support only to the poorest, and the local health and hospital services, which had provided lower standards of service to those who could not pay for themselves. The idea was that these would all be replaced with public services, universally available to all.

The postwar NATIONAL HEALTH SERVICE therefore provided free public services to all, financed out of taxation. Similarly state education was also provided free to all children, in schools run by LOCAL EDUCATION AUTHORITIES. Health and education services were universal in the sense that they were equally available to all. They also provided, in theory, the same standard of service to all. Universalism therefore applied both to service ACCESS and service standards.

Universalism is also sometimes used to refer to the principle upon which the SOCIAL SECURITY reforms introduced following the proposals in the BEVERIDGE Report were based. The reforms were based on a SOCIAL INSURANCE model of ENTITLEMENT, which was not genuinely universal as it only paid BENEFITS to those who had made prior contributions to the scheme – although all those who did receive BENEFIT got the same amounts of support. The FAMILY ALLOWANCES introduced at the same time were universal as they paid BENEFIT to all parents of more than one child.

Universal health and education services have remained key features of British SOCIAL POLICY development, although CHARGES have been introduced for some services (such as prescriptions for medicines) and MEANS TESTING used to exempt some poor people from paying these charges. More recently, however, universalism has been criticized for providing public services to those who do not 'need' them – in practice those who could perhaps afford to pay a commercial fee for them. And many services are now TARGETED on those thought to have the highest priority NEED for public support. (PA)

University

A self-governing institution of HIGHER EDUCATION established by Royal Charter or Parliamentary Statute. Traditionally universities engaged in research and the provision of degree-level and postgraduate programmes, but increasingly also offer sub-degree and professional courses. (DEG)

Uprating (of benefits)

See INDEXING OF BENEFITS

Urban policies

Policies developed as a response to the identification of specifically urban problems, originally associated with inner urban areas policy introduced in 1976. A succession of subsequent measures has followed. A review of urban policy carried out in 1996 summarized this range of policies and concluded that they had not had any major impact. Following this the Single Regeneration Budget (SRB) drew together the different elements in urban policy and provided a focus on economic outputs rather than property development. Urban policy has tended to be associated with area-based approaches focusing upon areas with high concentrations of social NEED and opportunities for economic development. (AM)

Users

An umbrella term with a variety of usages. Most commonly, it denotes groups of people who may receive welfare services and are affected by official policies that characterize these. However, many people we might think of as users, who have, for example, serious physical IMPAIRMENTS, may not be service users most of the time. Others who have rejected services because they see them as damaging, such as survivors of MENTAL HEALTH services, are still characterized as 'users'.

The term may also be seen as derogatory – 'substance users' is not the sort of LABELLING most people want; it may also imply a DEPENDENCY on services that users seek to reject. The social model of DISABILITY argues that many people are reduced to DEPENDENCY by their physical and social environment, rather than by their physical and mental IMPAIRMENTS.

Users are often talked about in the same context as CARERS, but this provokes tensions. Service-users' groups argue that emphasis on CARERS has overlooked the complex interaction between users and CARERS at the expense of users' NEEDS. RESPITE CARE, for example, is more often construed as 'giving the carer a break' than giving the user a break from care at home. (SB)

Utilitarianism

A nineteenth-century philosophical theory based on two leading principles associated particularly with JEREMY BENTHAM. The first is that the motive for all human actions is the pursuit of pleasure and the avoidance of pain, with pain and pleasure capable of quantification by the so-called felicific calculus. Second, whatever measure maximizes pleasure over pain in a population is what is good and, therefore, right. Consequently, the greatest good was defined as the greatest happiness of the greatest number. It thus raises issues about the RIGHTS of minorities and the risk that rulers would pursue their own self-interest rather than the greatest happiness principle. BENTHAM addressed the latter by advocating parliamentary reform and the extension of representative democracy through the introduction of universal suffrage, the secret ballot and annual elections. His practical reform programme also emphasized the importance of a centralized and ACCOUNTABLE administration in social affairs as well as particular proposals for prisons, the POOR LAW and education. (DEG)

V

Value Added Tax (VAT)

A form of INDIRECT TAXATION dating back to the early part of the twentieth century in the US. It taxes all forms of economic activity at the same rate and minimizes interference with the market. It is now used as the main indirect tax in the European Union, with tax levied at each stage of the production process of goods and services. (HG)

Vertical redistribution

See TRANSFERS

Vocationalism

A notion traditionally associated with those entering a religious order or ministry through a 'calling', which since the nineteenth century has also been linked to the semi-professions of teaching, nursing and SOCIAL WORK in which the central value is to put others first. It is often contrasted with PROFESSIONALISM and thought to emphasize practical, non-academic skills, the unimportance of material rewards, obedience and acquiescence to discipline, and general rather than specialized skills. Sociologically, therefore, it can be identified as an ideology used to justify women's continued segregation into relatively low-paid, stressful jobs with limited career structures, little authority and a poor public image. As a result, the drive to professionalize occupations like those above has met with resistance. In SOCIAL WORK genericism was valued over specialization in the 1970s and 1980s and a national system of registration not established until 2001. In nursing there has been hostility to the establishment of nurse practitioners. The conflict between the two concepts has yet to be resolved, but they should not be seen as mutually exclusive. (SB)

Voice

A term coined by Hirschmann to describe the pressure individuals can exert on an agency to change the service or object to the standards offered. It can take the form of USER committees or surveys of consumers' views, although in such fora some USERS may be more active than others. It is often contrasted with EXIT as a means of USER control. (HG)

Voluntary organizations

See VOLUNTARY SECTOR

Voluntary sector

A generic term used to refer to those organizations operating on a collective basis to provide goods or services, which do not distribute any profits and are not agencies of the central or local state. They also rely, in part at least, upon the support of voluntary labour or voluntary donations. They are sometimes also referred to as the THIRD SECTOR, the non-profit sector, or the non-statutory sector. Voluntary organizations vary considerably in size, scale and scope and accurate definition and measurement of the sector is therefore often disputed. However, four key features distinguish the sector:

- a degree of formality;
- relative AUTONOMY from government;
- a degree of self-government;
- commitment to non-profit distribution.

In Britain it consists mainly of a large number of organizations and associations whose income ranges from virtually nothing to less than £10,000 per annum. At the opposite extreme are a small minority of very large, formal organizations whose central management comprises full-time paid professionals, many on salaries commensurate with their commercial sector peers, handling tens of millions of pounds per annum. Voluntary organizations include those engaged in service provision, SELF-HELP, PRESSURE GROUP activity and advocacy, as well as those acting to provide co-ordination and infrastructural development for others. Despite the variety and diversity of voluntary activity some attempts to quantify its scale have been attempted. Estimates for total income vary from £13–14 billion, while the monetary value of VOLUN-TEER activity varies from £8–12 billion.

The voluntary sector has always been significant in SOCIAL POLICY development and delivery in the UK and all other advanced WELFARE CAPITALIST nations. However, in recent years increased PARTNERSHIP between the voluntary sector and other sectors, especially the state, has been openly promoted. Many voluntary organizations now receive funding from PUBLIC EXPENDITURE to provide services, in some cases under contractual arrangement with state agencies. Relations between voluntary agencies and the state are also governed by COMPACTS, which seek to ensure that both parties have clear RIGHTS and responsibilities. See also CONTRACT CULTURE (DWS)

Voluntary welfare

A collective term for a family of organizations characterized as formally organized, separate from government, non-profit distributing, self-governing and involving VOLUNTEERS. A narrow definition of these would include social services (particularly COMMUNITY CARE), health, housing and education. A broader view would include cultural and leisure activities and the work of religious congregations of all faiths. Perhaps more contentious are those activities centred on advocacy and campaigning; for example, many organizations have been established to redefine or extend the definition of social NEED. Typical among these would be those challenging INSTITUTIONAL RACISM and SEXISM and arguing for new forms of service provision. Governments have increasingly sought to engage service-delivery voluntary welfare agencies in more prescribed (contractual) agreements, often justified by reference to WELFARE PLURALISM. Mainly as a consequence of contracting, many welfare agencies experience growth, more formal work practices and greater numbers of paid professional staff. While such pluralism has often been described as a PARTNERSHIP, there is evidence that voluntary elements can become marginal and the innovative capacity of agencies diluted. (DWS)

Volunteer

Someone who freely chooses, without direct material reward, to help an individual or group beyond the immediate circle of family, neighbours and friends; in practice, both the motivation (why do people begin and continue as volunteers?) and the objects of the volunteering (known social worlds or strangers?) are less clear-cut. Volunteers may give their time to an activity, but they may also donate money, materials or expertise. (DWS)

Vouchers

Tokens issued by public authorities to give holders the right to 'buy' services, such as education at a state or a PRIVATE SCHOOL. They operated briefly in the UK in the 1990s for pre-school facilities. Quasi-vouchers are similar but do not involve actual tokens; rather, government promises to pay providers for each USER of their services, such as pupils in a school. (HG)

W

Wages Councils

Workers in some industries used to have legal MINIMUM WAGES and other minima, such as holiday entitlement, set by Wages Councils. However, the coverage of Wage Council regulation was reduced in the 1980s and abolished in the 1990s. (JC)

Webb, Martha Beatrice (1858–1943) and Sidney James (1859–1947)

In the early part of her life Beatrice Webb was a member of the CHARITY ORGANIZATION SOCIETY (1883) and a rent collector in one of OCTAVIA HILL's housing schemes. Subsequently she worked on Charles Booth's major study on *Life and Labour of the People in London*, leading her to adopt a more critical stance towards PHILANTHROPY.

Sidney Webb was a civil servant in the Colonial Office and joined the FABIAN Society in 1885. He served on the London County Council from 1892 to 1910 and was MP for Seaham from 1922–9, serving as President of the Board of Trade in 1924. He was largely responsible for the drafting of the Labour Party's constitution in 1918 and served on the National Executive Committee from 1915 to 1925. He became Lord Passfield in 1929 and served as Secretary of State for the Dominions and Colonies from 1929–31.

After marrying in 1892, the Webbs devoted their lives to social reform. They believed that society would advance by means of the collective ownership of capital, municipal provision of social services, state REGULATION of private property, REDISTRIBUTIVE taxation and the establishment of a social minimum. They worked together on the Minority Report on the POOR LAWS in 1909 that recommended the break up of the existing relief and its functions transferred to specialist LOCAL AUTHORITY committees. In the latter part of their lives they expressed their admiration for developments in the Soviet Union, which they believed exemplified a FABIAN SOCIALIST approach. The prodigious writings of the Webbs included *The History of Trade Unionism* (1894), *English Local Government* (1906–29) and the more controversial work *Soviet Communism: A New Civilization?* (1935). They helped to establish both the London School of Economics (1895) and *The New Statesman* (1912). (RMP)

Welfare

At the heart of SOCIAL POLICY is a concern with the factors that improve the welfare of people and conversely with those that undermine this and create DISWELFARE. Welfare is a difficult concept to define. There is no common conception of such welfare and no agreed way of analysing it. It involves social and individual well-being, but economic, political, moral and ethical definitions of well-being differ. Economists might point to wealth as an indicator of a society's welfare. A political scientist might be concerned with SOCIAL CAPITAL and democratic PARTICIPATION. Moral and ethical commentators might ask questions about the distribution of resources, opportunities and LIFE CHANCES as indicators of societal well-being. Psychologists might focus upon an individual's physical and MENTAL HEALTH.

Although welfare is generally used in all of these approaches in a positive context, as a social good, it is also sometimes used to refer to an undesirable dependency upon public resources. For instance, high numbers of SOCIAL SECURITY CLAIMANTS have been referred to as a problem of welfare DEPENDENCY, particularly in the US. (AE)

Welfare capitalism

The historical development of capitalism has resulted in markets becoming universal and the COMMODIFICATION of productive forces, including labour. Welfare capitalism has maintained markets as the economic basis for democratic and industrial societies, but has transformed capitalism into welfare capitalism via the introduction of social RIGHTS to BENEFITS and services. (JC)

Welfare effort

Measured as the proportion of gross domestic product (GDP) spent by governments on social programmes such as health, education, SOCIAL

SECURITY and PERSONAL SOCIAL SERVICES. Measures of welfare effort do not necessarily reflect the degree of welfare enjoyed in any particular country, since expenditure may be wasted or social programmes may be supported by finances that do not count as part of government expenditure. (AE)

Welfare pluralism

A term used to indicate that there are (or ought to be if the commentator is a 'welfare pluralist') multiple (plural) sources for meeting health, SOCIAL SECURITY, education, housing, care and welfare NEEDS generally. At its core, particularly if the term is being used prescriptively, is the idea that 'welfare' does not only have to be delivered by the WELFARE STATE on a collective basis. Instead there is the view that there are multiple sources of welfare, including the PUBLIC SECTOR, the PRIVATE SECTOR, the VOLUNTARY SECTOR and the family, which can be mixed and matched through policy. Hence the meaning of what constitutes welfare is crucial, as is the question of whose welfare counts most. Welfare pluralists tend to support EVIDENCE-BASED policy, on the grounds that it is immaterial what the sources of welfare are, so long as those sources are EFFECTIVE and efficient. Many would also favour policies promoting a MIXED ECONOMY OF WELFARE. (CU)

Welfare regimes

Central to Esping-Andersen's comparative analysis of WELFARE CAPITALISM. Rather than postulating degrees of social RIGHTS on a continuum, the concept of welfare regimes is based on the premise of qualitatively different arrangements between state, markets and the family as the principal sources for SOCIAL PROTECTION in modern WELFARE STATES. It is the respective roles of those three social institutions that produce specific configurations and thus allow a clustering of countries according to different regime types. Esping-Andersen identified three clusters. In the 'liberal' WELFARE STATE, UNIVERSAL but modest and largely MEANS-TESTED forms of SOCIAL SECURITY prevail, combined with a substantial level of market-provided PRIVATE WELFARE. The 'corporatist-statist' regime type provides BENEFITS which serve to maintain status and income differentials, promote family-work and motherhood rather than paid employment as the prescribed role for women, and leave markets with a marginal role in providing SOCIAL PROTECTION. In the SOCIAL DEMOCRATIC regime UNIVERSAL welfare BENEFITS and services promote EQUALITY, crowding out both markets and families as principal sources of social welfare. Other writers have since proposed the existence of other regimes, such as the Latin-rim or Mediterranean, and the Pacific-rim or Asian-tiger models. (JC)

Welfare rights

The existence of RIGHTS to welfare which can be legally enforced, and in particular RIGHTS to SOCIAL SECURITY BENEFITS, has led to the development of a group of workers and VOLUNTEERS providing advice and assistance to those who might be ENTITLED to such rights. This activity is referred to as welfare rights work. It is carried out by officers in LOCAL AUTHORITIES and by workers and VOLUNTEERS in independent ADVICE CENTRES. One of the main focuses of welfare rights work is on the encouragement of CLAIMANTS to TAKE-UP BENEFIT ENTITLEMENT which they may not be fully aware of, and sometimes workers organize take-up campaigns to promote this, using leaflets, posters and other publicity media. Welfare rights workers also provide advocacy services to support CLAIMANTS pursuing legal appeals against BENEFIT decisions that they wish to challenge. (PA)

Welfare society

A WELFARE STATE should be distinguished from a welfare society. The establishment of the former does not necessarily give rise to the creation of a fairer society. According to TITMUSS those nations which introduced integrative, progressively funded, UNIVERSALIST welfare provision for their own CITIZENS and who assisted less prosperous neighbouring countries were more entitled to be regarded as welfare societies. (RMP)

Welfare state

In the British context the term is inextricably linked with the 1942 BEVERIDGE Report on Social Insurance which promised cradle-to-grave protection for all CITIZENS. It describes the process whereby state power is used to modify the impact of market forces by guaranteeing a minimum income for all, a reduction in insecurity and the provision of a range of social services for all without regard to status or class. The origins of the welfare state can be traced back to the latter part of the nineteenth century, when a number of European and North American nations introduced various types of SOCIAL PROTECTION. There were differences in the pattern and pace of development, but growing expenditure levels were a common feature in these countries. It rose from around 3 per cent of GDP before the First World War to between 10–20 per cent in the 1950s, and finally to somewhere between 25–40 per cent in the 1970s.

Various explanations for the development of the welfare state have been put forward, including the impact of war, industrialization, growing humanitarianism and the need to forestall working-class unrest. British commentators such as TITMUSS have contested the assumption that the coming of the welfare state has resulted in sizeable gains for the poor at the expense of the rich. The term 'classic' welfare state has often been used in reference to the period from 1945 to 1975, when more extensive and more UNIVERSALISTIC forms of SOCIAL PROTECTION were introduced. See also BUTSKELLISM; KEYNESIAN WELFARE STATE. (RMP)

Welfare to work

The generic term used to refer to the NEW DEAL and other policy measures designed to support moves into employment introduced by the Labour government after 1997. Welfare to work schemes include job-search assistance, training or education, wage SUBSIDIES for taking on unemployed people, and intensive counselling, advice and guidance. Compulsory participation in a programme is a condition in some schemes. (JC)

White Paper

A UK government document, now published electronically as well as on paper, presenting new policy initiatives and proposals for legislation. It provides a more accessible account of such proposals than BILLS and may be preceded by a GREEN PAPER. (MJH)

Widows/widowers benefits

The provision of widows BENEFITS under the NATIONAL INSUR-ANCE system in the last century can be seen as part of the MALE

BREADWINNER MODEL, whereby married women were entitled to a PENSION based on the contributions paid by their dead husbands. Provision for widows with children is generally better than that for other LONE PARENTS.

More recently, with the introduction of BEREAVEMENT ALLOWANCES and SURVIVORS BENEFITS, some provision for widowers has been introduced and support for women and children revised. (DM)

Wilson, James Harold (1916–1995)

After a short academic career, Harold Wilson was propelled into public life as an Economic Assistant to the War Cabinet (1940–1) and then as Director of Economics and Statistics in the Ministry of Fuel and Power (1943–5). He was Labour MP for Ormskirk from 1945 to 1950 and for Huyton from 1950 to 1983. He was President of the Board of Trade from 1947 to 1951, but resigned after the imposition of NATIONAL HEALTH SERVICE CHARGES in 1951. He became Labour Party leader in 1963 following the sudden death of HUGH GAITSKELL. He achieved more electoral success than any other Labour leader to date, serving as Prime Minister from 1964 to 1970 and subsequently from 1974 until his abrupt departure in 1976. At the time both these Labour administrations attracted considerable criticism from their own supporters for pursuing moderate modernizing policies rather than bringing about more fundamental forms of economic and social change. However, the SOCIAL POLICY achievements of the Wilson governments have come to be viewed in a more positive light in recent times, not least because they were achieved against a background of economic turbulence. (RMP)

Women's refuges

The establishment of women's refuges arose directly out of the women's liberation movement of the 1960s and 1970s. The first UK refuge was set up in Chiswick in 1972, providing a safe haven for what were then referred to as 'battered women'. The movement grew rapidly in the 1970s and by the end of the decade there were about 200 refuges in operation. In 2000 there were about 250 and around 50,000 women and children spent at least one night in a refuge in England during 1994–5. Refuges are locally based, not-for-profit organizations usually run by women, and which provide advice, support, information and emergency temporary accommodation for women and children experiencing violence from someone, usually in the home, and often a male partner. The 1995 Home Office circular on inter-agency co-ordination on domestic violence recommended the inclusion of women's refuges in local projects alongside statutory bodies such as the local SOCIAL SERVICES DEPARTMENTS and police and probation services. As well as providing immediate help and support the women's refuge movement has also played a wider campaigning role in respect of issues of domestic violence, especially in relation to the legal framework and to the support available to the victims. (JM)

Wootton, Barbara Frances (1897–1988)

Worked for the research department of the Labour Party and the TUC. She was reader, then professor, of Social Studies at Bedford College. Wootton's main interests were in the fields of criminology, penal policy and SOCIAL WORK. The UTILITARIAN and positivistic underpinning of her work is much to the fore in her most influential publication, *Social Science and Social Pathology* (1959). (RMP)

Work–life balance

See FAMILY-FRIENDLY POLICIES

Work test

ELIGIBILITY for UNEMPLOYMENT-related BENEFITS depends on being out of work and capable and willing to take up paid employment. One of the tasks of JOB CENTRES is to control the latter by offering, for example, employment or participation in a training programme. Refusal on the part of BENEFIT CLAIMANTS might constitute failing the work test and risking BENEFIT reduction or withdrawal. (JC)

Workfare

Originally developed in the USA, workfare makes the receipt of SOCIAL SECURITY BENEFITS conditional on unemployed CLAIMANTS accepting temporary work or participating in training or preparatory work-experience courses. Other countries also have the option of requiring

UNEMPLOYED BENEFIT CLAIMANTS to take part in work or training programme with, in case of refusal, the risk of losing or deducting BENEFIT
payment. This applies particularly to those UNEMPLOYED who have been
receiving BENEFITS for long periods and/or are claiming SOCIAL ASSIS-
TANCE rather than INSURANCE BENEFITS based on previous contributions
made. Critics argue that the WELFARE TO WORK programmes introduced
by the Labour government after 1997 indicate a shift from a WELFARE
STATE based on the notion of CITIZENSHIP RIGHTS towards one which
is inspired by the idea of workfare. See SCHUMPETERIAN WORKFARE
STATE. (JC)

Workhouse

A feature both of the Old and New POOR LAW. Under the former, it was
envisaged as an establishment, distinct from the poor house for the aged
and disabled and the house of correction for persistent idlers, where the
poor would be set to work at appropriate rates of pay on a residential
or non-residential basis. A concern with rising costs in the late seventeenth century led various towns and cities to make relief more conditional through the application of a labour test, and the system more
financially self-sufficient through the work done by PAUPERS in new
workhouses established for the purpose. This local practice was confirmed in legislation in 1722. Under the New POOR LAW it was used as
a deterrent to the able-bodied poor. The physical and psychological
characteristics of the institution were designed to ensure it was less desirable than low-paid work, that it was a last resort. In this it appeared to
be successful. By 1860, for example, able-bodied labourers accounted
for just 5 per cent of workhouse inmates. By the time of the *de facto*
abolition of the POOR LAW in 1929, the remaining inmates were a combination of the most 'UNDESERVING' and most helpless – vagrants,
unmarried mothers and the aged poor. (DEG)

Working age

Used to refer to the period during an individual's life when they
might normally expect to be engaged in paid employment – generally
16 or 18 to 60 or 65. In the UK the term is incorporated into references to policies or institutions focusing on provision for people at this
stage of their lives, such as the Working Age Agency in delivering
BENEFITS. (PA)

Working time

Refers to the hours of work per week. With the aim of protecting workers against excessively long working hours and the organization of working time that could be detrimental to HEALTH AND SAFETY, the European Union has repeatedly formulated directives and legislated in the area of working time. (JC)

Y

Yearbook of Labor Statistics

A reference source produced annually by the International Labour Office (ILO). Based on national data, it presents the principal labour statistics for over 190 countries, including information on employment, UNEMPLOYMENT, wages, hours of work, labour costs, inflation, occupational injuries, strikes and lockouts. (JC)

Younghusband, Eileen Louise (1902–1981)

One of the leading figures in the development of SOCIAL WORK in Britain. In her report on the role of social workers in LOCAL AUTHORITY health and welfare services (1959) she recommended the establishment of training courses in colleges and UNIVERSITIES. This gave rise to the establishment of the Council for Training in Social Work and the National Institute for Social Work. Her publications include *Social Work in Britain 1950–1975: A Follow-Up Study* (2 vols, 1978). (RMP)

Youth services

Mostly operate from a centre or club to which young people are invited, although outreach workers interact with youth in their own territories. Functions include recreation, education and social welfare. Approaches range from uniformed to highly informal. Access may be open to any local young person or restricted. (MH)

Z

Zero-tolerance

A style of policing that deliberately targets incivilities and petty offences in public places, such as begging, street drinking and vandalism. The premise that informs this approach involves a particular interpretation of what has been called the 'broken windows thesis'. The idea is that just as the prompt repair of broken windows prevents a house or a neighbourhood from spiralling into greater dereliction, so by analogy decisive action against minor offences will lower the public's tolerance of crime and DEVIANCE in general. This will inhibit the escalation of crime and disorder. While successes have been claimed for zero-tolerance policing in the United States, the evidence has been subject to challenge and debate. More recently, the term 'zero-tolerance' has been adopted and used to refer generally to heavy-handed policing methods. It is also used whenever policy makers seek to advocate drastic remedies for particular kinds of anti-social behaviour or to justify the investment of resources in measures to combat FRAUD within welfare systems. (HD)

Index

References to main dictionary entries are in bold type